Do you **hear** the
people sing?

Do you hear the people sing?

The Male Voice Choirs of Wales

Gareth Williams

Gomer

Published in 2015 by
Gomer Press, Llandysul, Ceredigion, SA44 4JL

ISBN 978 1 78562 060 7

A CIP record for this title is available from the British Library.

This book is published with the financial support of the
Welsh Books Council.

Printed and bound in Wales at
Gomer Press, Llandysul, Ceredigion
www.gomer.co.uk

in memory of

Bryan Davies (1934–2011)
master musician of Ferndale

and

Philip Griffith Jones (1937–2015)
of Rhymney and its Silurians

CÔR MEIBION

Dod at ei gilydd –
Chwarelwyr, glowyr, siopwyr,
Dynion y diwydiannau newydd, rhai athrawon –
Dynion yn rhengoedd
A'r gwahaniaethau'n plethu'n gân,
Yn gytgord.

Ar y bŷs, bras –
Straeon coch, galanas
O chwerthin, sgwrsio, tynnu coes.
Ac wrth gwrs, y stopio
A'r rhelyw'n pwyso fesul un
O'r bŷs am ddiferyn.

Ond wedyn eu gweld nhw,
Ddynion yn eu siwtiau yn lân ar lwyfan –
A'u hwynebau'n myfyrio'r gân,
Eu llygaid yn astud
A grym eu cerdd –
Yn dangnefedd, yn orfoledd, neu'n alar –
Yn fflam drwy'r neuadd,
Fel einioes yn llosgi mewn diffeithwch o nos.

Gwyn Thomas

MALE VOICE CHOIR

They come together –
Quarrymen, coalminers, shop-keepers,
Workers from new industries, and some teachers –
Men in rows
And the differences between them
Woven into song,
Into harmony.

On the bus, coarse –
Saucy tales, shambles
Of laughter, talk and leg-pulling.
And, of course, the stopping
With the majority pushing one by one
From the bus for a pint …

But then, to see them,
Men, smart in their suits on the stage –
Their faces meditating the song,
Their eyes attentive
And the power of their singing –
Serene, or glorious, or sad –
A flame through the hall,
Like life burning in a desolate night.

(trans. GT)

Contents

Foreword by Tim Rhys-Evans

⟨❦⟩

I'm sure I won't be betraying my roots when I say that there weren't a lot of opportunities to hear live classical music in 1970/80s New Tredegar. However, thanks to the male choirs that proliferated in our valleys, I got to experience the thrill of hearing ordinary men uniting in song to make extraordinary things happen.

With every fibre of their being, they would commit to a sound that was both powerful and virile but yet moving and beautiful. Men who mostly did impossibly physical jobs underground and who would never have expressed their emotions in words felt no embarrassment in standing in front of hundreds of people and singing of their love, faith, joy and pain.

As a non-Welsh speaker until my 30s, I wasn't an active participant in the Eisteddfodau tradition growing up, but thanks to the male choir I learned of my language, of my culture and of my heritage years before I knew what it truly meant.

Not only did I get to experience 'that sound' in close quarters but I also got to hear world famous singers who, as soloists with these small local choirs, would fit in guest appearances at annual concerts between their operatic commitments at Covent Garden, La Scala and The Met. By the time I was 12, I had heard Sir Geraint Evans, Stuart Burrows, Dame Gwyneth Jones and Dennis O'Neill, mostly in the now-closed Central Hall in Bargoed. How many other nations can claim to have given that musical education to their people?

With there being so many more eminent champions of the Welsh male choir than me, I feel honoured to have been asked by Professor Gareth Williams to contribute to this comprehensive and compelling account of Wales's most famous musical export. I never actually intended to become a male-choir conductor, but, like so many others mentioned in this book, once it got into my veins it was almost inevitable that it would remain with me forever.

Like the Rev. Eli Jenkins, I praise God that we are a musical nation and, as much as I am proud of our past, I dearly hope and pray that through the perseverance of our male choirs, we may always be able to claim that we are, as our anthem proclaims, a 'Gwlad beirdd a chantorion'.

Author's Preface

'Tenors, baritones, sopranos, came and went: all developed in face and stance as well as in voice, used to travelling from distant villages and from the mining valleys' to the Glynmawr eisteddfod, affectionately recreated by Raymond Williams in his novel *Border Country* (1960):

> … It was time now for the choirs … Each choir moved into position, into dark settled rows, and the set faces turned to the conductor, eyes widened and lips poised … asking for movement and control. The drop of the raised hand, and then not the explosion of sound that you half expected, but a low, distant sound, a sound like the sea but insistently human: a long, deep, caressing whisper, pointed suddenly and sharply broken off, then repeated at a different level, still both harsh and liquid; broken off again cleanly; then irresistibly the entry and rising of an extraordinary power, and everyone singing; the faces straining and the voices rising around them, holding, moving, in the hushed silence that held all the potency of the sounds until you listening were the singing and the border had been crossed. When all the choirs had sung, everyone stood and sang the anthem …
>
> (R. Williams, pp.257–9)

In this vivid portrait of a rural eisteddfod, warm without being sentimental, we can see why Raymond Williams (1921–88) is so highly regarded as a novelist as well as a cultural critic. But there is, in this account, something missing. 'When all the choirs had sung, everyone stood and sang the anthem,'- and that's it? What was the result of the competition which, after all, was the eisteddfod's climax?

Those choirs had been practising for weeks, probably months, for that evening, and like their listeners, would have been agog for an adjudication or at least a result. But the audience, here, has apparently no interest in the outcome; it has dispersed and gone home.

Perhaps to Raymond Williams the novelist, to dwell on this would be to impede the narrative. Perhaps Raymond Williams the socialist intellectual is here indicating his disapproval of the competitive urge which, with its stress on rivalry and struggle for primacy among ordinary people, is a ploy to divert and divide the unity of an egalitarian working class.

The historical experience over the centuries suggests otherwise, and so does this book, which pulses with choir rivalries, adjudications, musical opinions and outcomes in more than a century of choral contests at the National Eisteddfod of Wales; in other words, the very element missing in the account of the Glynmawr eisteddfod is, here, central. In the introduction to Part Three I explain why I have chosen this device as a means of tracing the historical geography of Wales' male voice choirs, and used it as a vehicle for identifying a people's cultural awareness and sense of distinctiveness.

In viewing the social history of Wales through this focussed lens of its male choirs, I have relied on the help and knowledge of innumerable correspondents and choir officers who must have come to live in trepidation of my late night texts and emails in the way that the victims of Stalin's purges came to fear the midnight knock on the door. Therefore I am particularly indebted to Dr Alwyn Humphreys, A.J. Heward Rees, Eric Jones (Côr Meibion Pontarddulais), Dr David R. Jones (Wrexham), Ann Francis Evans (National Library of Wales), Tom 'TC' Jones, Huw Tregelles Williams, Terence Lloyd, Professor E. Wyn James, Gareth Pritchard Hughes and Geraint Phillips (Côr Meibion y Rhos), Gareth Reese (Bridgend), J. Vince Roberts (Trelawnyd), Roy Pugh amd Alan Lewis (Morriston Orpheus), John Wines (Maesteg Gleemen), Wyn Lewis (Ar Ôl Tri), John Parry and Gwilym Williams (Hogia'r Ddwylan), Creighton Lewis OBE, Gavin Parry and Rhydfen Morgan (Pendyrus), Dean Powell (Treorchy), Carl Llewellyn (Dowlais), Paul Rogers (Mynydd Islwyn), Ralph Williams (Rhymney Silurian), Emyr Evans (Penrhyn), Nia Clwyd (Bois y Castell), and Gwyn L. Williams and Caio Higginson (Tŷ Cerdd).

I doubt if I could have written the book at all without the kindness and sustaining care of friends and family. Gill Thomas of Treorchy Reference Library and John Jenkins of Bow Street have known me long enough to be able to deal patiently with my endless requests, and to pass on to me stray references and nuggets of information likely to interest me. Gill's bibliographic skills proved invaluable, and I cannot thank Maldwyn Pate enough for the generous tuition he gave me at the keyboard of my gleaming but often infuriating new laptop, preserving my sanity but in the process endangering his own. Diolch yn wir, Mal. His lasting friendship, along with that of Ken and Eluned Richards, John and Susan Hollyman, Chris and Sara Williams, Cyril Jones, Dai Smith, Trevor Herbert and Gwyn Prescott, has mattered more to me than they probably realise. Daniel Williams – you can't call your own son 'Professor' – has been a constant source of intellectual stimulation, critical comment and good humour, and I hope he and Sioned and her family in Rhymney will like the dedication; the late Philip Jones, her father, was a staunch Silurian, a resonant 'down bass,' and, most of all, a fine man. Mary, Tomos and Zoe cared for me with unstinting love and devotion when I ran into a little local difficulty in the heart-stopping second half of 2013. And as I was writing my 'Conclusion' in June 2015, Lefi Wyn Williams arrived to mark a new beginning, and join Aneirin and Hana in Canton and Lowri and Dewi in Alltwen to become the fifth beat in the bar of their Tadcu's contentment.

Dr Rhidian Griffths very kindly read the entire typescript and I benefited enormously from his sharp eye, unrivalled knowledge of Welsh music, and much else besides. That he had a script to read at all was due to the tireless word-processing skills of my indispensable typist Dorothy Evans in Aberystwyth (with assistance from her daughters Menna and Meryl). It was my notorious handwriting, however, that resulted in the distinguished former Director of Music at St. John's College, Cambridge, George Guest, appearing in an early draft as George Best.

At Gomer Press, Ceri Wyn Jones, who, as a Crowned and doubly Chaired Bard and member of regular National winners Côr Meibion Ar Ôl Tri, knows the Eisteddfod stage better than most, guided the entire operation with the utmost professionalism. Special thanks go to Professor Gwyn Thomas for allowing me to use his poem 'Côr Meibion' and for making his own translation of it; and to Tim Rhys-Evans for finding time, among his many commitments ensuring that the past of our male voice choral tradition has a future, to write a generous Foreword.

My thanks are heartfelt.

I bawb, diolch – o galon.

Gareth Williams
September 2015

Introduction: 'The Soft Sweetness of B-flat'

You see them in their blazers on the field before kick-off at the Millennium Stadium, or grouped around some rusting pithead gear in a heritage park where many think they should be among the exhibits. Right on cue they will sing 'Bread of Heaven' and 'Arglwydd, dyma fi', two hymns known in the business – but rarely outside it – as 'Cwm Rhondda' and 'Gwahoddiad', which can always be relied on for an ovation that sometimes disguises little more than a lachrymose sentimentality. Seen as throwbacks to a more patriarchal society, pale, male and stale they are the frequent object if not of scorn then of cliché, cartooned and caricatured near to death. Except they are far from dead, though their passing has been predicted for the last sixty years; they are a feature of public life.

The Welsh male voice choir is alive and well and impervious to cliché. Age has weathered but not withered it; its roots are too deep, continually watered by the loyalty and genuine affection of most of the population of Wales, and by the tears of exiles. At the same time it often evokes among thousands of people who are less Welsh than King Offa and who think 'calon lân' is a heart condition, an admiration tinged with incomprehension because somehow they can be unbearably moved by the distinctive sound of what is still one of the most popular and enduring emblems of Welsh identity. We need to begin by asking not why the Welsh male voice choir so doggedly defies its sell-by date, but where did it come from in the first place. In other words, this thing the Welsh have about singing – how did it start?

Some think we should go back to Gerald of Wales (Giraldus Cambrensis) who in his *Description of Wales* (1193) wrote that 'when they come together to make music, the Welsh sing their traditional songs not in unison as is done elsewhere but in parts .... When a choir gathers to sing, which happens often in this country, you hear as many different parts and voices as there are performers, all joining together in the end to produce a single harmony and melding in the soft sweetness of B-flat.' But to interpret this in terms of the four-part harmony of the 19th century is like claiming Boadicea (Buddug) was a suffragette. It is nonsense. Yes of course there had been singing in Wales for centuries, formally in monasteries and churches, informally on festive occasions, at work, in the fields and in alehouses, but it is with the industrial history of Wales that the popular mind associates the Welsh male voice choir, and the popular mind is right.

It was in the wake of the double triumph of the men and women of the South Wales Choral Union at the Crystal Palace in 1872–3 that Gerald's testimony was seized on to claim that the Welsh had always sung, just as they were good at rugby, another new activity in the late 19th century, because in the reign of Elizabeth the First they had indulged in some brisk shin- and skull-cracking in pursuit of a ball called a cnapan. They were keen on finding precedents in Victorian Wales for the simple reason that so much in that century *was* new, and people have a psychological need to explain novelty by appealing to the past for precedents, if only to convince themselves, and others, that this apparent innovation – the Welsh appetite for choral singing – was as old as the hills.

The fact is, there were *no* precedents for what happened to Wales in the 19th century. Its population doubled in 50 years, and doubled again during the next 50, quadrupling from barely half a million in 1801 to over two million by 1901. Within that increase, some places saw quite staggering growth. Most spectacular was the Rhondda, a tree-lined valley of fewer than a thousand souls in 1851, but which by 1911 – only 60 years later – had exceeded 150,000 and was still growing. The engine of this growth of course was the sudden growth of the south Wales coalfield which transformed the valleys into one of the great fuel-producing regions of the world and made the Bristol Channel as economically significant as the Gulf of Oman is today.

Into this region, to dig the coal and operate the mines, become shopkeepers and shop assistants, school teachers, policemen, surveyors, solicitors, doctors, railwaymen, clerks, publicans, drinkers, Christians –

and others, you name them, they arrived, in their thousands. Most were in search of higher wages than they could command in the agricultural counties of the rest of Wales and the west of England. There were soon more men than women, and seeking a recreational outlet, one of the spheres they found was that expression of multi-voiced music, the choir, and the surplus of men meant a male choir. This was in the main a man's world, and it explains much about the masculine culture of the south Wales valleys where there are still clubs that will not admit women, physical strength is valued, and sports like boxing passionately followed.

When these rural migrants poured in from west, mid and north Wales to the valleys and ports, they brought with them their language, their Nonconformist religion and their fondness for congregational singing, and the more receptive incomers from further afield adopted this culture and became assimilated by it. In their unfamiliar new surroundings, they found solace and sociability in song, for in a materially poor society the voice was the most democratic of instruments; most of us have a voice and it costs nothing. Men and women found comfort from the daily industrial grind in their chapels, which were opening in Wales at the rate of one every eight days – that's nearly one a week – throughout the 19th century; by 1900 there were over five thousand of them, over 150 in the Rhondda alone, dominating both the skyline and, in large part, the social and cultural life of the people. They were places of song as well as worship. This was where choirs took shape, rehearsed and performed, for where else was there? In the early industrial years, before welfare halls and workmen's institutes were built, chapels were also the people's theatres, their venue for entertainment. And this had consequences, for even out of hours you couldn't sing music-hall ballads, popular ditties and street doggerel in the sanctuary, the music had to be suitably respectable. But this didn't mean it couldn't be enjoyable, and the beefy cheerfulness and rousing choruses of Handel, Haydn (both soon to be popular names in Wales) and Mendelssohn, with their compelling narratives of the Israelites fleeing captivity from Egypt and their wars with the Philistines and with the followers of Baal, these and their thrilling climaxes captured the passions of their audiences.

Male choirs were originally offshoots of the large mixed choirs which could number between 150 and 200, but as the gender imbalance kicked in they became increasingly independent, self-standing organisations often linked to the workplace: the colliery, the quarry, the railway, the works, the docks. And the emphasis, as it was in industrial life itself, was on struggle, conflict, and the unity that hopefully would overcome all odds. We have only to consider some of the staples of the standard male choir repertoire, much of it still popular today: along with the operatic choruses that Bellini, Verdi and Wagner wrote for assorted soldiers, gypsies, pilgrims, sailors, and slaves, there were Christians to be martyred in the arena, plains to be crossed, and sandy wastes where 'the desert's dusky sons' met their comeuppance. And there was the Charge of the Light Brigade, the Destruction of Gaza, the Soldiers of Gideon, the War Horse, and battles right, left, right and centre fought by Comrades in Arms, precisely the bellicose items that the writer Gwyn Thomas, born in Cymmer in 1913, recalled from his Rhondda upbringing as 'pieces of vocal artillery that headlined menace and ruin and reconciled thousands to the Social Insurance'. For with the sole addition of songs from the shows and musical theatre, the repertoire of the Welsh male choir today has changed little over the years: the dramatic choruses and melancholy part-songs, rousing hymns and roof-raising anthems that rang out when Welsh miners, steelworkers, quarrymen, foresters and farmers, as choristers became, in an instant, Soldiers, Pilgrims, Martyrs, Bandits, Slaves, Sailors or Crusaders, and then all passion spent, reverted just as quickly to being their ordinary selves.

And not only south Wales contributed to the rich weave of this choral tapestry. The rich musical traditions of north-east Wales would find expression in the famous choirs of Rhosllannerchrugog, Froncysyllte and Trelawnyd, while to the north west the renowned choristers of Penrhyn and the Brythoniaid testify to the contribution of the hardy quarrymen of Bethesda and Blaenau Ffestiniog. Some have claimed that while coal produced the ringing top tenors of south Wales, it is to slate that the thunderous basses of the north owed their comparable resonance. Similarly, in west Wales the poured molten metal of the tin and copper works of the Swansea district contributed to the mellow tones we associate with the historic choirs of Dunvant, Morriston, Manselton and Pontarddulais. And of course along the northern rim of the east Glamorgan and Gwent coalfield the choirs of the once world famous iron-making townships of Dowlais, Rhymney, Tredegar and Beaufort are reminders of that ruthless exploitation which nevertheless gave birth to a workforce that found powerful comfort in the comradeship of song.

Apart from the fellowship and the pride in asserting local and working-class identity, another inducement was the opportunity to travel. Competing in semi-national and National eisteddfodau took men out of their dark and narrow valleys; this was a competitive society based on delivering and rewarding productivity, and on beating rivals. Travel not only took choristers to other parts of Wales and England but much further afield. We ought not to think that the overseas tour is a modern phenomenon made possible by transatlantic air travel. The Rhondda Glee Society toured the Welsh settlements of North America for six months in 1888–9, and returned there, along with the Penrhyn quarrymen, to compete (and in the case of the Gleemen, to win) at the World's Fair Eisteddfod in Chicago in 1893. The Treorchy male choir in 1908 embarked on an 18-month round the world tour of over 300 concert engagements. Their venues included the Neuberg Asylum in Pennsylvania and the Cleveland Penitentiary, where at least they were guaranteed a captive audience. Add to the mix invitations to sing in front of Queens and Presidents, at Windsor Castle and the White House, and we see that by the turn of the century the Welsh male voice choir had become a means to showcase Welsh identity and respectability.

> Listen …
> 'On the breeze a sound is stealing,
> That sweetly each ear charms;
> Let no clamour rudely pealing
> disturb the strain melodious …'

In the soft sweetness of B-flat perhaps? Anyway, this is what happened. For by tracing the chronology, geography and social origins of Wales's male voice choirs we are charting the contours of modern Welsh history.

COMRADES IN ARMS.

CHORUS FOR MEN'S VOICES.

GEORGE LINLEY.   ADOLPHE ADAM.

1st Tenor.

2nd Tenor.

1st Bass.

2nd Bass.

PIANO.
(ad lib.)

On the breeze a sound is steal - - ing, That sweet-

ly each ear charms; Let no cla - mour rude - ly peal - - ing Dis-

J. CURWEN & SONS LIMITED

(A Division of Music Sales Ltd.)
8/9 Frith Street, London W1D 3JB

Part One

Chapter 1

'On the Breeze a Sound is Stealing': 1840–1870

There are male voice choirs in Wales today that call themselves 'glee singers' or 'gleemen', but they owe little apart from their conviviality to the original gentlemen's glee parties of 18th-century England. The glee was an unaccompanied part song (i.e. a song that combined various vocal parts) for, generally, male voices, and it was an offspring of the round and the catch, where the voices appear to chase each other (from the Italian *caccia,* the chase) but never catching up. The posh London Catch Club, founded in London in 1761 for sociability and singing, was a pretext for drinking and dining, essentially song-and-supper occasions where inebriation and jocularity of a peculiarly male and lavatorial kind predominated. The glee was altogether more moral and modest than the increasingly obscene catch, and as it might include female voices, the more salacious material was rejected.

The tendency of the English glee to divide the text into small sections with different emotional colouring, detailed dynamics, chromatic harmonies and some basic counterpoint was inherited by the larger scale male voice choruses of Welsh composers from Joseph Parry onwards, but there the similarity ends. The glee did sometimes go beyond romantic love, the hunt and the fairies to more topical even mundane subjects like 'My pocket's low and taxes high' (Samuel Webbe, c.1800), but after dabbling with the seasons ('Yr Haf'/'Summer', by Gwilym Gwent c. 1863) and nature ('Y Gwlithyn'/'The Dewdrop', Alaw Ddu, c. 1864), which were ideal for the smaller vocal groupings that were by then springing up across Wales, Welsh composers would soon be drawn to write meatier choruses that larger ensembles relished and were already picking up from the French repertoire like Adolphe Adam's 'Comrades in Arms' which dates from the 1830s and which smaller glee groups were already singing.

The vocal grouping was different too. The most popular deployment of voices to sing English glees was male alto, tenor, tenor, bass (ATTB) or TTB, with the male alto singing falsetto, or counter-tenor; composers also wrote for sopranos and female altos as well as men (SATB and SSATB) with one voice to a part. The glee more often than not was for unaccompanied solo voices. It happened differently in chapel-going, hymn-singing Wales, which never wholly embraced the glee in its pure form, any more than it took to its heart what Mendelssohn called 'the bearded alto' which was chiefly associated with cathedral and courtly milieus in England. The glee was cheery, light and decorous. The Welsh were not.

Essentially, what prevented the English-style glee tradition from planting deep roots in Wales, apart from the inherent melancholy of its inhabitants, was the strength of religious Nonconformity and the encouragement it gave to harmonised congregational singing. The popularity of four-part hymnody in the chapels of Wales produced a fondness for SATB anthems and choruses which dispensed with the bearded alto. Glees and catches were unaccompanied rounds for three to five solo voices, less commonly six to eight. But in Wales, with its enormous parallel growth of population and Nonconformity, John Curwen's tonic solfa system, which reached Wales in the 1860s, nurtured collective harmonised singing. And whereas in England glees tended to be the preserve of the comfortable class, the Welsh male voice choir has its roots in the working class and working-class conditions.

The first known example of a Welsh glee is a 'Canig Ddirwest', a temperance glee of 1845. The Merthyr and Dowlais Temperance Choir sang glees in 1862 at a local abstinence festival and, we can safely say, brought to them the muscularity which would always characterise the singing there and was far removed from the more refined English style. Similarly, while the pre-eminent Welsh exponent of the English type of glee was Tredegar-born Gwilym Gwent (William Aubrey Williams, 1834–91), one of his first compositions was the robust 'Chwi Feibion Dirwest' ('Ye sons of temperance') for the Aberdare Temperance Eisteddfod in 1860. If Samuel Webbe brought the glee to perfection in England, Gwilym Gwent was his equivalent in Wales, to the extent that the Rhondda publisher Isaac Jones of Treherbert thought it worth commissioning work from him even after Gwilym had migrated to Pennsylvania in 1872.

Temperance retained its influence longer than the glee, whose compositional popularity was short-lived but intense, in Wales peaking in the 1860s and 1870s. The English glee, compositionally, had dried up in the 1830s; it reached Wales later. It seems to have appealed little to mid-century composers like John Ambrose Lloyd and Tanymarian (Edward Stephen) whose output was mainly hymns, anthems and oratorios, but the next generation responded enthusiastically albeit briefly. Joseph Parry entered three glees for the 1863 National Eisteddfod in Swansea, beating Gwilym Gwent's 'Yr Haf' in the process. The glee exercised the compositional skills of others like Alaw Ddu (W. T. Rees), John Thomas, D.W. Lewis and D. Emlyn Evans. Rees's 'Y Gwlithyn', particularly, was a popular test piece up to 1914 and 'glee' ('canig') was the name given to compositions for smaller choirs of 20 to 30 voices well into the 20th century. The glee, 'a much neglected style of composition in Wales,' Dr T. Hopkin Evans told the National Eisteddfod audience at Cardiff in 1938, 'is not a laboured trick effect for competitive singing; it should be a graceful story told in melodious harmony with all the delicacy and strength suggested by words and music'.

By the 1870s we detect a shift: the Welsh preference was increasingly for full-blooded European choruses influenced more by the flourishing *orphéoniste* movement of male choirs in France than by jolly English glee clubs. These were better suited to the well-drilled choir that reflected the equally well-disciplined workforce found in the rapidly industrialising Wales of the 19th century with its premium on teamwork and co-operation. But the distinction wasn't clear cut. The ambivalence of the Welsh situation is illustrated by the difficulty we have in seeking to distinguish between the glees and part-songs of Joseph Parry. Most of the part-songs he composed in the 1860s are glees: his 'Sleighing Glee' of 1873 was written for SATB with accompaniment, but while his 'Sailors Chorus' or 'Cytgan y Morwyr' (its refrain 'Codwn hwyl' dubbed 'Cod in Oil' by more irreverent choristers) and sung by Welsh – and Cornish – choristers a century later also dates from that time, it can hardly be described as a glee for it is one of his more robust men's choruses, its virility anticipating his later 'Pilgrims Chorus'

CARADOC.

"He led them on to Victory."

Yours faithfully
Griffith R. Jone
(Caradog)

('Cytgan y Pererinion', c.1886) and 'Iesu o Nazareth' (1898). The 'Sailors Chorus' was signposting the direction the Welsh male voice choir was ready to take, and in Haverfordwest, for instance, they knew the difference: a glee society was already in existence when the Haverfordwest male voice choir was formed independently of it in 1896.

Clearly, therefore, glee societies were common in Wales by the 1860s. The Merthyr Glee party entertained the Cymreigyddion of Abergavenny in 1839, and we hear of an Abersychan glee party in 1847. The Twyn Carno Musical Society of Rhymney (Cymdeithas Gerddorol Twyn Carno) had been in existence for at least fifteen years when the monthly journal *Y Cerddor Cymreig* ('The Welsh Musician'), in the first year of its appearance, reported on its concert of four-part glees in 1861 and it was in no way the first example of such activity. In January 1849 the 'celebrated glee singers from Rhymney' gave a concert in Tredegar Town Hall under the patronage of the ironmaster Samuel Homfray. Glee groups competed at Lady Llanover's Abergavenny eisteddfodau in the 1830s and 1840s. There was glee singing at the Aberafan eisteddfod in 1853, and the following year the local Band and Glee Club sang at Dowlais station for the families of soldiers 'engaged at the seat of war' in the Crimea.

We notice the link with the seats of industry too, and it is in the iron, coal and copper towns almost without exception (the announcement in 1849 that a glee society was to be formed in Chepstow being one of them) that this small-scale form of choral singing is to be found. In July 1856, at about the time the Pontypool Glee and Madrigal Society came into existence, the Brynmawr Glee Club was entertaining the clientele at the Rock and Fountain Inn in Clydach (Gwent). Throughout the 1860s the Monmouthshire press reports the activities of glee parties in Blackwood, Rhymney, Gilwern, Beaufort, Tredegar, Ebbw Vale and Craigfargoed; by the end of the decade the infection has spread beyond the industrial south to Llanddewi-brefi (Cardiganshire) and to Rhydymain, Corris and Dolgellau (Merionethshire). Further north again, there were glee parties active, in a mostly genteel environment, in Ruthin, Denbigh and Pwllheli. North met South when the the Mountain Ash and Merthyr Glee Parties combined singing with a seaside visit to Tywyn and Pwllheli in 1866, while the Blaenau Ffestiniog Glee Party is in 1867 performing a varied programme in both languages by Henry Bishop, Rossini, Joseph Parry and Alaw Ddu, in support of a concert tour to raise money by Miss Megan Watts Hughes of Dowlais to further her musical education, an early hint of singing's role in fostering a nationwide musical identity. This was an indication, too, of the choral vibrance of this quarrying district that would assert itself even more strongly in years to come. Gentility was not a characteristic of the working class-singers of Blaenau any more than of industrial Mountain Ash and Merthyr.

The process of industrialisation in Wales is mostly associated with the development of iron smelting along the northern rim of the southern coalfield and the export of steam coal from the south-eastern valleys. But there were significant industrial developments, too, at the south-western extremity of the coalfield, in particular copper smelting and tinplate manufacture in the Swansea/Neath region. For most of the first half of the 19th century, John Hugh Thomas tells us (in Griffiths, ed., 1990), 'Swansea relied for its music almost entirely on a succession of visiting musicians, some passing through like migratory birds, others settling in the town for most of their working lives'. From the 1850s its musical life began to be built on more solid foundations as chapels organised their own singing classes and choirs, and a town choral society was formed. By then the

The early Welsh glee parties were found in the seats of industry, like Dowlais, whose blast furnace site is seen here under construction in 1865.

(*Western Mail*)

metallurgical industries of west Glamorgan were generating considerable vocal activity. Mid-century saw dramatic expansion in tinplate: where in 1840 there were around 30 tinplate works, extending in an arc from Llanelli through Swansea and its hinterland to Neath and Port Talbot, by 1890 there were over a hundred. The lower Swansea Valley in particular was one of the most important industrial centres in the kingdom and Swansea itself, 'Copperopolis', the centre of the global copper trade.

The population of the Swansea district increased from 6,631 in 1801 to 19,115 in 1851; it was 65,000 in 1881 and had more than doubled to 134,000 by 1901. By 1860 15 of the 18 copper works in the UK were in the Swansea area, and the peak of activity they reached in the decade before 1914 was reflected in the vigour of the region's musical life, just as it was in the pre-war success of Swansea's 'All Whites' champion rugby XV. While tinplate works tended to cluster around the ports or along the river valleys, inland too the Ystalyfera Iron Company had diversified into tinplate with numerous furnaces, mills and forges. Morriston's Forest, Dyffryn and Worcester works sprang up in the midst of the Lower Swansea Valley collieries. Tinplate was manufactured in Cwmafan from the 1820s and Briton Ferry from 1850, with further expansion in the 1880s. The Gilbertsons were the princes of Pontardawe's tinplate mills and steel furnaces while smelting was carried on in Landore and Llansamlet. In this sulphurous, foul-smelling setting the choir, like the chapel, offered an escape from industrial squalor.

Not coincidentally, here, in mid-century, glee parties take off. The Landore Tinplate Glee Party, Oystermouth Glee class, Mumbles Glee class drawn from the Wesleyan chapel choir, Swansea Orpheus Glee Society, Llansamlet and Neath Abbey glee parties were all spawned in that hyperactive decade by Copperopolis' rich industrial heritage. They offered a platform to famed soloists like Eos Morlais (Robert Rees) and Llinos y De (the Southern Linnet, Lizzie Williams), and when the Morriston and Landore Glee Party gave a concert in 1873 they were accompanied by the ardent tonic-solfa propagandist W. T. Samuel, with 'Mr. G. R. Jones in attendance', none other than the burly Caradog, hero of the South Wales Choral Union's victories in 1872–3 at the Crystal Palace.

The Margam Copper Works Glee class met in a chapel schoolroom in the 1860s, with an emphasis on the educational, the learning of the parts and musical notation, and the Cwmafan Works Glee Club, in existence from at least the early 1860s, was still active in the next century. The Swansea Glee and Madrigal Society sang in Swansea Town Hall in 1862, the year we also start to hear of Morriston Glee Party, a precursor of the great male and mixed choirs that would in time make that densely populated township a byword for choral excellence. It is clear that at this stage too women sang with the men. In this regard Welsh towns were perhaps influenced by the occasional incursions by English societies, like the visits to Newport in 1848 and 1849 of the Clifton Orpheus Glee singers, and of the Lady and Gentlemen Amateurs of Bristol and the London Glee and Madrigal Union to the Assembly Rooms in 1857 and 1866. It was a development to be welcomed for, writing in 1869, a self-styled 'Professor of Music' as was the Welsh way, wished that male glee societies 'be leavened by female voices. Concerts would be much better attended and the performances give greater satisfaction [for] without female voices the singing sounds both dull and disagreeable' (*Cardiff and Merthyr Guardian,* 8 December 1869).

As regards dullness the professor was seriously wrong, as the emergence of the fully-fledged Welsh male choir was about to show. He was wrong on the gender exclusivity of the glees as well. The Libanus (Morriston) Glee Party included Mrs. W. A. Davies and Miss S. Abraham, and while Swansea's Crystal Glee Society consisted of seven men and three women, some of their names tell us something of their character and social origin: Messrs Routley, Prater, Cowman, Buse and Marton, and Misses Huxtable and Prucelle. The Temple Glee Society, also of Swansea, included Miss Puxley, Mrs Parker and Miss Southwell. We cannot be sure they sang Gwilym Gwent as well as Samuel Webbe, but around the copper works and in the thoroughly Welsh-speaking valleys of the Tawe, Nedd and Afan rivers, his compositions would certainly have had an airing.

A further influence were the Christy Minstrels, after Edwin P. Christy (1815–62) and also known as 'nigger minstrels', the generic name for black-faced groups of singers popular in the USA in the 1840s and 1850s, whose tuneful songs featuring allegedly African-American harmonies soon caught on in the UK. We hear of concerts by Christy Minstrels in Cardiff and Newport in 1860, while another at Taibach in 1861 included selections from a repertoire that was condemned outright by the religious and musical reformer Ieuan Gwyllt (Revd John Roberts) as nothing less than 'sensation music … feeding the most debased instincts' (*Y Cerddor Cymreig*, March, 1867).

A more significant portent of things to come was that while, at a Temperance Festival at Tabernacle, Merthyr, in 1862, local choirs sang glees and part-songs, they also performed larger choruses like the 'Credo' from Mozart's (attributed) Twelfth Mass. By 1869 the appeal of substantial works solely for male choirs as opposed to small glee parties had reached north Wales too, for that year the men of Engedi, Caernarfon, who constituted the male section of the mixed Eryri (Snowdonia) Musical Union, were getting their teeth into 'Martyrs of the Arena' and 'Comrades in Arms'. Much more would be heard of these particular choruses in the years ahead but for the present, the Welsh male choral tradition was slow in finding its feet. For all the heroics of the Côr Mawr there were no Welsh entrants in the competition for male choirs at the Crystal Palace in 1872 or 1873; they left the field to choirs from Bristol, London and Liverpool. It couldn't have helped that the test pieces by Mendelssohn and Schubert were then wholly unknown in Wales. Though Schubert's 'Gondolier's Serenade' would eventually become familiar from the 1950s, it did not feature as a National test piece until 1984. When it did, it was for 'glee' choirs under 40 voices, while the test for the 'second' competition of 40–70 voices that year was a TTBB arrangement of 'Sound an Alarm' from Handel's 'Judas Maccabeus', and for the 'chief' Joseph Parry's 'Pererinion'. That was an indication in a nutshell of what glees could and could not do.

It was an indication, too, that the Welsh experience was part of a wider pattern. Male choirs emerge in Europe from the early 19th century. Initally they were associated with democratic and nationalist sentiment, as in Austria. In countries like Serbia and Bulgaria the movement had an explicit political agenda, an element in a nationalist project. When from mid-century male choirs became a feature of public life from Spain to Scandinavia, too, the emergence of choirs was simultaneous with a growth of a less assertive national consciousness which triggered a musical awakening, especially on the edge of Europe. In these countries, as well as in established states, choirs and festivals became important vehicles for the expression of national and regional identity (Lajosi etc., 2015). Wales was no exception.

Chapter 2

'Heard Ye that Ringing Cheer': 1870–1890

From the 1860s male vocal ensembles of a different character from the glee parties were emerging on the Welsh musical scene. We see recognisable forerunners of the Welsh male voice choir – 'côr meibion' was a phrase in use in Wales well before it first appeared in English in London's *Musical Times* in the 1880s – taking shape as the male sections of existing mixed choirs start to perform as self-standing ensembles. Glee parties had been similar off-cuts of, for instance, the Swansea Harmonic Society and Newport Philharmonic Society in the 1830s, and the Mold Choral Society and Haverfordwest Harmonic in the 1840s. The first male voice choir competition to be held at a National Eisteddfod (an unofficial institution before the 1880s) took place at Swansea in 1863, for a prize of seven pounds and open to the male sections of mixed choirs numbering between 20 and 40 voices, so we are moving ahead of pure glee singing. It was won by the men of Ivander Griffiths' Swansea Valley Choral Union, with Aberdare second. Choruses from Pencerdd Gwalia (John Thomas)'s cantata 'Llewelyn', much influenced by Bellini and Donizetti, were the test pieces for the Swansea Music Festival of 1864, for men's choirs of between 30 and 50 voices. Two years later, Brymbo, laying the foundations of the fine male choral tradition of north east Wales, won on 'Y Gwlithyn', the test piece for men's choirs, at the National Eisteddfod in Chester.

It is impossible to keep the name of Caradog out of any meaningful account of the beginning of the choral movement in Wales. He is best known for his leadership of the mixed voice South Wales Choral Union at the Crystal Palace in 1872 and 1873. The Côr Mawr, as it was known, is commemorated by W. Goscombe John's statue of Caradog, baton aloft, erected in 1920 in Victoria Square, Aberdare, and rightly so, for although it contained choral units from across industrial south Wales from Brynmawr to Llanelli, its nucleus was the Aberdare Choral Union. In the late 1860s the male section of that choir was holding concerts in its own right, featuring 'Comrades in Arms' and Gounod's 'Soldiers Chorus', and these popularly dubbed 'war-horses', sung at the very outset of the male choral tradition in Wales, still feature permanently in the programme of any self-respecting Welsh male choir in the 21st century. Twenty-odd men of the Aberdare Choral Union under Caradog constituted a choir confident enough to sing a varied programme at Pontypridd in 1866 that included those two items plus 'Men of Harlech' and glees by Henry Bishop and Alaw Ddu. The following year the men of Dowlais Temperance Choir No. 2 sang 'Comrades' and 'Soldiers' in Bethania, Dowlais. In 1869 in a Whitsun Eisteddfod in Swansea they won on 'Comrades' in front of an audience of 2,500. When in 1870 Caradog moved from the Fothergill Arms, Cwmbach, to the Treorchy Hotel in the Rhondda, one of his first actions was to form a male voice choir, one of the very first that was from the outset independent without being an offshoot of a mixed choir. He was thus the pioneer of a mighty tradition, a forerunner of the famous Treorchy choir founded 13 years later.

Further west, one of the earliest self-standing male choirs could in the 1870s be found in Ystalyfera under Morgan Morgans (1839–94), perhaps consisting of survivors of the Swansea Valley's Dyffryn Tawe Choral Union that had disbanded following Ivander's departure for Treforest, then Cumbria, in 1869. This group, the Ystalyfera, or Swansea Valley Orpheus Glee Society, competed at the South Wales Chair Eisteddfodau in Cardiff in 1879 and Swansea in 1880, winning on both occasions, their rivals including the Gwent Minstrels, Aberdare Minstrels, Cardiffians, glee parties from Taibach, Aberaman, Ton (Pentre), Neath, Llansamlet, Cwmbran, and, to break the southern monopoly, Meibion Eryri ('Sons of Snowdonia'). For by now there was, especially in south Wales, a profusion of formal and informal combinations, some of which, like contemporary rugby teams, would have been specifically 'got up' for the occasion. Glee societies, mixed and male but mostly the latter, would continue to be formed, disbanded and reformed as the occasion demanded, adopting the designation of 'glee' until well into the next century, like the Garndiffaith

Gleemen founded in 1948, or the Maesteg Gleemen (1958), National Eisteddfod regulars – and winners – from the 1980s. Such parties had abounded in Wales for well over a century, and 'glee' is still the name adopted by many male voice groups of between 20 and 30 choristers, though it was not until the 1960s that the National Eisteddfod decided to recognise this category with a dedicated competition.

As much as 80 years earlier, Welsh glee choirs had, in size and repertoire, become increasingly distinct from their English counterparts. At the Merthyr Musical Festival in August 1884 the chief competition of the day was for glee parties of no fewer than thirty voices. Against opposition from Brynmawr and Gilfach Goch, the winners were Tom Stephens' Ton Glee Party who had made their mark by winning out of 17 choirs at the Cardiff National in 1883. They certainly impressed the man from the *Daily Telegraph* who 'did not expect to hear better singing in London than that of these miners from the Rhondda. Power and delivery, precision and artistic freedom were conspicuous to a degree which filled strangers with amazement.' The chief adjudicator, Joseph Barnby (1838–1896) director of music at Eton College, and later principal of the Guildhall, reminded the eisteddfod audience gathered in the temporarily converted Cathays railway sheds that 'glees were essentially English [and] should be sung by one voice to each part'. It was advice that went unheeded by Welsh choirs. After Cardiff competitions for male voice choirs became the rage and larger prizes offered. At Liverpool in 1884 the Arvonia choir of Llanberis quarrymen conducted by Dr Roland Rogers (1847–1927), organist at Bangor Cathedral, and winners two years earlier at Denbigh, won out of twelve entrants on 'Martyrs of the Arena' – incredibly, the only time this totemic item has been featured as a National Eisteddfod test piece (and of which more, much more, later).

In London in 1887 the prize for male choirs was an unprecedented fifty pounds, shared by the Rhondda Gleemen and John North's prestigious Huddersfield choir, beating eight others on test pieces by Beethoven, Arthur Sullivan and David Jenkins. Entrants included Tredegar Orpheus, London Welsh (conducted by Joseph Parry's son, J. Haydn Parry), Dowlais Glee (conducted by Eos Myrddin, father of Harry Evans) and Rogers' Arvonia. Prize money was generally far more modest than the metropolitan munificence on display in 1887; in the early 80s it varied from five guineas (at Merthyr in 1881) to 25 pounds (at Caernarfon, 1886). A cautious 25 pounds was generally the norm, the measly fiver at Wrexham in 1888 a reaction to what was seen as London's showboating which was eventually exceeded by the sixty pound prize at Llanelli in 1895. There was judge inflation too, with now six adjudicators, one of whom, Sir George Macfarren (1813–1887), remarked that it was 'wondrous that in the remote Principality where small opportunities for hearing excellent performers prevailed, that such high merit in singing should have been developed as it had been their great privilege to hear that day'. Male voice choirs were here to stay and have been a feature of every National Eisteddfod, and the national landscape, from that day to this.

Though they rarely ventured south, on their own patch choirs from the modestly industrial fortresses of the mountainous north west (Arvonia, Penrhyn, Moelwyn) gave as good as they got, for slate-quarrying districts like Dinorwig, Penrhyn (Bethesda), the Nantlle valley and Blaenau Ffestiniog (whose population had within a few decades mushroomed to 11,000 by 1881), with outcrops in Abergynolwyn and Corris in southern Merionethshire, were bastions of a virtually monoglot Welsh-language musical and literary culture. 'Gellir tybio mai ar ganu yn unig y mae y Ffestinogiaid yn byw,' mused the music journal Y Gerddorfa ('The Music Place') in 1874 – 'one might think that the Ffestiniogites live on music alone.' In terms of competitive male voice choralism, however, the pressure points were in the more industrialised south, as we contrast the single entrant (Nantlle) at Bangor in 1890 with the ten choirs at Swansea the following year. For by now the male voice choir had become one of the principal events of the week's proceedings and in 1891 it was for choirs of 60 to 80 voices, with a thirty pounds prize (clearly the monetary reward fluctuated) and a gold medal to the winning conductor. The immense audience, in excess of 15,000, were enthralled by this first of several subsequent 'battles of the giants', with five adjudicators listening to Port Talbot, the Rhondda Gleemen, Treorchy, Pontycymer, Glantawe Glee Society, Myrddin (Carmarthen), Treherbert, Cynon Valley United, Rhondda Fach Glee and Brynaman United Glee, essentially male voice choirs in a rivalry which most English glee parties would hardly have understood. Surveying the scene from Lancashire, though, choirs like the 80-strong Nelson Arion Glee

Society would have recognised kindred spirits, and would in time want to test themselves against them.

The competition of 1891 was by any measure a pulsating contest, with the ten choirs on their toes, especially the top tenors with which south Wales choirs were – many still are – well-endowed: Signor Alberto Randegger (1832–1911), Italian-born professor of singing at the Royal Academy of Music remarked that Treorchy's tenors at Swansea 'were superior to anything he had ever heard in England or on the continent'. The struggle for mastery turned on Joseph Parry's 'Pilgrims' ('Y Pererinion') and de Rillé's 'Destruction of Gaza' in a contest that lasted five hours. Pontycymer took the honours under T. Glyndwr Richards (1859–1935) who later guided the Resolven choir from the vale of Neath to victory at Mountain Ash 1905 and in Swansea in 1907, and took the Mountain Ash choir to the White House in 1908 to sing before President and Mrs Theodore Roosevelt.

The fare on offer at Rhyl in 1892 satisfied the subscribers too. Choirs from Ebbw Vale, Cefn Mawr (Rhos), Penrhyn, Treorchy and Manchester Apollo were in the frame, but first prize went to Caernarfon, with Middlesbrough on their tails. This was a foretaste of what would become, for the next 40 years, a feature of the event when held in north Wales, namely the temerity of English choirs in venturing onto the stage of the

Penrhyn's slate quarrymen, conducted by Edward Broome, 'National' winners in 1894 after coming second at the World's Fair Eisteddfod in Chicago the previous year. *(Gwynedd Archives)*

16

Tom Stephens' Rhondda Gleemen, winners at Chicago in 1893 and who sang for Queen Victoria at Windsor Castle in 1898.

(*Courtesy of Treorchy Male Choir*)

premier Welsh festival, and confident choirs like Manchester Orpheus and Nelson Arion began showing their Welsh rivals how it should be done through the disciplined singing, secure pitch and pure intonation which often eluded their Welsh rivals.

Whereas the competition in Rhyl was for choirs of 30 to 40 voices, the Pontypridd National in 1893 upped the ante, now for 60–80 voices, with five adjudicators headed by the Scottish composer and choral specialist Alexander Mackenzie (1847–1935) who heard five choirs and didn't mince his words ('the Maerdy choir would have been better without certain of their second tenors and second basses', though he was careful to add that 'some of their voices were very good indeed'). Three were from the Rhondda, and between two of them, Treorchy and the Gleemen, the decision lay, for Rhondda choirs were now as unstoppable as the valley's exponential industrial and demographic growth, which stood at fewer than a thousand in 1851, had exploded to 88,351 by 1891 and was still rising. Treorchy gave 'an admirably crisp performance' despite their conductor William Thomas having to stamp his foot as he beat time towards the

17

end of his French namesake Ambroise Thomas' 'The Tyrol' when his choir were 'evidently in difficulties'. For that reason the palm went to Tom Stephens' Gleemen, whose choir 'exhibited a great amount of sustained power exceedingly perfect in its intonation and did not force its voices out of tune by over vigour'. And the Gleemen had an ace up their sleeve, for Tom Stephens, landlord of the Blacksmith's Arms in Treherbert, had received first-hand information from a brewery representative who had visited Switzerland regarding the vocal effects produced by the yodellers of the Tyrolean mountains, and the Gleemen's execution of this piece of alpine realism helped swing the decision in their favour.

Their next assignment was at the World's Fair Eisteddfod in Chicago later the same year where they won again. Taking second place in the White City that September were the Penrhyn quarrymen. Conducted by Edward Broome (1868–1932), they hoped for revenge at Caernarfon in 1894. But the Rhondda colliers did not enter the lists that year, and the *chwarelwyr* of Bethesda had to content themselves with beating an equally formidable outfit, Pontycymer, victors at Swansea in 1891. It was Treorchy who exhausted the superlatives of the adjudicators at Llanelli in 1895, each independently writing 'wonderful' on their notepads and sitting back to listen in admiration. Joseph Barnby remarked on this occasion that while he thought it 'generally understood that the Germans had what might be called the copyright in male voice singing,' nevertheless 'he had never heard any male voice singing that would come within easy distance of this performance by Treorchy.' Coal was on a roll, though Tal Hopkins' Porth and Cymmer choir did not have it all their own way at Llandudno in 1896, being forced to share the prize with Cadwaladr Roberts' Moelwyn slate workers from Blaenau Ffestiniog.

Ffestiniog was a crucible of choralism and hosted the National itself in 1898 where not Moelwyn but another north Wales choir won, from the mining village of Rhosllannerchrugog under the musicianly Wilfrid Jones. The *Daily Telegraph*'s correspondent Joseph Bennett reckoned that Rhos 'had the delicacy of a Damascus blade and the strength and energy of a Nasmyth steam hammer'. Founded in 1891 and spearheading a whole clutch of choirs in this coal and iron making corner of north-east Wales in the 1890s – Ponciau, Penycae, Rhiwabon, Cefn-Mawr – Rhos would make infrequent but decisive interventions on the National stage for the next century and more, earning the plaudits of partisan south Wales audiences for their winning performances at Cardiff (1938), Llanelli (1962), and a notable hat-trick in 2012, 2013 and 2014.

Crucial to the spread of competition were the railways that enabled the Welsh to imagine themselves as a nation and brought Wales together as never before. They were constantly being rolled out since the first 2,000 kilometres of track had been laid between 1840 and 1860, so that by the end of the century the rail network was, per head of the population, more dense in Wales than anywhere in the world. With the railwaymen and dock workers of Barry achieving their one and only win at Cardiff in 1899, the coal and iron workers of Dowlais (under Harry Evans at Liverpool in 1900) and Rhymney (Dan Owen at Merthyr in 1901) shifted the focus to the valleys east of the Rhondda. Never was there more tangible proof of the maxim that economic growth produces cultural energy, and with the emergence of Moelwyn's quarrymen and Rhos's miners we can see ever more clearly the map of industrial Wales reflected in the topography of its male choirs. A tradition, once established, generates its own momentum, and these areas, along with the choirs born among the tinplate and copper, coal and iron works founded in the 1880s and 1890s like Dunvant, Tredegar and Beaufort, whose national fame was yet to come, would uphold the male choral tradition even when the industrial and religious fervour that created them had receded.

For these thickly-populated districts could boast the largest chapels too, Nonconformist cathedrals like Capel Mawr, Rhos, Noddfa in Treorchy, Hermon and Bethania in Dowlais, and Morriston's Tabernacle, where the pews in the gallery sweep around behind the pulpit purposely to accommodate the large choirs that served to increase these communities' sense of themselves *as* communities. A concentration of population, industry and a Welsh-language Nonconformity were the three pillars on which the Welsh male voice choir tradition was built, and we cannot overestimate the influence of the congregationally sung, richly-harmonised hymns and anthems that sonorously filled Welsh chapels, in the making of that tradition.

Chapter 3

'Sound an Alarm' – a tradition takes off: 1890–1900

Welsh choirs moved in rhythm with their communities in adversity as well as in prosperity, becoming multi-purpose, or as sociologists say, polyfunctional organisations, appearing on all kinds of public occasions from the celebratory to the solemnly commemorative. Tom Stephens assembled his Gleemen twice a day during the hauliers' coalfield strike of 1893 in preparation for their journey to Chicago, and during their hour-long practices no-one but Tom Stephens was to speak. In 1900–1 twenty members of the Penrhyn choir of Caernarfonshire toured the industrial districts of north Wales and the north of England to raise money for their striking fellow-quarrymen, and raised what was then the substantial sum of fifty pounds one Sunday night in a chapel in Rhos. They were warmly received in the valleys of the south too, where many of their fellows and families had migrated during the traumatic Penrhyn lockout that lasted until 1903; similarly Porth and Cymmer and other choirs visited towns in England during the strike of 1898. Choirs from Bethesda and the Rhondda visited Cornwall between 1900 and 1910, often providing a kick-start to the formation of local male choirs there (Skinner, pp.108–10).

From the outset Welsh choirs travelled far afield. This was not a Welsh thing. Visiting Norwegian choirs were always assured of a warm welcome by the Scandinavian diaspora in Wisconsin, as were touring German singers in Minnesota. The Rhondda Gleemen visited the USA twice in 1888–9 and 1893. Performing a staggering 140 concerts on the first occasion, on the latter visit to compete at Chicago they were joined by Penrhyn. Most of these choristers had never left their villages before, let alone Wales. One Penrhyn chorister assured his anxious mother that his ship would never be out of sight of the coastline and would put into harbour every night on the way across so that he could sleep on shore (Elfed Jones, 1989, p. 11). The choirs of Resolven and Mountain Ash were both in the USA in 1908, 'Mount' again in 1911 and 1912, when their eighteen trained vocalists were hailed as 'Wales' greatest male chorus'; the 'Cambrian National Glee Singers', in fact no more than a dozen or so vocalists from the Swansea-Llanelli area, were there in 1909–11. Moelwyn, founded in the late 1880s and under Cadwaladr Roberts (1854–1914) National winners in 1896, became the first north Wales choir actually to *tour* in the USA, Penrhyn having travelled there only to *compete* at the World's Fair in 1893. That was in 1910 when, having already sung before royalty in 1907, they were one of seven Welsh choirs in the home of the brave, giving rise to complaints in the Welsh-American press of a surfeit of choirs from Wales. Undeterred, Moelwyn returned there the following year, though they were forced to abandon their trip halfway through when their arrangements fell apart.

The 50-strong Rhondda Male Chorus, an *ad hoc* choir assembled for the sole purpose of an American tour, had a similar experience in 1913. Having won the prize out of 14 choirs at the Pittsburgh International Eisteddfod on Daniel Protheroe's 'Castilla', they were stranded in New York, 'their purse having failed. Twenty of the sixty sang at Ocean Grove, New Jersey, a great seaside assembly, on an agreement that they should have any receipts over $300. After singing they were told that the receipts had not reached $300. They have since been singing here and there trying to make money to get them home who must return'. (*Musical Herald*, Sept. 1913). It was not finance but an outbreak of flu that prevented the Gwent Gleemen who had in May 1913 sung at the White House, from returning intact from a later visit; some were forced to stay in the US to recover while nine sailed for home. The year was 1915, their ship was the *Lusitania*, and three of them including their conductor were lost when it was torpedoed off Kinsale. Among the six Gleemen saved was the subsequently famous tenor Parry Jones (1891–1963) of Blaina (Llewellyn, 2004).

Episodes such as these remind us that men were freer to travel than women since they had more opportunities to do so. The performances of 'ladies choirs' were strictly for domestic consumption, if they had time to sing at all, tied as they were to sink and scullery, maintaining a tidy home, and meeting the demands of their menfolk in constant daily, and unpaid, 17-hour shifts. In 1891 there were in the Rhondda 50,000 men to 38,000 women, and many of these men were young, single lodgers given the room next to the front door through which they went, if they still had the energy, in search of the recreation and company they found in the workmen's institute, the men's fellowship, the club, the pub, perhaps the band, more often the choir. These were male pursuits and this man's world was symbolised by its male choirs, refined by its mixed and ladies' choirs who brought a visual as well as admired vocal counterpoint to what was a predominantly male discourse and its necessarily limited musical compass. Exceptionally, Madame Clara Novello Davies' Welsh Ladies' Choir, drawn from south-east Wales, did everything the male choirs did and more: they won at the Chicago World's Fair in 1893 and again at the Paris *Exposition* in 1900, where they received far more favourable reviews than the Welsh male choristers there; they were invited to the *Exposition* again in 1937. In the meantime they had sung at Windsor Castle in 1928. But this was 33 years after the 'Treorky boys' had received their Royal Command in 1895. It was for its male choirs that Wales was known.

Perhaps the earliest photo of any Welsh choir, Treorchy in 1885.   (*Courtesy of Treorchy Male Choir*)

Treorchy conducted by William Thomas, in 1895, when they won the National at Llanelli.
(*Courtesy of Treorchy Male Choir*)

This was particularly true of the Rhondda valley where, although mixed choirs of men and women abounded, male choirs became a speciality. They were the most widely travelled too. The Rhondda Gleemen, re-badged after the death of Tom Stephens the previous year as the Rhondda Glee Choir, landed in the USA in October 1907 and over the next two months sang a total of 74 concerts. William Thomas' Royal (Treorchy) Welsh – 17 choristers, all unmarried miners – visited North America in 1907 and the following year embarked on a round-the-world tour that took in South Africa and New Zealand. William Thomas' diary for 1908–9 contains heart-rending accounts of tearful Rhondda emigrants, by then settled in the Antipodes, bidding an emotional farewell to choristers who were sailing home to villages which those settlers knew so well, and were unlikely ever to see again.

At home these choirs constantly competed at local eisteddfodau, which were the nationwide base of a pyramidic structure that extended through 'semi-nationals' to the National itself, underpinned community life, and were a godsend to chapel treasurers. They were forever raising money for charitable causes while contributing also to a wider musical life, with essential female support staging operettas, cantatas and even more ambitious works. To take some Rhondda examples, Porth and Cymmer's male voice choir did 'Il Trovatore' in 1897, David Jenkins' 'David and Goliath' 1898 and Joseph Parry's 'Blodwen' in 1899. With the female roles more than adequately filled, in 1900 Treherbert men's choir were able to produce T. Mee Pattison's 'Sherwood's Queen', while the Royal Treorchy's 26 choristers did Prout's 'Damon and Phintias' in Pentre, with one of Wales's finest tenors, the legendary Todd Jones, and Llew Bowen in the title roles. In December 1905 the Mid-Rhondda male voice party joined the members of Ebenezer chapel, Tonypandy, to do Maunder's cantata 'The Martyrs' (not to be confused with de Rillé's masterpiece of the same name) though it was the New Zealand All Blacks who were martyred that month in the arena of Cardiff Arms Park.

The experience of this Mid-Rhondda party tells us that these choirs were not always the most reliable examples of what students of human development have called 'the civilising process'. They could be boys behaving badly, for boys some of them were. 'As a precaution against over-exuberance, it should be borne in mind that among this choir are several very young men and mere lads, every one of them belonging to the working class', the Windsor-bound Treorchy choristers were warned by their secretary W.P. Thomas in 1895. It was therefore gratifying to read reports that they 'behaved like gentlemen and sang like angels' on that royal occasion. It was not ever thus: the Gleemen and Treorchyites came to blows on more than one occasion and the tent pegs loosened, threatening Treorchy with its collapse, during a performance on another. Three Porth colliers who were tenors in the Cymmer choir sued the conductor of the Mid-Rhondda male voice party for breach of contract when he reneged on a promise to pay each of them 15 shillings (75p, a meaningless conversion today when a miner's weekly wage was two pounds) to sing at the Mountain Ash National in 1905 and another in Neath, on the understanding that they attended two practices a week. The Porth 'professionals' were dismissed for failing to attend a part-practice from which they thought themselves exempt. The judge agreed with them and found in their favour.

Springing up in every town and village of 5,000 or more inhabitants, male choirs proliferated in Wales in the years between 1890 and the Great War, precisely as the percentage of those men working in the heavy industries of coal, slate and steel rose from 35% to 43% of the occupational population. In 1892 the monthly magazine *Y Cerddor* ('The Musician', founded three years earlier) proclaimed that 'in the last twenty years no branch of music has seen greater advance in Wales than male choirs'. Within a span of twenty years the face of Wales became freckled with them. Even rural Wales was infected; a widely dispersed agricultural population could not easily assemble for regular practice, yet Cardiganshire's small market towns like Lampeter, Llangeitho and Tregaron, and the scattered lead-mining communities in the north of the county all boasted their local choirs. Dolgellau's New Year eisteddfod (Eisteddfod Calan Dolgellau) became an annual fixture from 1898 when Abergynolwyn's male party beat Talsarnau, Machynlleth, Corris and Aberystwyth. Further north again, Moelwyn, Criccieth, Nantlle, Padarn, Llanberis, Llanrwst, Trefriw and the busy copper-exporting, shipbuilding port of Amlwch on Anglesey all ran small competing choirs. To the north east Rhos, in existence from 1891, gained their first National win in Ffestiniog in 1898, and won again ten years later at Llangollen in the second competition, with neighbouring Cefn-mawr on their tail.

'The prairie is ablaze with light', sang choristers jubilantly, with a nod to Haydn's 'Creation', in T. Maldwyn Price's 'Crossing the Plain', a chorus particularly popular in the south Wales coalfield where there were few prairies or plains but where by 1911 70% of the entire population of Wales lived and where colliery and works choirs were common. Today's Cambrian Male Voice Choir based in Tonypandy began life in the 1890s as the Cambrian Colliery choir of Clydach Vale. The Ocean Coal Company which employed 11,000 men in eight collieries, in July 1902 held its own eisteddfod that year to celebrate the coming of age of 'the young squire of Llandinam', David Davies, who, since the early death of his father Edward in 1898, already owned them. The thought might have lurked in the back of the mind of a shrewd company and choir secretary like W.P. Thomas that is was no bad thing for its workforce to be expending its energies in singing than in potentially more disruptive activities. There was no dearth of miners, men or male choirs in the Rhondda where 70,000 males aged 12 or over were employed in 1911. One in every three occupied men and boys in Wales was a miner, over a quarter of a million of them on the eve of the First World War, neighbours thrust together in those Rhondda ribbon-developed houses and streets, working alongside each other, worshipping too in any one of the valley's 151 nonconformist chapels, dependent on each other in an often perilous environment which bred familiarity, interdependence, unity of purpose, sympathy and rivalry. And revelry too, for the choir was a valve for the release of steam and high spirits.

In addition to providing later commentators and cynics with a catalogue of cliché about laddish camaraderie, the male choir underpinned a sense of belonging, community and identity, and reinforced the patriarchal norms of a society thinly veined with misogyny. It met significant needs. Before the introduction of safety precautions and regulations, men employed in coal, iron, copper and tin had to trust each other to make the correct sequence of movements at the right time, for not to do so was to risk serious injury or death. What a later generation would label their 'inter-active skills' were honed in adverse circumstances and derived from their pride in what the historian John Davies called 'their understanding of the ways of the furnace and the vagaries of the seam'; this was the essence of their comradeship and the basis on which they defended their rights as a group, a Federation, and as a Union when necessary against their employers. It was not a coincidence that the Williamstown choir of Clydach Vale was formed during the Cambrian dispute of 1910–11, nor that the Cwmbach male choir was formed during the coalfield lockout of 1921.

In its stress on practice, endeavour, achievement, discipline and the acceptance of leadership, the choir replicated the world of work. The Welsh male choir emerged where large numbers of men worked generally in the same location of heavy manual industry. The connections between a workforce and its recreation are intricate, but inescapably the well-disciplined choir was as much an extension of the workplace as an escape from it: choristers were told what to do and they did it, and did so more cheerfully than the obligations of work. But the south Wales coalfield was also the most dangerous in the UK. South Wales accounted for a fifth of the output but nearly half the fatalities of the British coalfield between 1880 and 1900, to the melancholy accompaniment of the steady 'drip drip' of individual death or crippling injury from roof falls and runaway trams that were in most colliery communities a weekly occurrence. These were exceeded only by the horrific explosions of gas and fire damp that claimed 114 lives at Cymmer in 1856, 290 at Cilfynydd in 1894, 119 at Wattstown in 1905 and worst of all, 439 at the Universal Colliery in Senghennydd in 1913. The repertoire of the Welsh male choir ranges from the melancholy to the dramatic because it emerged from an environment that bred faith and fellowship and where lives were lived in valleys where the shadow of death, distress and bereavement were ever present. In such circumstances 'the consolation of music' was more than a cliché: singing together, like working, worshipping and playing together, provided what a later generation would fashionably call a 'bonding' experience. Singing in a choir was to participate in a social relationship based on a mutual interaction between singers and audience that was understood by both.

This experience found its highest form of expression in the local, semi-national and National Eisteddfod. The eisteddfod, Ieuan Gwynedd Jones has written (1990), was 'the most typical product of the chapel-oriented working-class culture of Wales in the nineteenth century ... the institution par excellence that shaped and gave direction to its mental and artistic progress.' This competitive culture raised the general level of participation, just as the musical life of towns and valleys raised standards of performance, public taste and discrimination. Competition offered the excitement of battle without the casualties: Orwell's 'war minus the shooting'. That is what drew the public. 'In the large populous centres of South Wales', observed the musician and critic D. Emlyn Evans in 1904, 'it is a well understood axiom that the crowds follow the choirs', and these more often than not were male choirs. He also observed that this was 'not entirely to our gain as a musical people' (D. Emlyn Evans, NLW 8034D, vol. 2, 12 March 1904). But a minority of educated critics apart, the musical people would have none of it. His cautionary words fell on the deaf ears of the vast majority for whom the male choir was nothing less than a vector of their identity.

Chapter 4

Martyrs and Crusaders: 1900–1914

Those musical people headed in their thousands to the National pavilion for battles of the giants like those at Swansea in 1891, Pontypridd (1893), Liverpool (1900) and Swansea again in 1907 when T. Glyndwr Richards' 100-strong Resolven choir won on 'Nidaros'. In 1913 12,000 sat for four-and-a-half hours on unrelenting benches to listen to 18 choirs at the perhaps unlikely venue of Abergavenny. By then that important railway junction and market town owed its familiarity with choral singing not so much to Lady Llanover's sedate upper-class gatherings of the 1840s but to the 'semi-nationals' regularly staged there in the decade before 1914. There in 1906 Beaufort, a Monmouthshire valleys' choir with 19th-century beginnings, re-founded in 1902, emerged as winners from 22 choirs who sang Daniel Protheroe's 'Crusaders' and Adolphe Adam's 'Comrades in Arms,' two pieces already condemned as hackneyed as early as 1901 by D. Emlyn Evans, though they would continue to be sung for the next hundred years. It is only fears of jihad being declared against choirs who 'prepare for bátt-le with the desert's dusky sons' that have persuaded male choirs to drop 'The Crusaders', composed in 1891, from their concert programmes. The same deference to political correctness has placed Maldwyn Price's 'Crossing the Plain' – which ascribes to 'the redman' a 'delight' in taking white scalps in what the *Amman Valley Chronicle* once described as 'the stirring North American Mabinogi' – under a similar embargo.

'Crossing the Plain' was one of the test pieces at Liverpool in 1900 when ten choirs competed, including the crack Lancastrian organisations,

Manchester Orpheus and Nelson Arion Glee Society. Competitions earlier in the week had seen English choirs take the honours in all the mixed and ladies' categories, leaving the Welsh press in despair at *cyflafan Llynlleifiad* – 'the Liverpool massacre'. The Welsh male choirs, especially those with National pedigrees like Dan Owen's Rhymney, John Phillips' Port Talbot, and Cadwaladr Roberts' Moelwyn, were resolved to redress the balance, but it was the dark horses from Dowlais under the master musician Harry Evans who registered a notable victory in front of 19,000 avid listeners. 'Dowlais saved Wales from utter obliteration' crowed the *Merthyr Express* with some justification.

Choirs formed, disbanded and reformed frequently in the course of the 19th century especially when their lineage was as long as Dowlais's. A more recent choir had been founded there in 1894 but this too had been short-lived, for the grandly named Dowlais Philarmonic Male Voice Society that won at Liverpool had been assembled by Harry Evans from Dowlais' abundant choral resources only nine months earlier. Had the entire 16 choirs who had entered their names in 1900 sung both test pieces, 'Crossing the Plain' and Boulanger's 'Cyrus in Babylon,' it would have been a long day indeed before closing. Fortunately several choirs withdrew and only the Boulanger was permitted to be sung. But after the verdict was announced the victorious Dowlais choir mounted the stage and 'to wild applause' sang their equally thoroughly-prepared 'Crossing the Plain', a recent composition now that the West had been won, its native peoples herded onto reservations and their leaders dead, killed or imprisoned; the Frontier was now closed and therefore safe to sing about. Harry Evans did not take exactly *that* Dowlais choir to compete again but persuaded most of them to join with Merthyr Ladies to form a mixed choir that won a major victory – they had been required to prepare the whole of Mendelssohn's 'St Paul' – at Llanelli in 1903. That year Manchester Orpheus gained revenge in an international male voice competition in Cardiff on Boxing Day. As Harry Evans had by then moved to Liverpool it was his accompanist of 1900, W. J. Watkins, who led Dowlais to another brilliant victory at the London National in 1909, with E. T. Davies now at the piano. True to Dowlais form this choir again fell on hard times, to be revived as Dowlais Penywern under Evan Thomas (Alaw Morlais, 1878–1948) who achieved several notable national and semi-national successes

PROGRAMME OF MUSIC

TO BE RENDERED BY THE

THE PENYWERN (DOWLAIS) MALE VOICE PARTY,

ON THE OCCASION OF THE VISIT OF

Their Majesties The King and Queen

TO DOWLAIS,

THURSDAY, JUNE 27th, 1912.

1.   ...   "GOD SAVE THE KING."   ...   ...

2. "Spartan Heroes"   ...   *Dr. D. Protheroe*

3. "Deryn Pur"...   ...   *(Specially arranged by E. T. Davies, Merthyr Tydfil)*

4. "Crusaders"   ...   ...   *Dr. D. Protheroe*

5. "Aberystwyth" (Welsh Hymn Tune) *Dr. J. Parry*

6. "Harlech"   ...   . *Harry Evans*

7. "Rhyfelgyrch Cadben Morgan"   ...   ...
    (Specially arranged by E. T. Davies, Merthyr Tydfil)

8. "God Bless the Prince of Wales" ...   ...
    Brinley Richards

9.   ...   "HEN WLAD FY NHADAU" ...   ...

CONDUCTOR,
EVAN THOMAS.

ACCOMPANIST,
ARTHUR HUGHES.

sxo Merthyr.

(Courtesy of the Author)

in the 1920s. Large-scale migration following the closure of the coal and steel works in 1930 forced the choir to disband once again until it was revived in the 1960s.

Boulanger's 'Cyrus in Babylon' which Dowlais sang at Liverpool in 1900 connected the Welsh tradition to the *orphéoniste* movement in France. The French word *sociabilité* enjoys a far greater leverage than its English ('conviviality') or Welsh ('cymdeithasgarwch') equivalents. As applied to associational life, in France it embraces recreation from sports to singing clubs, and the *orphéon* movement developed in this contex. Essentially a phenomenon of small towns, and middle and skilled working-class in composition, the first *orphéon* male voice choir society was established in Paris in 1833 and grew rapidly among the smaller municipalities and larger villages (Gumplowicz 2001). Promoted with an explicit agenda of nation building that aimed to subordinate the more spontaneous, oral traditions of France's many dialects to a standardised national 'French' culture (Weber, 1977) – this ideological element was absent in countries like Wales and Norway, where the folk tradition was (allowed to be) more highly regarded – by 1860 there were 700 provincial societies in France and their cross-Channel influence can be discerned from mid-century in the popularity of Adam's 'Comrades in Arms' and Gounod's 'Soldiers Chorus' from his opera *Faust*, first performed in Paris in 1859. The Gounod was a compelling, forceful operatic chorus, while 'Comrades', available from mid-century with George Linley's English words, soon established itself as a concert favourite, its appeal lying in its martial rhythm and frequent changes of tempo and dynamics, its attractive harmonic structure punctuated by spirited antiphonal passages. There were over 2,000 societies of male choirs affiliated to the French *Orphéon* by 1900, and while Wales with its much smaller population could not hope to match these numbers, the descriptive choruses, hymnic and military in nature, of Gounod, Adam, Boulanger, de Rillé (director of the Paris Orphéon 1852–60), Saint Saëns ('Soldiers of Gideon'), de Saintis ('On the Ramparts'), Ambroise Thomas ('The Tyrol') and Dard Janin 'King of Worlds' (still a National test piece in the 1980s), ideally suited the fervent Welsh style of singing.

In their tripartite sonata-like structure most of these choruses were written to the same formula: the opening scene with its hint of trouble ahead, followed by a more meditative movement consisting of the prayer beseeching divine aid, and then the dramatic finale. Welsh masters of the craft like Joseph Parry, Daniel Protheroe and T. Maldwyn Price wrote with an assured awareness of the strengths and foibles of the amateur choirs available to perform their works, and in their vocal settings, as Gareth H. Lewis notes, 'knew exactly which vowel sounds fell most easily into each part of the voice' (*Welsh Music*, Winter, 1976/77, pp. 61–2). They were all influenced by the Gallic dramatic style, with a nod also to the German *Männerchöre*, whose choruses Joseph Parry ('Pencerdd America', after all) had heard German immigrants sing in the USA and whose fondness for music of a militaristic kind was matched by a sensitivity in execution that other choirs were not always so adept at imitating. It is worth reflecting therefore that the roots of the Welsh male choral repertoire which by 1900 was enthralling audiences from Hengoed to Holyhead, and soon would from New Tredegar to New Jersey and New Zealand, had been watered and nourished in Prussia and Paris, for as we have seen the glee tradition which tempered its bellicosity in England hardly existed in Wales.

For popularity and excitement combined, nothing could match Laurent de Rillé's choral epic 'Martyrs of the Arena', whose rising diminished chords announce the bloody saga of the dying Christians as they submit to Great Caesar, Lord of Life and Death. Such was its appeal that de Rillé was invited to Cardiff to adjudicate at an International Male Choir competition at the 2,500-seater Park Hall (now Thistle Hotel) in Cardiff on Boxing Day 1903. The test pieces set for the 13 competing choirs – one from England – were two compositions wholly representative of the French Ophéoniste repertoire, 'King of Worlds' by Dard Janin, principal of the St. Etienne Conservatoire, and de Rillé's own specially commissioned 'Song of the Crusaders', a piece designed both to create interest and give trouble ('the diminished fifth in bar eight is … to be dealt with cautiously' warned the *Western Mail*, 24 Dec. 1903)

M. de Rillé and his wife, 'a vivacious and fascinating lady,' were the guests of the mayor of Cardiff at Christmas, in preparation for the Boxing Day Festival. Disappointingly the verdict went to the sole English entrant, Manchester Orpheus (conducted by Walter Nesbitt), ahead of Cardiff (Roderick Williams) and Mountain Ash (Glyndwr Richards, third), but the French composer-adjudicator mollified his audience by declaring that

Martyrs of the Arena.

J.M. Staniforth's cartoon shows Laurent de Rillé, composer of 'Martyrs of the Arena' and guest adjudicator at the Cardiff International Male Choir competition in Cardiff on Boxing Day 1903, awarding the prize to Manchester Orpheus, with Cardiff second and Mountain Ash third.

(*Western Mail*)

'even the smoke of the Rhondda could not eclipse the beauties of the fine arts' and that 'it was wonderful how men who exhausted themselves in the pursuits of hard employment such as mining regained their strength in the bright intellectual pursuit of music'. He was not in the hall to hear the massed rendition of 'Aberystwyth' in memory of Joseph Parry who had died earlier in the year, but Mme. De Rillé 'was carried away with the prevailing enthusiasm and although knowing neither the words nor the music she joined in the singing' (*Western Mail*, 28 Dec. 1903), a technique famously brought to a fine art by an English Secretary of State for Wales some 90 years later.

A glance at the occupational composition of Nesbitt's Manchester Orpheus Choir indicates that it had more of a lower middle-class profile than that of its resolutely working-class Welsh opponents: within its ranks were seven teachers, three organists, tradesmen and clerks. When

Manchester won at the Llangollen National in 1908, the contrast in social origins was noted by the chief newspaper of its own city:

> The Welsh choirs are virtually self-taught. Often they are isolated and far away from opportunities of gaining musical experience. The native conductors are not musically educated in the strict sense ... And the choirs are democratic in a far stricter sense than are the English choirs. English bricklayers, iron puddlers and quarrymen do not sing and pick one from their number to lead them. When a picked body of educated and generally intellectual singers with a skilled musician to lead them go to compete against choirs having comparatively so limited an outlook, the terms are unequal. The surprise ... was not that the Manchester Orpheus won but that the Welsh choirs did so well against them.
>
> (*Manchester Guardian* quoted in *Y Cerddor*, 1908, p. 113)

Not that Manchester Orpheus always had it all their own way against socially lower class, less educated singers, and Moelwyn, Mountain Ash and Dowlais lowered their colours on more than one occasion in these years. Still, a social disparity existed. It is reflected in the fact that in Tonypandy in 1899 the prizes for the conductors of the first two male choirs included a pair of boots and a pair of trousers. Musically it is reflected in a comparison of the test pieces set for the Blackpool Festival of 1907 and the National Eisteddfod of 1908. At Blackpool the tests for male choirs were all unaccompanied, two by Cornelius and one each by Granville Bantock and Edward MacDowell, whereas for Llangollen the following year they were J. H. Roberts' 'Treasures of the Deep', and David Jenkins' 'Sons of Gwalia,' both with accompaniment. Peter Cornelius acquired sudden prominence in Britain in 1905 when Novello published fifteen of his compositions for male choirs. The National Eisteddfod eventually cottoned on to them and selected two for Colwyn Bay in 1910, when Nesbitt's Manchester Orpheus won again, finding Cornelius more to their taste than the third piece by T. Osborne Roberts which better suited their Welsh opponents.

Neither Manchester nor even Moelwyn took to de Rillé's 'Martyrs' with the same enthusiasm as choristers from south Wales, where it had a magnetic effect on choirs and audiences, however minor the occasion. In

1890 eight choirs competed on it at a Whitsun eisteddfod in Caerphilly, won by Treherbert: in July twelve choirs sang it at Bridgend's more prestigious semi-national, won by Pontycymer with Treorchy second. For nothing could match, let alone diminish, the appeal of the 'Martyrs'. The broadcaster and writer Wynford Vaughan Thomas (1908–87), son of the eminent Welsh musician D. Vaughan Thomas, remembered it as 'a musical folk ritual' of his boyhood when

> at the small eisteddfodau [which] were one of the joys of our lives
> ... we waited breathlessly for the inevitable Battle of the Parties.
> The Party, outside South Wales, conjures up pictures of grim-faced,
> padded-shouldered Iron Curtain massmen ... But in the South Wales
> of my youth, the Party was simply the male voice choir. Like the local
> rugby team, they symbolised our pride of defiance against the rows
> of slate-roofed cottages, the unpaid-for welfare halls and the coal tips
> perched on rain-sodden mountains which were the background of
> our lives. We gave the Party a fierce loyalty and the Party, in return,
> attacked the music as if they were exacting revenge at last for the
> defeat of Owain Glyndŵr. In the battles that formed the male voice
> competitions there were no holds barred ...

This was especially the case when the test piece was the 'Martyrs' – as it was at a small eisteddfod in rural Carmarthenshire during the war years, when such eisteddfodau and the 'Martyrs' were still in their prime, and where the competing choirs warmed up beforehand in the clearings in the surrounding woodland.

> But our local choirs were facing those formidable songsters the
> Penybont Gleemen, and everyone realised that the battle was going
> to turn on that vital phase just before the end 'and when their life-
> blood is pouring'. Should the choir pour its life-blood *mezzo-forte*
> or *double forte*? The adjudicator was known to have strong views on
> this point.

It was to resolve this agonizing problem that the young Thomas and his chum were asked whether they were 'prepared to take a risk for the honour of the choir'.

'Oh, of course, Mr Rees', we hurried to declare.

'Then will you crawl through the undergrowth and find out what Penybont are doing about the *forte* in bar eight after the *Tutti* before the end? Our fate depends upon it!'

Like Red Indians we slipped from the tent. We crawled through the brambles, slid on our stomachs amongst the heather and became spies for the cause of art. We came back dirty but triumphant. 'Mr Rees, it's a *double forte*! Mr Rees raised his eyes to the hills in the mood of Cromwell before Dunbar, 'Pouring out their life-blood *double forte*. The Lord hath delivered them into our hands.' Indeed he had.

(Vaughan Thomas, pp.215-7)

As for the piece itself, De Rillé maintains the tension by skilful alternation of *soli* and *tutti* passages and imitative sections between tenors and basses; second tenors particularly relish their declamatory 'God of the martyr and the slave' as the climax approaches. The purists' view that the paucity of the 'Martyrs' musical ideas is well matched by the doggerel of the improbably named J. C. Stallybrass's words has never commanded any support in Wales where its fruity harmonies and deathless climax have endeared it to generations of choristers. Welsh male choirs, historically well-endowed with short, stockily built tenors with compressed but powerful necks, have been drawn as much by physique as by temperament to the distinctive and stirring Gallic style, and Welsh composers were not slow to follow suit: David Jenkins's 'The War Horse', D. Christmas Williams's 'Charge of the Light Brigade' and 'Destruction of Pompeii', Daniel Protheroe's 'Spartan Heroes', 'Invictus, 'Nidaros', 'Castilla' and 'The Crusaders', Cyril Jenkins's 'Fallen Heroes' and 'The Assyrians Came Down', T. Maldwyn Price's 'Crossing the Plain' and 'Y Pysgotwyr' (The Fishermen) and T. Osborne Roberts's 'The Battle of the Baltic' were all composed in the 30 years before 1914 and were all test pieces at the National Eisteddfod for which, with technical assurance and melodic accessibility, many of them were specifically written. Foregrounding features which Welsh choristers savoured – reiterated words and repeated musical phrases, passages built around ascending scale figures and imitative entries – these pieces cumulatively constituted a relentless catalogue of blood-and-thunder choruses with in-your-face dynamics and hair-raising climaxes, most of them with a tell-tale pause on the penultimate dominant chord, a sure signal for the premature rapturous applause which composers like Parry, Protheroe and Maldwyn Price expertly milked. 'Death or glory' items of this kind raised concert and eisteddfod audiences to a pitch of barely contained excitement, though more detached observers could be less enthusiastic. A favourite de Rillé piece never heard today, 'The Destruction of Gaza', was reckoned by an English critic in the 1920s to be 'the sort you need to hear if you are in search of evidence to disprove the assertion that the singing male is an intelligent animal' (*Birmingham Post*, 10 October, 1927, quoted in Wiltshire, thesis, p.294). The detached professional view that sumptuous sound is almost by definition musically questionable had already been expressed by the *Musical Times* in 1903 with the 'Martyrs' in mind: 'The fondness of Welsh male choirs for realistic and picturesque music of a rather low art-value is remarkable', it observed, 'the hurly-burly of a battle with its moans and gasps of the wounded, the roaring of the lions – if not of the wagging of their tails – earthquakes, hurricanes, catastrophes are the subject matter over which the fervent Welsh choralist loves to vent his tense emotionalism and to tear his passions to threads'. The Welsh male choralist did, and still does.

Unsurprisingly, the detached professional view cut little ice among Welsh choristers, least of all when they were attacking a meaty chorus like Daniel Protheroe's rousing setting of H.W. Longfellow's 'The Nun of Nidaros'. Known in all Welsh male voice circles as simply 'Nidaros', the medieval name for Trondheim in Norway, composed in 1902 and rarely correctly pronounced 'Nidarósh', it featured, with its magnificent climax 'The dawn is not distant, nor is the night starless,' as a test piece at the Swansea National in 1907. Ten choirs turned up and if the 12 original entrants had appeared and all also sung the second test piece, the competition would have lasted six hours. It was won by the coal and tinplate workers of Resolven, an exceptionally musical village in the vale of Neath, who secured a victory that was the embodiment of what Dai Smith has aptly described as 'the working-class triumph that was South Wales at its collective peak and moral best' (Smith, 2010, p.x).

As happened to organised sport, the religious revival of 1904–5 caused only a minor irregularity in the choirs' regular heartbeat. Some clubs temporarily disbanded as crowds fell away and fixtures were cancelled,

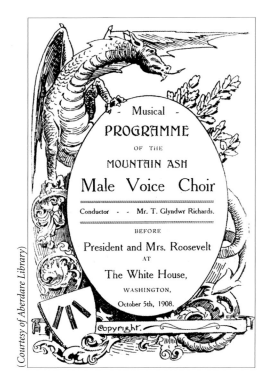

but the visit to Wales of the hitherto invincible New Zealand All Blacks was still in late 1905 awaited with choking anticipation. Gloomy forecasts that the Revival would adversely affect the Eisteddfod were not entirely proven unfounded. Seven choirs competed at the Mountain Ash National in 1905 to see Resolven and Rhymney share the prize, but it was generally held to be a lack-lustre contest in a festival that lacked the customary 'hwyl', one of the flattest in memory. The Revival *did* make itself felt, as with club rugby, at the local level where it was reported that 'scores, if not hundreds' of small eisteddfodau were postponed across the country as chapel schoolrooms and halls where choirs practised were occupied throughout the week by revivalist meetings. In 1905 the *Musical Herald* reported that only four Welsh choirs turned up at the customarily well-attended London Welsh eisteddfod in the Royal Albert Hall in February, many others having intended competing, 'but the Revival in Wales prevented proper rehearsal'. The number of sol-fa certificates issued in Wales, another reliable indicator of musical activity, sharply declined in 1905. But the Revival's social impact proved short-lived, just as its preference for what were seen, by some, as meretricious hymn tunes ensured that its musical influence would be no more than superficial. All the same, Ebenezer Mission Choir, reputedly formed from converts made of those taken in from the streets of Swansea in 1905, won out of 18 choirs in a gruelling contest at the Abergavenny National in 1913.

In north Wales, with some notable exceptions like Dowlais' victory in 1900, the first four decades of the 20th century, competitively speaking, saw English choirs in the driving seat. Outside the competition arena they sang a repertoire that would have been unrecognizable to a contemporary

Welsh chorister. From the West Country to the West Riding, a survey of concert programmes suggests that few pieces would have been familiar in Wales outside evergreens like Hiles's 'Hushed in Death', Sullivan's 'The Long Day Closes', and Richard Genée's 'Italian Salad', though it is also true that in Cornwall Protheroe's 'Crusaders' was as popular as 'Comrades' and 'Martyrs'. Elsewhere in England, Palestrina motets and new works by Elgar, Bantock and Delius were being taken up for festival competitions at which the progressive Harry Evans frequently adjudicated.

By the end of the decade Elgar had joined Cornelius in the National Eisteddfod schedule. As tough tests went, none was tougher for amateur working-class choirs than Elgar's setting of Bret Harte's poem 'The Reveille,' a challenge posed to eight male choirs of between 75 and 100 voices, an indication of choir size inflation, in London in 1909, and successfully executed by Dowlais under Harry Evans' successor W.J. Watkins. Elgar, with his striking range of harmonic colour, subtle changes of tempo, quasi-orchestral detail to interpretative markings on individual parts and carefully chosen words, saw vocal writing as an aspect of his symphonic output and made stern demands of amateur choristers. In 'The Reveille' (1907) he dispatches the basses to bottom B flat, and requires the tenors in 'Feasting I Watch' (1903) to start on top A.

The prolific Celtophile Granville Bantock, stylistically influenced by the late German Romantics, who succeeded Elgar as professor of music at Birmingham in 1908, was another whose unaccompanied part-songs called for textured singing of a symphonic kind, and the Rhondda émigré Llew Bowen's Swansea and District Choir proved equal to it at Wrexham in 1912 when Bantock adjudicated performances of his own 'Glories of our Blood and State'. His 'Ballade' was the test at Barry in 1920, and his setting of Robert Browning's 'Paracelsus' in 1955 and 1964. Welsh choristers preferred the noisier Bantock to Elgar.

Another newcomer in the Eisteddfod's lists was the German Friedrich Hegar (1840–1927) whose thickly-woven 'Phantom Host' and 'Walpurga', first published in the UK in 1909, were similar in style to de Rillé's and therefore commended themselves to Welsh choirs, though Hegar has more harmonic flair than the Frenchman. The other test piece, with 'Walpurga', at Carmarthen in 1911 was by David Jenkins (1848–1915), who often used his joint editorship with David Emlyn Evans of the *Cerddor* to complain that the test pieces for male voice choirs were too warlike and militaristic. A more disciplined style, he felt, would be encouraged if they sang about 'y wawr' (dawn), 'y nos' (night), 'y sêr' (the stars), 'heddwch' (peace), 'cwsg' (sleep) and 'blodau' (flowers), all hoary glee subjects. Jenkins himself was the composer of 'Men of Philistia', 'The War Horse', and 'Sons of Gwalia'!

Other newcomers could be heard off-stage. 'The Song of the Jolly Roger' by the splendidly named C.F. Chudleigh Candish was first published in 1911, Wilfred Shaw's 'Evening Pastorale' three years later, and both became immediately popular for the rest of the century – generally as concert rather than competition pieces – as did the German Richard Genée's 'Italienisch Salat', a musical jest in the form of the finale to an Italian opera demanding a sense of fun and the articulation of musical terms like *pizzicato*, *sostenuto* and *sforzando*. An earlier and far superior German work, Schubert's 'Song of the Spirits over the Waters', first published in England in 1905, provided with its unaccompanied eight parts a far sterner challenge. Its chromaticism made it more difficult to translate into sol-fa than Cornelius or Hegar whose harmonic shifts seemed cleaner, and this, added to its inherent difficulty, militated against its overnight acceptance in Wales. It was performed in concert in 1914, as was Brahms' 'Alto Rhapsody' for soloist and male choir, by Llew Bowen's enterprising Swansea and District choir, who had come second to Nesbitt's Manchester Orpheus in 1910, and captured the first of what would be several subsequent National firsts at Wrexham two years later.

If the emergence of a choir in the village of Dunvant, to the west of Swansea, drawing its members from two collieries that at the turn of the century employed 770 men (from which the original Dunvant Ebenezer Excelsior Male Voice Choir was founded in 1895 under T.C. Richards, father of Ceri Richards, the artist, who in the early 1920s accompanied them) was typical, then the result at Carmarthen in 1911 was a further classic but unexpected example of the link between choir, community, and determining economic context. In the late 19th century a mini-industrial revolution turned the picturesque vale of the River Teifi in Cardiganshire into a significant centre of woollen manufacture. In 1895 the railway whose expansion was so crucial in rolling out an eisteddfod network across Wales reached Newcastle Emlyn, bringing coal for the fulling mills in and taking woollens and flannels out, chiefly to meet the demands of the insatiable south Wales market. These demands brought startling technological and social change to the rural hamlets of Drefach Felindre, Henllan and Llandysul. Mills and factories employing up to a 100 people at a time sprang up, power-driven equipment was installed, and handloom weavers were converted into factory operatives. By the turn of the century the Teifi valley had the appearance and features of an industrial community with a billiard hall, football and cricket teams, thriving chapels, bands and choirs (Jenkins, pp.5–6). It could have been Rhymney or Rhosllannerchrugog, Blaina or Blaenau Ffestiniog. It could have been Bargoed. It *was* Bargoed: Bargoed Teifi, Cardiganshire.

In the pre-1914 decade the Bargoed Teifi male choir moved confidently up the competitive ladder from the rungs of local and semi-national level to pose a challenge to choirs from the more established industrial areas of the country. At the Llangollen National in 1908 they came hard on the heels of Manchester Orpheus, sharing second prize with Moelwyn. In 1911, at Carmarthen, the main competition for male choirs of up to 80 voices required, under the critical eyes of Drs Walford Davies, Daniel Protheroe, David Vaughan Thomas and their fellow composers Samuel Coleridge Taylor and David Emlyn Evans, the execution of pieces by Hegar and David Jenkins. Conducted by Daniel Jenkins of Henllan, Llandysul, the Bangor Teifi choir beat nine other choirs, were awarded a full one hundred marks on the Hegar, and snatched the winning prize from under the noses of seasoned veterans from Glamorgan. With Newcastle Emlyn's mixed choir and Cardigan ladies winning their respective sections too, Bargoed sealed a triple choral triumph for the Teifi valley, one made possible by its sudden industrial spasm among the gentle fields that joined Carmarthenshire and Ceredigion.

The male voice tradition survives and still thrives a hundred years later because it draws upon the accumulated capital of a process of cultural production that was moulded by, and in turn contributed to, the shaping of a new society between 1850 and 1914. It had in the space of a few decades shown a capacity to provide hundreds of thousands of the working people of Wales, and thousands again beyond its shores, with a satisfying and enriching social experience. That capacity would be severely tested in the next 30 years.

Chapter 5

'Brethren, Be Strong': 1914–1930

The outbreak of war postponed the National Eisteddfod scheduled for Bangor in 1914 until the following year, when the inescapable military context virtually ensured that the male voice choir winners would be the Royal Welsh Fusiliers (16th Battalion). As the war unfolded some choirs disappeared – lost to the historian is any knowledge of a myriad choirs that have gone unrecorded and left no substantive evidence of their existence a hundred year ago – but more choirs survived to give concerts for relief funds and entertain wounded soldiers; in Monmouthshire a choir like Blaenavon, founded in 1910, made many visits to St Woolos Hospital in Newport. Abroad, this by now familiar symbol of Welsh identity found expression wherever there were concentrations of Welshmen in the armed forces, particularly in 'Pals' battalions of men from the same locality. For some there were opportunities to be seized; the later famed conductor of the Morriston Orpheus choir, Ivor Sims, gained vital choral experience with the Glamorganshire Yeomanry in Greece. The 53rd Division Welsh Fusiliers' 110-strong Welsh male voice choir in Egypt and Palestine was conducted by Second Lieut. W. Bradwen Jones (1892–1970), later a well-known adjudicator and composer. Côr Meibion Cymraeg Alexandria, one of several Welsh choirs formed in Egypt during the war, began life on a troop ship in 1916 and was made up of men posted to Egypt as replacements for casualties suffered by the 53rd. Forty strong, they sang in Cairo and in military hospitals along the Nile, their soloists including Privates Parry from Penygroes, Elias from Pwllheli, and Jones (A.) from Pontypridd. A matching choir was formed by men of the Welch Regiment conducted by Lieut. the Revd. W. Davies, a nonconformist minister from Aberfan.

'The Welshmen', reported the *Manchester Guardian* from a training camp in the south of England, 'bring with them into their lonely exile a certain homely warmth and clannishness which you do not find in [other] communities. To feel how the Welsh bring their own atmosphere with them into an alien land you must be there as I was, when the weary route-marchers swing back to camp in the twilight singing "Sosban Fach".' The writer Llewelyn Wyn Griffith (1890–1977), an officer in the 15th R.W.F., recorded a moment when a company of the Welsh Guards, waiting to go up to the trenches on relief, started singing in harmony. The Brigadier-General wanted to know, 'Why do they always sing those mournful hymns? Most depressing – bad for morale. Why can't they sing something colourful like other battalions?' Griffith tried to explain to him that what they were singing was what they sang in their chapels and choirs 'in the world to which they belong. They are back at home, in their villages. But he does not understand. Nor can he with his background. I do not think I "understand" it myself … While they sang they, and I, were in another country' (Hughes, 1990, pp.38-39).

Naturally there were plenty of soldiers who knew concert pieces like 'Comrades in Arms' as well as hymns. Dudley Ward, the historian of the Welsh Guards, tells us that the 'really effective singing' came not from the choir standing in a body on the concert platform but from the heart of the battalion going into battle or after the fight. Their rendition of Daniel Protheroe's 'O mor bêr yn y man' ('In the sweet bye and bye, we shall meet on the beautiful shore') after the bloody engagement at Gouzeaucourt when the shattered battalion withdrew to a wood behind the village, 'brought a hush over the camp. The singers were hidden amongst the trees in the moonlight and the air was frosty and still. This was not a concert but a song of hope and faith. There were many similar dramatic moments.' (Ward, 1920, pp.392–96)

Eisteddfod contests paled in these circumstances. In any case there were no choral competitions in the 1916 or 1917 National Eisteddfod but it was noticeable that the war years seemed to have further sharpened civilian appetites to sing; there were more small-sized choirs in Glamorganshire than ever, with weekly concerts and eisteddfodau in the populous industrial areas exceptionally well-supported by choirs and audiences, often for war charities. The coming of peace in 1918 signalled an initial burst of industrial prosperity that was reflected in booming eisteddfodau local and nationally which perhaps masked the degree of uncertainty that existed within the social and economic structure, of Wales especially. Immediately post-war an eisteddfodic frenzy, reflected in a calendar of almost weekly concerts by the Rhondda's formidable roll-call of choirs, gripped the entire valley which had remained industrially active throughout the coal-hungry war years and now testified to a reviving communal and musical life.

Both the continuity and the vigour were embodied by the Williamstown choir, founded by the 29-year-old Ted Lewis during the Cambrian Combine Collieries strike of 1910–11. Having shown their mettle in the National Eisteddfod at Abergavenny in 1913 where they had come third, Williamstown had stayed together to develop an *esprit de corps* that won first prize at the Neath National in 1918 out of 14 entrants, five of them from the Rhondda alone. In keeping with the sombre times, the test piece was D. Vaughan Thomas's defiant 'Here's to Admiral Death'. Even more in keeping, the second prize went to the 60-strong choir of the Welsh Guards who had been active throughout the war raising money for prisoners of war and other funds, with 'Y Delyn Aur', 'Comrades' and 'Martyrs' particular favourites in their repertoire. They were good enough to win on 'Admiral Death' at the Maesteg semi-national in 1918, and were given an overwhelming reception at Neath where the composer himself was one of an imposing five-man panel of adjudicators, alongside Granville Bantock, E.T. Davies, Dr David Evans and Dr Caradog Roberts.

David Vaughan Thomas (1873–1934) was a gifted musician and mathematician whose elevation to the professorship of music at Aberystwyth, that many thought should rightly have been his, never happened, courtesy of an influential cabal consisting of Thomas Jones of Rhymney, the Davies sisters of Gregynog who endowed the chair, and the Prime Minister David Lloyd George, all of whom were determined to appoint Henry Walford Davies. Vaughan Thomas' 'Y Gariad Gollwyd' (The Lost Love) was the test piece along with Daniel Protheroe's setting of W.E.Henley's 'Invictus' (1915) at Corwen in 1919, where 18 choirs competed in an atmosphere described by the *Musical Times* as 'almost terrifying'.

Williamstown on this occasion came third behind Tredegar Orpheus who could claim to be the premier Welsh choir that year. But they in turn were beaten by Lawson Berry's Nelson Arion choir from the Lancashire cotton mills, formed in 1887 and therefore in age and background not dissimilar to many Welsh choirs. But there the similarity stopped. The smallest in size – just over 60, when most of their opponents numbered over a hundred – they were commended for their 'cultured tone' and 'fine artistry' that carried the adjudicators 'far beyond the realm of pen and ink'; even their performance of 'Invictus' which should have better suited the impassioned Welsh style, was 'a perfect study.' This result sounded the tocsin for the next decade when English choirs would dominate the choral competitions whenever the Eisteddfod was held in north Wales.

Their reluctance to compete in south Wales was regretted but understandable, since even for the Corwen event the Nelson choir had left home in a fleet of charabancs at five in the morning (though, of course, so did choirs from south Wales heading north). English choirs won on every occasion when the Eisteddfod visited north Wales in the 1920s, and

Williamstown (Rhondda), founded during the bitter Cambrian Collieries dispute 1910-11, winners out of 14 choirs at Neath in 1918 and out of 12 at Barry in 1920.

(Courtesy of Richard Burton Archives, Swansea University)

another twice in the 30s. At Holyhead in 1927 Alfred Higson's Manchester CWS choir and Scunthorpe took the first two places, making a better fist than their sole Welsh rival Caernarfon (there were only three entrants) of what was an invitation to a morris dance by the Elizabethan composer Thomas Morley (not the Welsh style), Bantock's 'Warsong of the Saracens' (which was), and J. H. Roberts' 'Treasures of The Deep' ('Trysorau'r Dyfnder'), dismissed by the *Musical Opinion* as 'a typical specimen of the platitudinous stuff which still finds its way in to the Eisteddfod lists'.

If such criticism rankled, at least there was comfort in the fact that the traditional bastions had survived the pummelling of the Great War. The choral crucible of Rhymney sent four choirs to compete in different categories at Barry in 1920, mixed, children, ladies and male voice. In the men's competition, listened to by an audience of between eighteen and twenty thousand, they came fifth out of 12, behind the winners Williamstown, ahead of Dowlais Penywern, Tredegar and Abertillery. E. T. Davies' 'Y Gwyntoedd' ('The Winds'), making its first appearance as a test piece, whose difficult enharmonic modulations can put choirs through a searching examination of their technical and musical abilities, would feature at regular intervals for the rest of the century. Accompanying it – though actually unaccompanied; both pieces were – was Bantock's equally testing 'Ballade', and Ralph Vaughan Williams, adjudicating, said he was 'thunderstruck and even terrified by the ease with which the choirs overcame its difficulties'.

The 1920s and 30s have been described by historians of the male voice choir in England, like Christopher Wiltshire (1993) and Susan Skinner (2014), as 'the golden age' of the male voice choir in England; in Cornwall, for example, many new choirs were established, there was significant expansion in choir membership, and competitive festivals flourished (Skinner, pp.276–7). In Wales, particularly in the southern coalfield, the picture was rather different. The economist Dudley Baines has defined 'the most important single characteristic of a depressed area' as '[being] dependent on a narrow range of industries' (Baines, p.175). No range was narrower, and no communities more dependent on it than coal, iron and steel-making south Wales: when in 1927 all work ceased at the Cwmbrân colliery, men left the district in droves and membership of the Pontnewydd choir founded in 1904 was halved. The Dowlais choir that won in London in 1909 had been 'almost entirely composed of working men who daily follow their employment at the Dowlais and Steel Iron works' (*Western Mail*, 19 June, 1909). The economic crash of the late 1920s and collapse of its heavy industries would now be keenly felt by choirs from historic industrial heartlands like Dowlais, whose choir was forced to disband in 1932 after the closure of the works in 1930, resulting in an unemployment figure of 73% by 1934. Two decades of success under Alaw Morlais (Evan Thomas 1878–1948) thus abruptly terminated, their glory days would be resumed in the 1970s under D.T. Davies (1900–83), accompanist to the Dowlais choir in the 1920s. A similar fate might have been expected to befall Tredegar whose Orpheus had enjoyed an unbroken history since 1909. There had of course been earlier formations in this pioneer industrial town, but contrary to all odds and expectations Tredegar Orpheus enjoyed success and growth in the inter-war period too. They absorbed a local rival choir and survived a near collapse in the early 30s to maintain a membership of over a 100. The Tredegar Coal and Iron Company, which employed most of those still in work, helpfully altered its shift patterns to accommodate Saturday travel to eisteddfod commitments and the hope of prize-money. That said, Tredegar's experience was the exception rather than the rule. The Blaenavon choir, more typically, played the role of a welfare organisation as somehow in the 1920s it still found funds to alleviate the condition of its more distressed members.

While English choirs swept the board in the alternating years when the Eisteddfod was in north Wales, taking the first three places at Mold in 1923, the major struggles whose high-voltage content pulled in tens of thousands of eager listeners occurred in south Wales, none more so than for the six-hour contest that took place in 1922. At Ammanford that year the chief male voice competition for choirs of between 60 and 100 voices drew, originally, 13 entries, though only eight appeared and were heard by a crowd of 30,000 inside and outside the Pavilion. Among those inside were the adjudicators Dr Henry Coward, Dr T. Hopkin Evans, E.T. Davies, and Ammanford's own *enfant terrible* Cyril Jenkins, who had drawn down hot coals of wrath on his head for attacking the reputation of 'y doctor mawr' (the great doctor) Joseph Parry: 'at its very best', he wrote, 'Parry's music is only second rate; at its worst it is beneath contempt'. Compositionally speaking the three test pieces brought all these threads together, for two of them were adjudicated by those who had written them, Jenkins' 'Sea Fever' and E.T. Davies' 'Y Deryn Pur'. On the day the latter had to be dropped owing to the length of the competition, for the third piece was Parry's well-muscled 'Iesu o Nazareth', first heard at the Cardiff National in 1899 and dismissed by the critic of the *Musical Times* as 'this feeble mixture of Mendelssohn and Taff water, sugary in its sentiment and flippant in its exultation'. To Cyril Jenkins' ally Gerald Cumberland, Parry's music was saccharine 'and often childish … no one save Welshmen would listen to it ['Iesu o Nazareth'] for more than a minute'. Welsh audiences were happy to listen to it for longer than that, and Welsh choristers, with their fondness for full-bodied, large-scale choruses with strong tenor lines, loved it.

The closeness of the final marks, carefully deliberate rather than arbitrarily decided on, saw the first four places awarded to Dowlais Penywern (183), Swansea (182), Barclays Bank, London (182) and Rhymney (180). It might have been some comfort to Rhymney that they scored best of all (96 marks) on the Parry. Dowlais people, who had turned out in their thousands to welcome their choir home at 12.30 in the morning with flags, bunting and detonators from the works, were particularly appreciative of the sporting gesture of the fourth-placed Rhymney choristers in cheering the victors as they passed through Dowlais on their way home, fully aware that they shared the same social and economic circumstances.

They shared similar admission policies too, for by this time entry to Dowlais, Rhymney and other leading choirs depended on the outcome of an audition in front of choir officials for sight-reading and voice tests, plus a character reference. It is embedded in Pendyrus folkore that some aspiring choristers, on being informed of this daunting process on arrival for the audition, chose to escape via a window rather than undergo it. Comment could be biting. An applicant to the Dunvant choir who claimed to have had his voice trained was told it appeared to have escaped and gone back to the wild. The chairman of a north Wales choir advised one hopeful warbler that it was 'just as easy to sing in tune as out of tune – try it sometime.' The more established and self-aware a choir was, the more formal its admission procedures; as late as 1980 their newly-appointed musical director Alwyn Humphreys felt obliged to tell the battery of Morriston Orpheus officials who lengthily interviewed every applicant with a rigour worthy of the Foreign Office that he was surprised anyone ever wanted to join the choir, so intimidating were its entrance protocols (Humphreys, pp.124-5).

Decisions could be difficult to make, and trying to find even the hair's breadth difference that separated the choirs in 1922 proved to be beyond the judges two years later at Pontypool, where the competition was now for choirs of 70 to 120 voices, and the first prize of a hundred pounds along with the coveted status of being a 'National Winner' was shared by Rhymney and Dowlais. The inclusion in 1924 and 1925 of pieces by Wales's new National Director of Music Henry Walford Davies, who now occupied the Aberystwyth chair, reflected his standing in the musical life of the nation even if it was still viewed contentiously in some quarters. By now too there were generally three test pieces, including at least one by a contemporary Welsh composer, and another unaccompanied. At Swansea in 1926 both elements were combined in 'Blow, blow, thou winter wind' ('Chwyth, chwyth aeafol wynt') by John Owen Jones, who according to A.J. Sheldon of the *Musical Opinion*, 'not content with assigning to the first line a melodic phrase one of whose closest parallels is to be found in a

Cwmbach Male Choir, seen here in 1925, fought a transatlantic battle for honours at the Treorchy National Eisteddfod in 1928. A choir born of industrial unrest, they were formed during the miners' lockout of 1921.   (*Courtesy of Cwmbach Male Choir*)

love song of Offenbach's ... built on it what was apparently intended to be a musical representation of a gale'. 'An absurd setting' it might have been to this English cynic, but the Eisteddfod's music committee was unmoved and 'Chwyth, chwyth' retained its status as a test piece long after World War II.

The seven month miners' lockout of 1926 caused six choirs to scratch, leaving a gap for the Cleveland Orpheus Choir from Ohio to swagger in. At first glance this might appear to be no more than an exotic intrusion into the incestuous rivalries of Welsh choirs. A second glance prompts the realisation that this was merely a reversal of an established transatlantic traffic, now symbolised by regular visits from the leaders of musical life among the Welsh communities in North America, spearheaded by Dr Daniel Protheroe (1866–1934) who had migrated from Ystradgynlais in 1886, had formed the 80-strong Côr Meibion Cymry Chicago in 1926, and was a frequent visitor and adjudicator at the National Eisteddfod. Nor was the choral scene among Welsh exiles entirely a closed book to those at home, for as we have seen Welsh choirs had been visiting the USA on a fairly regular basis since the late 1880s.

It might also be thought that the onset of the Depression would have militated against transatlantic jaunts in the inter-war period, but several small-scale groups of singers continued to find their way West. The best-known were the Welsh Imperial Singers assembled in 1926 by Trawsfynydd-born, but since 1908 U.S. resident, R. Festin Williams (1870–1944). Between 1929 and 1939 this group of 17 singers, drawn mostly from north Wales but with a sprinkling of south Walians to leaven the dough, dressed in red swallow-tailed jackets, brocaded waistcoats, frilly shirts and light grey drainpipe trousers, made five tours of the USA, singing in most of the northern states, and performing over fifty concerts in Chicago alone, where their resonant but disciplined singing won them many admirers. Other vocal globe-travellers included the Royal Welsh Choir (the result of William Thomas' culling of his original Treorchy choristers), who visited Australia in 1922 and South Africa in 1938, and 'Professor' Tom Morgan's Rhondda Welsh Male Voice Glee Party, a different entity, who visited the USA and Canada in the early 1920s. At home, Treorchy's own male voice choir struggled to keep alive, stumbling from conductor to conductor as its numbers fluctuated. This was not unrelated to the fact that the unemployment figure for the Rhondda in 1934 stood at 60.8%; the choir's own figure was 85%.

The Cleveland Orpheus' feat in 1926 was emulated in the second competition for choirs between 60 and a 100 in number at the Treorchy National two years later by the Anthracite Male Chorus of Scranton, Pennsylvania, conducted by Kidwelly-born Dr Luther Bassett and representing the single largest concentration of Welsh exiles anywhere in the USA. There were 20 male choirs at Treorchy, ten of them in the chief competition for choirs above a 100 voices, won by Llew Bowen's Swansea who had come bottom of the poll two years earlier and where two of Wales's later most famous conductors made their first appearance, Ivor E. Sims conducting Morriston United (later *dis*united by the breakaway Orpheus), and the Rhondda Fach's Pendyrus, making their first National appearance under 34-year old Arthur Duggan. The main test piece in the 'chief' was Schubert's eight-part unaccompanied 'Song of the Spirits over the Waters,' while choirs in the second competition were required to sing two somewhat insipid part-songs by Protheroe and Dan Jones. Scranton were 62 on stage, their dapper white check trousers and blue serge jackets a marked contrast to the dowdy Sunday suits, black bows and Lloyd-George style collars of the Welsh choirs. This was Depression Wales, and most of the 3,000 miners employed at the local Parc and Dare and Abergorki pits chose to listen to the competition from the hillside above rather than pay the price of admission. The verdict in Scranton's favour was followed by 'promiscuous kissing by the winning choir of the conductor, each other, and any young girls in sight', to the distaste of staider eisteddfodwyr. In second place behind Scranton were Cwmbach, founded during the miners' lockout of 1921, by which time the Cynon Valley, thanks to the discovery of the four-foot seam, had seen its population increase nine times over to 54,000. In the choir's own telling, some of the onlookers at a cricket match had lost interest in the play and joined with members of the recently disbanded Cwmbach Excelsior Glee Party in singing hymns and part-songs, and the Cwmbach Male Choir was born.

We should bear in mind that not all parts of Wales endured unremitting distress in the inter-war period. While the closure of the steel works in Brymbo caused considerable hardship and brought local choirs to their knees, others parts of north-east Wales benefited from new developments like the Courtaulds rayon factory in Flintshire. Among the beneficiaries of this localised economic recovery were Trelawnyd, some five miles inland from Rhyl and Prestatyn, future National winners who were founded in 1933, while other notable choirs dating from the early 1930s include Llangwm and C.H. Leonard's Dyffryn Nantlle. After hearing seven choirs from the Penrhyn quarries competing at an eisteddfod in 1934, the adjudicator, Dr Caradog Roberts, urged them to combine into one choir. This they promptly did and before the year was out the historic Penrhyn choir of Bethesda was revived.

In south Wales, for the most part, it was a different story.

Chapter 6

'Nor is the night starless': 1930–39

From the late 1920s the Depression tightened its grip. In 1929, the year the Rhymney choir disbanded with Dowlais facing similar closure, the *Merthyr Express* tried to keep spirits up. 'The lack of enthusiasm in our choral societies,' it opined, 'lies in the fact the members have not, for some time, had any cause to sing. But with the return of prosperity they will lift up their voices joyfully and thankfully.' Or so it was hoped. 'Prosperity? What prosperity?' its readers might have asked. There were 13,000 unemployed in Merthyr and Dowlais in 1934, 60% of the insured population (74% in Dowlais) having been out of work for the last ten years. The industrial crisis of the Depression, in Gwyn A. Williams' dramatic comparison as devastating in Wales in the 1930s as the Famine had been to Ireland in the 1840s, caused immense social dislocation and bore heavily on the collective institutions of the coalfield from chapels and trade unions to football clubs and choirs. What is surprising is their resilience and determination to keep going.

Pendyrus, founded in 1924, like the Morlais choir formed in the adjacent village of Ferndale in 1928, was based in the Rhondda Fach, in the mining village of Tylorstown just as the valley was about to enter the bleakest period in its history. Within a few years Pendyrus had a membership of 160, making it one of the largest in Wales, but in the upper Rhondda Fach in 1934 63.7% of the workforce was registered as unemployed, and by the end of the decade 75% of Pendyrus' membership, mostly coal miners, were out of work. Their conductor Arthur Duggan, 'the young man from the 'Cop' – he was a baker – would muster some 70 to 80 choristers in the morning, deliver his bread, call in the band room for rehearsal, then resume his morning round. Test pieces like 'The Arsenal at Springfield,' with orchestral accompaniment (a death-defying challenge to a sol-faist), 'Sons of the Desert' and ' The Charge of the Light Brigade' (1911) – known in the Duggan era as simply 'The Charge' – could well have been written with Pendyrus' robust style in mind.

Having made their National debut at Treorchy in 1928, Pendyrus under Duggan's leadership (1924–60) would prove themselves fiercely competitive at almost every National throughout the 30s, north or south, a ferocity derived from the idle pits and social dereliction they knew at first hand. You could not fail to 'hear the people sing, singing the song of angry men,' and Pendyrus had a lot to be angry about; they sang with a fervour and intensity that staggered both audiences and adjudicators. Typical were the revealing comments, after the five-hour competition for choirs of 80 to 120 voices at Neath in 1934, of Dr Hopkin Evans, adjudicator and composer of one of the test pieces, 'Sons of the Desert' – the others were 'Apollo and the Seaman' (Josef Holbrooke) and 'Crossing the Bar' (Caradog Roberts) – that Pendyrus, in coming second, were 'generous where great sonority was required … [with] a strong tendency to fierceness … when nothing more than fine luminous tone was required … the volume of tone seemed out of proportion to the inherent nature of the music and words. There was a certain lack of perspective. Contrasts were too violent and the choir seemed to be spending themselves in the *fortes* … While the ending of the first piece was very beautiful and ravishing in its sweetness, in the third piece they worked up a terrific climax …'

Clearly, the role of conductor was vital: the interpretation was his, and the fate of his choir was bound up with him. Ever greater demands were placed on the conductor in the inter-war period by pieces that were technically more advanced, more challenging, and demanding a higher level of musicianship than hitherto. Arthur Duggan confronted the adjudicators' criticisms and addressed them sufficiently to win at Caernarfon in 1935 on Mussorgsky's 'Rise Red Sun', a fitting test piece for a choir with a core contingent from the mining village of Maerdy whose much publicised communist sympathies in the 1920s had led to its being known as 'Little Moscow'. Such was the excitement that one of the choir's eight homeward-bound buses crashed in Tremadog in the early hours of

Sunday, seriously injuring some travelling supporters. When Pendyrus next won, at Rhyl in 1953, the test piece, 'Meibion yr Anial' ('Sons of the Desert') was sung with particular feeling by those choristers who recalled the misfortune which had occurred 18 years earlier in Tremadog, the birthplace of T.E. Lawrence (of Arabia).

This encapsulates the competitive male voice scene in the inter-war period, and highlights its salient features: the adjudicators' attention to detail, the crucial role of conductors, the fervent, occasionally 'terrifying' atmosphere, the immense crowds of rarely less than 15,000 in the packed pavilion, the high-intensity five-hour competitions, a demand for contrasting pieces to offset against the dogged preference for essentially dramatic test pieces in what was still a slowly expanding repertoire, the determination of competing choirs, in the face of often abject circumstances, to travel at dawn to compete and return overnight, the defiant appearance of choristers in sombre Sunday clothes and tweed suits which had been 'patched and darned bravely in places' (as was noted at Wrexham in 1933) – and through and above it all the sheer electrifying passion of the singing which even the Depression could not quell. The composer Arthur Bliss, in the course of a musical pilgrimage through

PENDYRUS MALE CHOIR, 1928.
Conductor - Mr. Arthur Duggan.

Pendyrus, formed in 1924, made their first National appearance four years later.
(*Courtesy of Pendyrus Male Choir*)

Britain in 1935, dismissed the Welsh as 'choir crazy'. The orchestral conductor Thomas Beecham's view the same year was even less nuanced, comparing the Welsh 'to the Negroes [sic] – simple, uncultured, musically a backwater – but can they sing!' Yes, Sir Thomas, they could. One wonders what conception he can have had of what being in a choir like Pendyrus meant, 75% of its members unemployed miners, when, in the recollection of a founder member, 'an excess of leisure time was thrust upon us [and] a life of idleness brought on by unemployment in the early thirties became a burden … the choir gave a fresh outlook on life, and provided us with a feeling that we counted in the scheme of things. It was a means of keeping alive … the wonderful spirit of comradeship that that was so essential in a world of unemployment and depression.'

Competition still involved personal effort for those who *were* in employment. Many of Llew Bowen's Swansea choir, like Pendyrus Eisteddfod regulars, would work the night shift at their iron and steel works until 6 a.m. on the Saturday, dash home to change, and just catch the 7 a.m. train north. In these challenging circumstances, the big male voice competition by now known as the 'chief', was from 1924 in Pontypool consistently for choirs varying in number from 70 to 120. The grandeur of this competition from then to the end of the 1930s is difficult to appreciate today. Between 1929 and 1932, there were never fewer than ten entrants when the supremacy of the Swansea choirs of Bowen and Sims would be challenged by the salutary intervention, in north Wales, of English rivals from the Potteries and Lancashire.

The changing musical culture which emerged in the 1920s and 30s and drew heavily on American jazz and dance via the radio and the gramophone, might be thought to have presented new opportunities to male choirs in terms of repertoire and new audiences. But the industrial depression in Wales was no time for innovation and enterprise. Survival was the priority; choirs dug in; a familiar repertoire was confirmed, and any new pieces in the competition lists were for the most part by pre-war composers like Bantock and Holbrooke. A dark year like 1932 when unemployment in the Rhondda stood at 52.9% still saw remarkable musical activity across south Wales. While Noddfa Chapel Treorchy pulsed to its choral society's ambitious performances of Bach, Dr Malcolm Sargent was guest conductor at the third Three Valleys Festival in the capacious Mountain Ash Pavilion, erected for the 1905 National Eisteddfod, and which had since echoed to the thudding of leather gloves. In the neighbouring village of Cwmaman where 90% of the male population was on the unemployment register, the local choral society did the Brahms 'Requiem' and Vaughan Williams' 'Towards the Unknown Region', with the composer himself conducting. In the course of a single month (February, 1932) Handel's 'Samson', Rossini's 'Stabat Mater', Mendelssohn's 'Hymn of Praise' and Hubert Parry's 'Job´ were performed in Llanelli.

It seemed right in a year so drenched in music that even as tides of economic misery lapped around those who performed it, the National Eisteddfod should be held in Port Talbot. When the Aberafan Male Choir was formed in October 1966 following the National held there earlier that year, the town already boasted two operatic societies, two choral societies, two male voice choirs and two glee parties (Tucker, p.11). The Afan larynx is a tireless instrument: in 1901 the Port Talbot Male Choir had performed David Jenkins' 'The Enchanted Isle' with orchestral accompaniment 'without a Lord, Lady or MP to cast their patronage over the proceedings', it was proudly noted. The intense musicality of the area meant that in the early 1930s there were, within a three-mile radius, two choral societies, two operatic societies, a ladies choir and three male voice choirs. Two miles up the valley at Cwmafan there was a choral society and another two male voice choirs. It was a kind of salute to this local profusion of musical activity that in 1932 eleven choirs entered the chief male voice competition for choirs of between 80 and 120 voices, with Sims' Morriston United, Duggan's Pendyrus and Ivor Owen's Swansea taking the first three places.

And as always by then, there were enormous crowds to hear them. At Swansea in 1926 those crowds, cheering, restless and expectant, demonstrated that they were informed too. When three of the male choirs came to grief on the third page of 'Blow, blow, thou winter wind', when the second tenors sing a G on the word 'Blow' and are immediately followed on a syncopated A flat by the top tenors, there was a noticeable shudder through large sections of the vast audience which indicated to one critic that 'they were possessed by a sense of "something wrong".' There *was* something wrong. There were parts of Wales where a man with a job was a rarity. At the Fishguard National in 1936 one choir was reckoned to consist entirely of unemployed members, the conductor of another was himself a redundant miner, and some choirs would not have even been there at all but for a fund run by the *Western Mail*. Grants worth seven hundred pounds (including £25 from the Ocean Coal Company) were distributed at Fishguard for bands, orchestras and choirs from officially designated 'special (i.e. distressed) areas.' In 1937 thirty six organisations received sums varying from five to sixteen pounds to enable them to compete at Machynlleth when the fund then closed. Seven of the eight choirs in the chief male voice competition came from industrial Glamorgan and would probably have been unable to travel without this relief.

In south Wales, it was choirs from the Swansea district, Morriston in particular, that enjoyed supremacy in the inter-war years, a domination that survived the next war, and it was not unconnected to the fact that the depression brought about by the pit closures and part-time working that befell the steam-coal industry of the eastern valleys of south Wales was less severely felt in the anthracite coalfield and the tinplate and copper industries further west. The employment figure for Wales, rising from 13.4% in December 1925 to 29% by July 1930, disguised pockets of severity: 59% in Merthyr and 80% in some of the valley townships of Monmouthshire, while the corresponding figure for Swansea stood at little more than 3% in 1923 and 8.3% in 1930. Just as rugby and football clubs collapsed in the valleys north of Cardiff, they thrived further west. It was not a coincidence that Swansea alone of the Welsh clubs beat the All Blacks in 1935, for in this relative prosperity lay the key to the Swansea sound of the inter-war period. The sporting vitality of the area mirrored the innovative literary, artistic and musical activities of the 'Kardomah boys' Dylan Thomas, Vernon Watkins, Alfred Janes and Daniel Jones. Not to be outdone, in August 1932 the Swansea and District Male Voice Choir performed Mendelssohn's 'Antigone' with full orchestra at Salem chapel Landore (Glyndŵr), certainly the first and probably the only performance of this work in Wales.

Llew Bowen had founded the Swansea and District male voice choir in 1905 and led them to victory before and after the war, at Wrexham in 1912, Pontypool (1924) and Treorchy (1928). It was a choir consisting of steelworkers, copper workers, miners, joiners, shopkeepers, solicitors and civil servants: socially and occupationally diverse, all human life was there. In the immediate post-war years their great rivals were Dowlais Penywern, coming second to them in 1922, sharing first prize in 1924, and finally beating them at Treorchy in 1928. The contrasting economic fortunes of west Wales were demonstrated at Llanelli in 1930, when Morriston United and Swansea triumphantly took the first two prizes. In the eastern valleys there was less to be triumphant about.

Swansea were now under Ivor Owen and the United under Sims, though not for long. As we have seen, male choral singing in the Morriston area, five miles north of Swansea, can be traced back to the late 19th century, and glee societies in the locality earlier again. The Morriston male choir, dating from at least 1893, emerged from the Great War as the Gwalia, became successful in the competitive field, and in 1924 changed its name to Morriston United, with its accompanist Ivor Sims becoming its conductor in 1926. The United made their first National appearance that year, and improved sufficiently to share second prize with Dowlais Penywern at Treorchy two years later. The adjudicators' perceived eccentricities consigned Swansea to last out of eleven on their home patch in 1926 only to promote them to first out of ten two years later. With the economic tide having turned against coal and iron further east, the great rivalry was now between Sims' Morriston and Swansea, conducted by Llew Bowen and then by its former accompanist Ivor Owen (1889–1968), brother of

The legendary Welsh scrum half Dickie Owen (fifth from left) came from a musically-gifted family. His brother Ivor led Swansea Male Voice Choir to 'National' success on three occasions before the Second World War, but like Dickie, he too had to take 'all the bumps that came his way'.

the international rugby scrum half and hero of Wales's first Golden Era, R.M. 'Dickie' Owen. Morriston's defeat of Swansea at Llanelli in 1930 was avenged at Bangor the following year. Morriston, Pendyrus and Swansea, in that order, took the first three places out of 11 choirs at Port Talbot in 1932, as they did at Neath in 1934, when their positions were reversed.

Morriston United were now conducted by David Rees, as a result of probably not the first and certainly not last rift in the choir's ranks. Ostensibly it occurred over whether to adopt a popularisation of its programme in order to increase revenue. But what could a more 'popular' programme have meant in the 1930s? A personality clash between Sims and a strong-willed secretary was the real issue. Sims surprisingly lost a vote of confidence 70 to 30 whereupon he resigned but requested his 30 followers to remain. By 1935 their loyalty and patience had worn thin and Morriston Orpheus was born, with around 50 members. The new formation could only manage fourth at Fishguard in 1936, but the following year with both Morriston choirs in the mix, Rhos now flexing their considerable vocal chords, and Pendyrus and Tredegar Orpheus capable of spoiling anybody's party, Machynlleth in 1937 would be the acid test. On three unaccompanied pieces by D. Vaughan Thomas, E. T. Davies and Granville Bantock, Sims' Morriston Orpheus, who that year gave the first performance in Wales of Cherubini's D Minor *Requiem* for male voices, brought off a great triumph, with the United in second place.

Rhos was the only north Wales choir among the eight entrants. With a population of 10,000, the mining village of Rhosllannerchrugog, Denbighshire, situated only eight miles from the English border, was virtually indistinguishable from many similar townships in south Wales whose cultural and social life turned around the Institute, the chapel, the football club, the choir – and in the early 30s an unemployment figure of 70%. It was arguably the most Welsh village in Wales, built on the collieries of Hafod, Bersham and Penycae, and had generated a Nonconformist, industrial, thoroughly Welsh-speaking culture. Since the previous century it had been a nursery of nationally known musicians like the singer and songwriter William Davies of 'O Na Byddai'n Haf o Hyd' and 'Nant y Mynydd' fame, the composer and organ recitalist Caradog Roberts, and the brothers John and Arwel Hughes.

There had been a male voice choir in Rhos since the early 1890s, an offshoot of a well-established competitively successful mixed choir founded in 1863. Led by eminent local musicians like Richard Mills, Wilfrid Jones, G. W. Hughes and Caradog Roberts before the war, there was some discontinuity between 1905 and 1911 until, successively, Dan Roberts, Ben Evans and J. Owen Jones of Penycae came to the rescue, enabling Rhos to take second prize in Fishguard in 1936, and a stunning first in Cardiff in 1938. John Owen Jones (1876–1962) composed the competition favourite 'Blow, blow thou winter wind' and lived long enough to see the young Colin Jones triumph at Llanelli in 1962, beating Treorchy, by then undefeated for ten years, Morriston and Manselton, and 'Chwyth, chwyth' again one of the test pieces. John Hughes of Rhos was an adjudicator on that memorable occasion (though also, and equally non-partisan, was Rhondda-born Mansel Thomas), as Hughes was at Wrexham in 1933 alongside J. Owen Jones himself, John Morgan Lloyd, Sir Hugh Roberton of the famous Glasgow Orpheus, and the ever-present Granville Bantock. Whether by now Bantock had become inured to the Eisteddfod style he poured a cold douche on Welsh ardour by awarding the first two prizes to the Potteries' Hadley and District, and Hebden Briercliffe from Yorkshire, while fellow-adjudicator John Owen Jones, addressing the audience in Welsh, told the Welsh choirs 'not to imitate the English.' Ivor Owen of the Swansea choir ruefully remarked that 'Dickie Owen the Welsh rugby international took all the bumps that came his way. His brother can also take his share' (*Western Mail*, 14 April, 1933).

Rhos's best known gift to Wales and the wider world is their accompanist John Tudor Davies's much-sung 1959 arrangement of Lewis Hartsough's hymn-tune 'Gwahoddiad' ('Mi glywaf dyner lais yn galw arnaf fi'). Until the 1980s Rhos had won more 'firsts' in south Wales than in the north; they did so again in 2012, initiating a hat-trick of victories which hitherto had eluded all choirs of their size, though this feat was less uncommon among smaller choirs like the Cambrian choir of Clydach Vale (Rhondda) in the early 1930s, Skewen's National Oil Refinery choir in the late 1940s, the Silurian Singers of Rhymney ten years later, Godre'r Aran (Llanuwchllyn) and Caernarfon in the 1990s, and Cardigan's Côr Undebol Ar Ôl Tri at the turn of the present century. But Rhos's habit of 'winning south' was first secured by their dramatic victory at Cardiff in 1938 as they beat seasoned champions Morriston United by a single mark, with Pendyrus, imdomitably loyal to the National festival through a decade of dire economic circumstances, way down the list gamely but disconsolately bringing up the rear.

The adjudicators' random roulette did not favour Rhos when it was on their doorstep in the last National before the outbreak of World War II held in Denbigh, which struck many of the dominant chords of the two decades 1919–39. The competition for large choirs was for between 80 and 120 voices, and there was no shortage of these, though only Rhos at that time was in that category among north Wales choirs. Indeed, Pendyrus withdrew as they wanted to stage 150. The competition was won, as it had been in 1919 – thus bringing the inter-war period full circle – by Nelson Arion who compensated for their relatively low number (87) by their restraint and purity of tone; the two bigger Morriston choirs were second and third, while Rhos came fifth but still ahead of Swansea whose long day was closing after more than two decades at the top. The Jacks' formidable musical tradition would reassert itself after the war, courtesy of the large choirs of Manselton, Dunvant, and, rising to a new level of excellence, Morriston Orpheus. The test pieces in 1939 were the still familiar blend of the tempestuous and the tender, Charles Wood's 'Paty O'Toole', Tawe Jones' 'Siege of Kazan' and T. Hopkin Evans' 'Mordaith Cariad' ('Love's Voyage'), a competition favourite down to the 1990s.

Much was made in the 1930 of 'the fighting south' who had found some consolation in music when the crisis their society faced all but deranged its inhabitants. During that decade Brynmawr was one of the worst hit areas, with an unemployed rate constantly above 70%, yet in 1939 the Breconian Choir from that beleaguered town, though numbed by the howling winds of recession and closures, travelled to Denbigh to win the competition for 40–80 voices, their second successive victory after winning at Cardiff the previous year. They had been in existence for five years and were nearly all unemployed miners, including their conductor.

Wales lost 440,000 of its people between 1920 and 1939. The Rhondda lost 50,000, a thousand people left Merthyr every year down to 1937. Little wonder that as choirs folded in Wales many sprang up in the centres of Welsh migration to England: the Midlands, the Thames valley and London. The Oxford Welsh choir was founded in 1928 and the Snowdown Colliery Welfare Choir in Kent founded by immigrant Welsh miners in

1929. In Gwyn Thomas' telling, Rhondda gravestones bore the inscription 'Not dead, gone to Slough.' Revealingly, the 1938 Cardiff National drew five entries for a competition for choirs of the unemployed, and another five for a new one for Welsh male choirs from outside Wales. There were by now plenty of them. It was won by the Hammersmith Welsh Male Voice Choir, founded and conducted by Dan Morgan Jones of Troedyrhiw near Merthyr, who beat Oxford Welsh, Welwyn Garden City, Coventry Welsh Gleemen and Luton Cambrian. These two competitions symbolised two decades of industrial devastation and choral defiance. By the late 1930s employment prospects in the 'special areas' of a distressed south Wales began to improve as the international situation deteriorated, and the two developments were not unrelated; arms and ordnance production became active and provided new jobs. The night, it seemed, was not entirely starless, nor was the dawn distant. But there was another war to be fought first.

Chapter 7

The Dog that Barked – Morriston Orpheus

As the experience of 1914–1918 showed, wartime brings its own peculiar opportunities, and even the Luftwaffe could not diminish the Welsh appetite for song. Singing is not implausibly reckoned to be a way of masking fear, a means of coping with – as we would now say, 'a strategy for managing' – danger, whether the peril is underground (the romantic image of singing miners comes to mind) or above it. In Swansea a group of air raid wardens discussed the possibility of forming a new choir even as the bombs fell. Their ambition was realised in 1946 when the Manselton male voice choir, described as 'a body of tinplate workers, commercial travellers and grocers,' arose from the ashes of the blitz, and its founder-conductor Emrys Jones found local fame with his choir's National wins in 1950 and 1951, and much wider recognition for his settings of 'The Lily of the Valley' and Isaac Watts' 'When I survey the wondrous cross' ('Morte Christe'), both of which continue to enjoy a huge popularity. When Manselton's choristers stood alongside local businessmen and shopkeepers to survey the ruined centre of Swansea in 1946, they must indeed, in the words of Isaac Watts, have counted 'their richest gain' a considerable 'loss'.

Abroad, determined to make their voices heard among the 123,000 servicemen resident in Cairo, a Welsh Society male voice choir and, with the obligatory split, a Cairo Welsh Glee Party, both conducted by Bargoed men, were active and popular. Given the success of north of England choirs in the National Eisteddfod between the wars, it was no great shock that the choral competition at the 1943 Cairo Eisteddfod, convened by the Right

Reverend Llewellyn Gwynne, Bishop of Cairo, and broadcast at home, should have been won by an English group, the Royal Engineers' Singers, conducted by a man from Bradford. It is difficult to decide which was the more bizarre: that 200 uniformed members of the armed forces assembled in the middle of a war should be asked 'A Oes Heddwch?' ('Is it Peace?') accompanied by a few isolated cries of 'Salaam' ('Peace'), that army nurses should have been coerced into converting purloined hospital sheets into a dozen bardic robes with Field Hospital Sister M. Davies Jones as 'meistres y gwisgoedd' (mistress of the robes), or that President Nasser should have sent anniversary greetings to the reunion of the 1943 Cairo eisteddfodwyr at the Llandudno National in 1963 (Wynne Jones, pp. 99-104).

After the many privations of the inter-war period the post-1945 decades witnessed a gradual transformation in Wales socially and economically. It did not happen immediately and many choirs' experience is represented by Blaenavon who were without a conductor and reduced to 16 members by the late 1940s. But that remnant 'fought tooth and nail' to keep the party in existence until the corner was turned with the appointment of Jean Willams in 1954, and the choir regrouped, recruited, began to compete, including at the National (Ebbw Vale, 1958), and went from strength to strength. In general terms the recovery in industry and employment brought a new confidence and optimism. Demobbed servicemen returned to civilian life and the institutions that had supported the deep-rooted associational and recreational male culture which had withstood the relentless buffeting of the inter-war years re-asserted themselves with renewed vigour. Industrial diversification saw the economic base of at least parts of the country transformed in the wake of new industries in the 1950s and 1960s, from Hoover in Merthyr Tydfil where new employment opportunities revitalised choirs in Cefn Coed, Dowlais and Treharris, to Hotpoint in Llandudno (Maelgwn), the new RTB steelworks at Llanwern (Caldicot) and tyre manufacture in Caernarfon (Ferodo).

Gradually (*poco a poco*) then more rapidly (*con moto*), post-war austerity gave way to the material improvement and changed lifestyles that brought with them money and more time and opportunity to spend it. The Welsh choral scene would in time feel the impact of this gradual social transformation but when hostilities ceased in 1945, Wales was still a country anchored to its recent past and the cables of continuity with the pre-war era were as strong as hawsers. The post-war success of the Hammersmith Welsh Male Choir at Bridgend in 1948 and of the Birmingham-based Côr Meibion y Canoldir (Midlands) in the 1970s and 80s were evidence of the lasting legacy of the mass emigration from Wales in the 1930s. In terms of chapel membership and regular attendance the grip of Nonconformity had been slackening since the 1920s, but many of its moral assumptions and social offshoots remained in place: the traditional institutions of chapel, club, cinema and choir were still the collective hub around which the recreational lives of most men and women in Wales still revolved.

Playing an active role was the re-activated round of eisteddfodau. The National Eisteddfod was not exactly mothballed during the war years, but prohibitions on large gatherings affected competition in front of several thousand spectators whether by singers or by sportsmen. A National Eisteddfod was scheduled for each of the war years, but it was severely curtailed by unfolding events, and while literary jousting continued, choral competition was rendered impossible, and the one-off 'Eisteddfod of the Air' of 1940, broadcast in the time-honoured first week of August from the BBC Welsh Region in Bangor, was an experiment not repeated. Still, the Archdruid Crwys seemed pleased that 'the pavilion was as big as Wales itself', adding, insensitively, that 'only the deaf would be unable to attend'.

The ties that bind still bound. Recovering from, by their standards, an ignominious sixth place at the 1936 Fishguard National, Morriston United, under a new conductor in Idris Evans, came runner-up three times in a row 1937–9, beaten by, in turn, their great rivals the Orpheus, the ever-formidable Rhosllannerchrugog (Rhos and Dinorwic, from Caernarfonshire's slate quarries, were the only north Wales choirs numerically strong enough to appear in the 'chief' at this time) and the always dangerous Nelson Arion, who were 15 decisive marks ahead of next-placed Morriston United in 1939. The United briefly returned in 1940 to the winning ways they had known under Ivor Sims in the early 1930s but they were not to last.

The United barely survived the war, and became finally absorbed in 1948 by the Orpheus for whom hostilities brought their own tribulations. During the war their rehearsal room became a canteen for HM Forces stationed in the Swansea area. It was to a similar room where one of Swansea's numerous choirs practised that 'Parker', a black American soldier, is taken in Ralph Ellison's semi-autobiographical short story of 1944, 'In a Strange Country.' Black GIs were stationed at Morriston – white soldiers in Swansea – and several attended choir practice. 'Parker' has been ashore barely an hour before he is attacked by white fellow-American soldiers ('It's a goddamn nigger') from which he is rescued by Mr Catti and some local men, who take him to a nearby pub to recover, then to choir rehearsal where

> … the well-blended voices caught him unprepared. He heard the music's warm richness with pleasurable surprise and heard, beneath the strange Welsh words, echoes of plainsong, like that of Russian folksongs …
>
> 'Do you see that fellow with the red face there?' asked Mr Catti.
>
> 'Yes.'
>
> 'Our leading mine owner.'
>
> 'And what are the others?'
>
> 'Everything. The tenor on the end is a miner. Mr Jones, in the centre there, is a butcher. And the dark man next to him is a union offical.'
>
> 'You'd never think so from their harmony,' he said, smiling.
>
> 'When we sing, we are Welshmen,' Mr Catti said as the next number began.
>
> Parker smiled, aware suddenly of an expansiveness that he had known before only at mixed jam sessions … He liked these Welsh.
>
> (Ellison, pp.142-3)

As happened across the country, every chorister who was not called up served with the Home Guard, Civil Defence, the Fire Service or in essential occupations like education, medicine and designated heavy industries. The Orpheus' rehearsals were not cancelled entirely but so few members were able to attend as to make meaningful practice virtually impossible. This must have been the experience of choirs more generally, if they managed to survive at all. In the case of the Orpheus, Swansea connections among the police force in Sussex lured the choir to Worthing, and about half the money raised during town's 'Aid to Russia' week in April 1942 came from a depleted Orpheus concert in front of an audience of 1800 hardy souls at the Assembly Hall. It is a safe assumption that politically conservative Worthing's wartime willingness to aid Russia, like the Morriston United choir itself, did not survive into the post-war era.

Morriston Orpheus celebrate their hat-trick at Bridgend in 1948, with David Grenfell MP standing alongside conductor Ivor Sims.

(*Courtesy of Morriston Orpheus Choir*)

Former conductor of the United, but since 1935 of the Orpheus, Ivor E. Sims (1897–1961) is one of the major choral figures of 20th-century Wales. Born in Bonymaen before his family moved to Morriston, he had served in Salonika where his conducting career began, after the war had qualified as a teacher of music and mathematics and taught from 1923 until 1953 at Pentrepoeth Senior Boys' School, Morriston. The school choir he founded there attained dizzying heights, extending far beyond winning at the Llanelli National in 1930 to the prestigious Three Choirs Festival at Worcester Cathedral, and to a famous wartime recording of Benjamin Britten's 'Ceremony of Carols'. Britten had composed this work in 1942 en route by sea to the USA, and originally scored it for female voices, soloists and harp. After hearing Sims' Pentrepoeth boys choir singing in

London, and astonished by their vocal purity and technical confidence, he rewrote the choral sections for three treble parts. Sims' boys gave their first performance of it at the Wigmore Hall in December 1943, and at Britten's request it was then recorded by Decca with Sims conducting and Maria Korchinska playing the harp, under the composer's watchful eye.

The Orpheus that Ivor Sims rebuilt after the war was composed mostly of manual workers in steel or related industries living in or near Morriston; still over 90% were Welsh-speaking, and the same proportion coming from a chapel background, able to read sol-fa comfortably, and familiar with choral music and harmonised congregational singing. With this choir Sims developed what became its exceptional velvety, mellow sound, mellifluous and burnished like the molten metal that so many of his choristers poured in their daily employment. This quite distinctive sonority, built on a rock-solid bass foundation, secure inner parts, and governed always by measured, even stately, tempi stirred a kind of subconscious melancholy that became the Orpheus' trademark. But it was not suddenly achieved. At Denbigh in 1939 the adjudicator Dr Wilcock could not but be impressed by the vocal material Sims had at his disposal, but he also noticed the first tenors missed many finer points, and a careless disregard of expressiveness that surprised the judges, given the excellence of the voices they were hearing. This want of attention to detail especially in the soft passages that occur in Hopkin Evans' summer love song 'Mordaith Cariad' led Wilcock to conclude that 'it was tragic that a choir with such power and intelligence should have neglected obvious marks of expression. The voices were most magnificent but they should have scaled down their immense vocal resources'.

Sims listened and learned. By the late 1940s the varnished Morriston sound was sweeping all before it, with an unprecedented four successive National victories between 1946 and 1949 that remains unequalled. 'What a splendid body of voices' remarked the adjudicators at Mountain Ash in 1946, 'their performance of [Vaughan Thomas'] 'Prospice' was outstanding; we got intensity without sacrifice of tone quality. One felt that intense feeling which can only be felt by a magnificent performance', while their 'intense and vivid' performance of Vincent Thomas' 'Y Carwr Ffyddlon' 'really made us sit up … the voices were always under control' in what was 'a revelatory performance.' At Colwyn Bay the following year they were again commended for their 'fine tonal qualities – like an organ.

Their singing was bold, brilliant, fervent and thrilling.' At Dolgellau in 1949 they showed mastery of every mood. The adjudicator referred to the choir's 'velvety voices and its scrupulous attention to detail', the basses 'sounded like cellos' in 'Mordaith Cariad,' while their performance of Dunhill's 'Full Fathom Five' was described as 'cheeky, impish and provocative.' The Orpheus' accumulating trophies electrified the Swansea valley just as the Ystalyfera mixed choir had done in the inter-war decades. Whatever the hour, on each occasion they were greeted back at Morriston Cross by a large crowd and police officers were called to control the traffic which stopped while occupants listened. Years later, the writer John Morgan (1929-88) recalled how the excitement generated locally by the Orpheus' return from their scenes of triumph would penetrate the whole community, and even teenagers like himself were not immune to:

> ... such excitement, and such cheering on those late nights in August in the 1940s as we welcomed the heroes at the Cross, back from the victories at the Eisteddfod. With my grandparents and one brother I'd set off down Martin Street and along Woodfield Street with what must have been most of the population of the town. It's true there had been some dissension at 9 Plas-y-Coed where so many of us lived in so small a house. My grandfather William Sayce was firm for the Orpheus. But would his son, my Uncle Stan, my mother's brother, transfer to the United? My mother, having been a life-long friend of Ivor Sims, believed only in the Orpheus. Even as a child I would follow the discussions with a curiosity that was to become an obsession. Strangely, it did not occur to me as at all peculiar that the two best choirs in Wales – which was itself the best country for choirs – should exist in the very same small community in which we lived, that our own household even should debate which choir we should support. Such easy familiarity with the best is a handy lesson for a child. Briefly I was tempted by the United, partly because they always kept on coming second to the Orpheus at the National. This may have been a natural sympathy for the underdog. I went to United rehearsals in the Horeb school room. My grandfather died in 1945 and men from both choirs sang at his grave in Llangyfelach, an experience as moving as any I can recall. I realized, though, that the Orpheus really was the choir to be near, even though they were the most successful. They

were the most powerful and made the loveliest of tenor sounds. Ivor Sims would always insist the choir was ahead of the note, and would permit no self-indulgence. He allowed me to take part in the famous recording of 'Y Delyn Aur' at Siloh in, I think, 1947, even though I had briefly been disloyal and was not truly fit to be a member of that memorable choir. But I had cheered the Orpheus with thousands of others on Morriston Cross on those famous nights; and cheer still ...

(Morriston Orpheus Golden Jubilee Brochure, 1935-85)

The reference to the Orpheus' famous recording of 'Y Delyn Aur' on a Columbia 78 rpm record before being transferred to one of the new-fangled extended play 45 rpm discs, suggests that John Morgan would also have known the choir's majestic rendering of Daniel Protheroe's robust arrangement of 'Pen Calfaria' ('Laudamus'), never a test piece but always a concert favourite, a haunting Tawe Jones carol 'Si Lwli' written just before the war, and best known of all a hypnotic performance of Parry's *a capella* song of unrequited love, 'Myfanwy,' with a barking dog providing a supportive yelp which can be heard, by listening carefully, between the two verses. The animal was brought by its owner to all practices, tied up outside and never uttered a sound. On this occasion, perhaps moved by the Orpheus' exquisite harmonies, it did so, but the sound engineer knew this was the 'take' he wanted and professed himself happy. When a perplexed chorister needlessly pointed out to him that there was a dog on it, the recordist replied that he 'didn't care whether it was a bloody elephant', that was the version he wanted. Time has vindicated his judgement. Morriston Orpheus' velvety 'Myfanwy' remains one of the two classic recorded performances of it, the other being by Glynne Jones's Pendyrus 40 years later.

The choir's participation in the extension of the audience for Welsh choral music via gramophone and radio saw the Orpheus featuring on popular weekly programmes like 'Welsh Rarebit' produced by Mai Jones who with Lyn Joshua (a descendant of the revivalist preacher Seth Joshua) composed 'We'll Keep a Welcome', guaranteed to jerk the tears of the Welsh in exile and which featured prominently in the Orpheus' concerts and recordings for Decca and EMI (Columbia). An appearance at the London Palladium in 1957 pointed a new direction for the Welsh male choir. But the

Morriston Orpheus are among the most recorded of all Welsh choirs; (below) in concert, building to a climax with Joy Amman Davies.

(*Courtesy of Morriston Orpheus Choir*)

incorporation into the established repertoire of challenging classical works like Cherubini's *Requiem Mass* in D minor for male voices (which the choir had first sung in the 1930s after Sims had found a copy on a second-hand book stall in Switzerland and brought back to transcribe and write out in sol-fa by hand), Max Bruch's 'Frithjof' and Schubert's 'Song of the Spirits over the Waters', performed on Sims' last appearance on the National stage in 1960 – these extensions to the familiar repertoire reassured purists that standards were not being sacrificed on the altar of commercial success.

At its peak in the post-war decade, Sims' Morriston Orpheus induced in its listeners arguably the most moving experience offered by any Welsh male choir either before or since. Singing it in a hushed tone, they could even make 'God Save the King' – or 'Queen' – sound like a prayer. According to Dr George Guest, Bangor-born director of music at St. John's College Cambridge (1951–91) and National adjudicator, 'every [choral] performance is a mixture of technique and emotion … It is in the relative proportion between the two that is found the true fundamental difference between choirs. And the really important question is this – do you wish your audiences to admire your performances or be moved by them?' Under Ivor Sims the Morriston Orpheus choir achieved both objectives.

After the purple patch of four successive victories in the late 1940s, National wins came the Orpheus' way less frequently, at Pwllheli in 1955, where they were unopposed, and at Cardiff in 1960. After Sims' death in 1961 they would never win again, a fact partially explained by the choir's decision to abandon competition altogether after coming second in 1969 and third in 1971 when they were conducted respectively by Sims' accompanist and successor Eurfryn John (1961–9), and Llanelli-born Lyn Harry (1969–75) who came to them from London Welsh, took them to Canada, and stayed there.

By then another champion choir which had reformed after the travails of the Depression to enjoy a decade-and-a-half of National glory had also decided to sheathe its competitive sword. It was a choir that the Orpheus had in that time faced only twice and beaten once (Dolgellau, 1949), and though Ivor Sims had seen them coming he would not live to see them equal Morriston's record of seven National wins, then surpass it. By the early 1950s the whooping braves of Treorchy were on the warpath and already crossing the plain.

Chapter 8

'To Take their Scalps is our Delight': Treorchy

The Second World War had not brought musical activity in the Rhondda Valley to an end – far from it, as the continuing round of concerts and *cymanfaoedd* (chapel singing festivals) testified – but it disrupted organised choral life sufficiently for the Treorchy and District male voice choir which had struggled to survive throughout the 1930s – in 1937 92% of its members were unemployed – and was now depleted by the call of National Service, to wind up its affairs in the summer of 1943.

Peace brought a revived optimism and in 1947 the miners of the Rhondda produced a souvenir publication entitled 'Rebirth of the Rhondda' to celebrate the long-demanded nationalisation of the coal industry, the introduction of the welfare state and a return to full employment. The Treorchy choir's own revival was part of that process of recovery. In October 1946, John Haydn Davies, a 41-year-old Caerleon-trained teacher from Blaen-cwm at the top of the valley, his family roots in Rhydlewis (Cardiganshire) and the Cynon valley, was approached by members of the disbanded choir to resurrect it. It was not a role unfamiliar to him, since in 1933 he had become conductor of the Glenrhondda Colliery Male Choir which met at the Miners' Institute, Blaen-cwm, and two years later of the Blaen-cwm Choral Society, a position he held until 1947, by which time he had already taken up the reins of the Treorchy and District Male Choir to launch a renaissance in Welsh male choral singing.

There was no shortage of new recruits, for young men turned up to the rehearsal room in clutches of seven or eight at a time, eventually requiring the books to be closed on 170. They joined older men of the inter-war generation who had been reared on the harmonies of the *gymanfa ganu* and were the beneficiaries of a regime in which singing was still central to their educational experience. The new members had come of age during the war and, while anxious to recreate some of the companionship they had known in uniform, had little knowledge of what being a chorister entailed. Half of them thought they were baritones, friends standing together irrespective of vocal compass. John Davies set about organising them by singing a note, and saying 'All those who can sing that are top tenors – stand there' and repeated the procedure for each section. Something similar must have happened in countless schoolrooms and vestries across Wales as musical life revived, though perhaps not all conductors would have shared John Davies' declared aim of fostering 'a sense of social awareness and responsibility' towards his young charges in a manner reminiscent of W. P. Thomas' stress on proper behaviour to the 'Treorky boys' on their visit to Windsor Castle in 1895. By the time the conductor reckoned they were ready for their first public performance in Ramah Chapel, Treorchy, in July 1947, they already numbered 154, the majority between 20 and 30 years of age, and an even greater percentage employed in the coal industry.

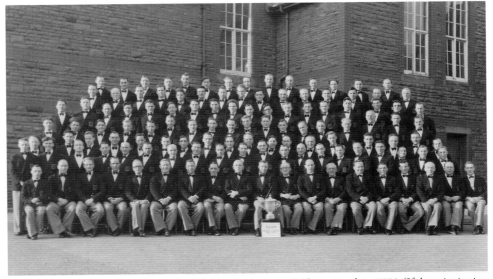

Treorchy's first National victory under John H. Davies, was at Aberystwyth in 1952. 'If there is singing like this in heaven,' said the adjudicator, 'I cannot wait to get there'.

(Courtesy of Treorchy Male Choir)

Treorchy's experience was again typical of choirs elsewhere as its members brought with them secretarial and financial expertise already acquired in the running of local affairs. A raft of organisational decisions had to be made, the lead taken by men familiar with the administration of miners' institutes, lodges and chapels. A full complement of officials needed to be appointed, subscription fees to be agreed (three pence, or 1½p), the transport and stage managers and the section attendance officers who in every choir carry out their duties with the seriousness of the quaestors of ancient Rome. And Treorchy signalled that a milestone had been reached in the development of the Welsh male voice choir by ending the pre-war habit of paying choristers from outside for attending a couple of rehearsals before a competition and being allowed to stand in the front row, once a regular bone of contention leading on occasion to legal proceedings. If the material legacy of the disbanded Treorchy choir was five pounds and a battered suitcaseful of music, the repertoire of the early post-war years set the pattern adopted by choirs throughout Wales for the next half-century, a mix of hymn-tunes like Mansel Thomas's arrangements of 'Llef' and 'Llanfair', opera choruses (especially Verdi), spirituals like 'Steal Away', 'Jacob's Ladder' and 'Were you There' (arranged by Maurice Jacobson when not by John Davies himself) and part-songs like 'The Jolly Roger', 'Cyfri'r Geifr' and 'Men of Harlech', all of which, given their natural appeal and the inherent conservatism of the medium, are still widely sung today. To list them further is to catalogue an inventory of the most frequently heard items in the Welsh male choir's song list. 'Close Thine Eyes', 'The Old Woman', 'All in the April Evening', 'The Holy City', 'Hava Nagila', 'Morte Christe', 'The Lord's Prayer', 'Calm is the Sea': all these were recorded by the Morriston and Treorchy choirs of the Ivor Sims/John H. Davies era, and when the list later lengthened with the addition of lighter and more agile numbers like 'The Rhythm of Life,' 'Memory' from *Cats*, 'Softly as I leave you', 'Some Enchanted Evening', 'There is Nothing like a Dame' or 'Bohemian Rhapsody', then the consummate musicians who respectively succeeded them, Alwyn Humphreys and John Cynan Jones, would record those too, forsaking the competitive stage to do so but perhaps reaching a wider world. One New Zealander who regularly led a small party to Europe would take them to visit only two places, Cordoba for the feria and flamenco, and Treorchy for the singing.

Choirs became associated with certain pieces, and with a style of singing them. South Wales choirs never quite managed the weighty sonority that Rhos or the Brythoniaid, founded in Blaenau Ffestiniog in 1964, brought to W. Bradwen Jones' interpretation of 'Oleuni Mwyn' ('Lead Kindly Light'), or T. Maldwyn Price's 'Y Pysgotwyr' (The Fishermen), though the redman's domain in the same composer's 'Crossing the Plain' was best left to the home-grown Indians of south Wales. Llanelli, established in the mid-1960s as Cwmfelin, became the specialists in the songs of modern Welsh light entertainers like Ryan Davies, while Glynne Jones' Pendyrus would move from Palestrina in one breath to Alun Hoddinott in the next. John Davies' Treorchy brought a trademark declamatory vigour to the Red Army's A.V. Alexandrov's adaptation of the traditional Russian melody 'The Silver Birch', found in Tchaikovsky's fourth symphony and set to Welsh words by D. Wynne Lloyd as 'Y Fedwen Arian'. This was the type of rhythmic item with its repetitive, accelerating phrases, mobile tempi and virile, animated tenor line that marked out Rhondda coal from Morriston tinplate. John Davies packed his choir with nearly forty top tenors and an equivalent complement of baritones, while the bottom bass section for their part could be relied on to be, in the words of a contemporary adjudicator, 'wonderfully effective'. They also had an emphatically accented delivery of phrases that some believe to have been an established characteristic of the congregational singing of the upper Rhondda more generally, and can even be detected in the earliest recording of Tom Stephens' Gleemen in 1899.

Enhanced by a touch of vibrato, it was their ringing tenor sound, reckoned by outsiders to be typically Welsh but achieved by only a few choirs, that was Treorchy's calling card and became more widely known from the late 1950s on the Qualiton record label of Pontardawe, founded by the musical entrepreneur John Edwards. Through being frequently aired on the BBC's Welsh Home Service, Mansel Thomas' arrangements of 'Llef' ('Deus Salutis') and 'Hyfrydol' ('Christus Redemptor'), the big 'Amen' – sometimes confused with the 'Amen' from Arwel Hughes' 'Tydi a Roddaist' – became taken up even by international rugby crowds. Genée's 'Italian Salad' and Maldwyn Price's 'Crossing the Plain' found themselves on the record shelves of countless Welsh, and not only Welsh homes as the novelty of 45 rpm vinyl extended-play 'singles' became complemented by ten- and twelve-inch long-playing 33 rpm discs.

The immediately recognisable, resonant Treorchy sound that now penetrated the collective Welsh consciousness via radio appearances had been honed on the eisteddfod stage, since competition, their conductor believed, 'rightly used shall stimulate us on the road to technical and artistic excellence'. Having come second to Swansea choirs in 1949 and 1950, John Davies set about correcting what he perceived to be an internal imbalance in the choral geography of Wales's most populous county. At Aberystwyth in 1952 Treorchy achieved their first National victory for over fifty years. Singing first of four choirs he adopted the perilous strategy of interpreting to the letter the adagio marking on Schubert's 23rd Salm ('Duw yw fy Mugail'), and underpinned by pianist Tom Jones' unfalteringly steady accompaniment it took over six minutes to perform and to overwhelm the adjudicators, who were moved to remark that 'it is only once in a century one hears such marvellous singing'. The entire performance was praised for 'the textured tone of the voices, the inner parts accurately executed, the climaxes gripping and artistic', even allowing for the also trademark Treorchy features of an excessive fondness for *sforzandi* and emphatic consonantal enunciation (a tendency that became even more pronounced under John Davies' successor John Cynan Jones). The near perfect 96 marks awarded for the Schubert said it all. The adjudicator W. Matthews

Williams' devoutly expressed wish that 'if there is singing like this in heaven I cannot wait to get there' confirmed John Haydn Davies in his belief that since all the angels have men's names the heavenly host must be a male voice choir, and the fast-track from Pentre to the pearly gates saw them get the better of Rhondda rivals Pendyrus each time they met between 1954 and 1964, defeating Morriston into the bargain. Aberdare in 1956 was the only time the recognised 'Big Three' of John H. Davies, Arthur Duggan and Ivor Sims met on the National stage, and it was Treorchy that emerged triumphant.

In terms of repertoire John Davies seasoned the familiar fare of hymn-tunes, part-songs in both languages, operatic choruses and warhorses of the 'Nidaros' variety with German folk melodies he himself had discovered and set to apposite Welsh words; his fusion of Silcher and Ceiriog made 'Nant y Mynydd' a 'must' for choirs of whatever size throughout Wales. At the same time, in 1955 he exchanged sol-fa transcriptions of Cherubini's D Minor *Requiem* with his great friend Ivor Sims who in this case had beaten him to it in performing it with Morriston; in 1960 both choirs combined to sing it with the BBC Welsh Orchestra at St Mary's Church, Swansea. In 1959 Treorchy had sung in English for the first time the 'Coronation Song' from Mussorgsky's *Boris Godunov*, transcribed into sol-fa by John Davies. For the Llandaff Festival that year he commissioned from the Rhondda composer Mansel Thomas (1909–86) a setting of Psalm 135 for male choirs and contralto soloist (who was Helen Watts on its première), which prompted the critic of the journal *Welsh Music* to declare that 'John Davies, the Conductor of the Treorchy Male Voice Choir, has developed a musical instrument which I would imagine is as near to perfection as one can get in concerted male singing.' In 1957 the choir had exchanged musical greetings with the legendary Paul Robeson, who was an outcast in his own country, via a telephone link-up paid for by Harry Belafonte and Robeson himself, from the Miners' Eisteddfod at Porthcawl to a studio in New York. This gesture of solidarity with the great black radical, reaffirming links between Robeson and the Welsh mine workers forged in the inter-war period – and many of the Treorchy choir were still miners – must have delighted the eminent Communist composer Alan Bush (1900–95) who in 1957 dedicated his 'The Dream of Llewelyn ap Gruffydd' to them. With the left-wing writer Randall Swingler's democratic words translated by Wil Ifan, it became a National test piece in 1978 at Cardiff, when Llanelli and Pontarddulais attacked it with the energetic vitality that had once been Treorchy's competitive hallmark but which they now reserved for the Palladium and the recording studio.

Their greatest competitive triumph was the Swansea National in 1964. The competition for male choirs of more than 80 voices attracted for an unprecedented £500 prize the six biggest names in Welsh choralism, all of them 'National winners': in the order in which they were to sing: Rhos,

Treorchy, Morriston, Pendyrus, Manselton, and the reigning champions after their unexpected win on their first appearance in the 'chief' the previous year, the young Turks of Pontarddulais, resplendent in green blazers – an indication perhaps of a youthful disregard for tradition – and with a bright, incisive top tenor sound they might have learned from Treorchy. They had; Bont's Noel Davies would always unstintingly acknowledge the personal and musical influence of Treorchy's John Haydn Davies on his own and his choir's development. In time-honoured fashion this was the closing competition that would bring the Eisteddfod to its climax. The pavilion was packed to its 8,000 sweaty capacity: outside another 30,000 strolled the field, basked in the Swansea sunshine, or clustered around the loud speakers that relayed the activities on stage to the enthusiasts outside. But few among those thousands knew that for the past week illness had confined Treorchy's conductor to bed, and from which he now crawled to be driven to Swansea.

So at 4.45pm the *Rhondda Leader*'s 'diminutive but mighty maestro of the baton' mounted the podium and surveyed his choir. A third of them still worked in coal-mining and its associated industries, but no miners ever entered the cage to meet the challenge of the shift underground more apprehensively than the 98 Treorchy choristers – numerically they were the smallest of the six choirs – who filed on stage that August afternoon. They felt more like martyred Christians than Roman gladiators but if they were nervous it was not for themselves but for their conductor: surely the previous two-and-a-half months of unremitting rehearsal three times a week, at the expense of all other engagements and diversions, would count for something? 'John, in bar 15 we're all to 'ell', one chorister had ruefully protested. Such was,

Treorchy's John H Davies keeps a close eye on the Welsh Guards Cup won in the epic contest at Swansea in 1964. *(Courtesy of Treorchy Male Choir)*

and still is, the price of National competition. At John Davies's signal conveying the required rhythmic urgency, three bars of energetic piano accompaniment from the dependable Tom Jones introduced William Mathias' witty treatment of 'Y Pren ar y Bryn', which the choir attacked with gusto. The modulation from the perky playfulness of Mathias to the reverential tranquillity of Tomás Luís de Victoria's motet 'Arglwydd Da nid wyf deilwng' ('Domine non sum dignus') was not easily managed – this was, after all, the Eisteddfod Pavilion not the Escorial Palace – but manage it John Davies did, though he was visibly wilting by the end of the last test-piece, Granville Bantock's setting of Robert Browning's 'Paracelsus'. He literally staggered off at the end to be bundled into the waiting car that whisked him back to Treherbert and bed, where news of the result reached him within ten minutes of its announcement around 6.30.

He never heard the other choirs, nor the arguments among the enthralled audience. Had the sonorous Rhos basses done enough to off-set the bright-toned young tenors of Bont? The influence of the late Ivor Sims could still be heard in the uniquely burnished sound of the Orpheus, while Glynne Jones had so authentically recreated the suave polyphony of the 16th century as to suggest that ripples of the Counter Reformation had eddied even as far as Our Lady of Penrhys. While the arguments went on, the only cardinals who mattered, the adjudicators, went into solemn conclave: the eminent choral and orchestral conductor Meredith Davies, Peter Gellhorn, Director of the BBC Chorus, and Elfed Morgan, music organiser for Carmarthenshire. Gellhorn stepped to the microphone to say 'Canu bendigedig' ('Wonderful singing') and Elfed Morgan delivered the adjudication which put Treorchy three marks ahead of a jubilant, because still apprentice, Pontarddulais, with a chastened Pendyrus third just ahead of Morriston.

The Mathias piece, it seemed, had 'unfolded in a most skilful manner while the inherent vitality and agility of the music was splendidly articulated' because, the adjudicators thought, 'every member had understood and been acquainted with the idiom. The cleanness of diction and phrasing in the interpretation of the motet went far beyond technique, while the Bantock demonstrated the talent and ability of the conductor to get the best out of every page of music. We felt that every section was in its place and moved towards some particular climax in every section of the work. Here was everything we could wish for and an abundance of vocal resources to sustain the piece throughout'.

If those words naturally pleased John Haydn Davies he kept his satisfaction to himself; his mantra was 'When you lose say little, when you win say less', and he was familiar with both. At an eisteddfod in Sennybridge in 1950 Treorchy had come fourth out of five; at the National three months later they came second to the choir placed fifth at Sennybridge by the same adjudicator. Before long they would be good enough to defy the slings and arrows of outrageous adjudicators. What most delighted John Davies about his choir's performance at Swansea was the accolade delivered the following week in a letter from William Mathias. 'It thrilled me considerably,' wrote its composer, 'to hear ['Y Pren ar y Bryn'] so finely done ... It had musicality, excitement and that necessary bit of dramatic point. Above all I admired the flexibility of the choir which, while taking in the various tempi nevertheless allows it to sing and react to your beat as though it were one man,' When Treorchy exposed a London audience that included members of the royal family to this piece in a sophisticated programme ranging from Palestrina to Bruckner's 'Consolation of Music' at the Royal Albert Hall in November 1966, they received the plaudits of the London press too. The *Times* commended their 'unshakeable intonation, precise and unfussy discipline and richness of sound in whispered pianissimos', while the *Telegraph* 'thought the Bruckner gave the basses an opportunity to produce a sonority which bade fair to rival the organ'.

When Treorchy sang 'Y Pren ar y Bryn' for the first time under the baton of John Davies' successor, John Cynan Jones, at the Cardigan semi-national in May 1967, the adjudicators there – Warwick Braithwaite, D. T. Davies and Leon Forrester – remarked that their performance was 'as rich as a fruity Christmas cake with glitter for icing on the top'. At the Bala National in August, in front of a capacity audience of 10,000, Treorchy's performance of Palestrina's 'Pueri Hebraeorum' had 'the fine control of a good organ playing', which must have delighted John Cynan Jones who, by a nice coincidence, had won the organ solo at Aberystwyth in 1952 on the morning of Treorchy's first National win in the afternoon. John Cynan was praised for the supple part-singing of his choir, and his attention to detail meant that 'there was something of interest all the time as it built up in waves to a crest'. The Palestrina was again lauded for its beautiful tone and sharply defined, flowing vocal lines, while Bach's 'Glory to God' ('Moliant fo i Dduw Anfeidrol') impressed by its rhythmic vitality, secure intonation and interweaving of the voices, and E. T. Davies' 'Y Gwyntoedd' by the sensitive rendition of the composer's delicate phrasing and expressive dynamics, the performance 'full of variety, colour and meaning'.

This would prove to be Treorchy's competitive 'end of', in modern parlance, a matter of regret not only to their many followers all over Wales, but also to a detached observer like George Guest in Cambridge, who deemed Treorchy's decision to withdraw from the competitive stage 'regrettable … an exact analogy would be the failure of Liverpool, Man U. and Everton [Dr Guest was born in Bangor] to take part in the F.A. Cup … One has to come to terms with the fact that there can be only one winner but it is … an error to suppose that there can be any losers in a real sense'. In 20 years of competition the choir had achieved eight National wins out of eleven, nine semi-nationals out of eleven, and five wins at the Miners' Eisteddfod. Where John H. Davies saw competition as 'a stimulant to technical and artistic excellence', John Cynan Jones believed that the social changes of the 1960s and 1970s were responsible for changing tastes among audiences and choristers, and he adapted the repertoire to reflect them. He added Brahms, Vierne and Fauré, but also began extending, some thought diluting, the classical Welsh and operatic chorus base with 'songs from the shows.' Medleys from musical theatre began nudging Mozart aside and by the 1980s Andrew Lloyd Webber, Paul Simon and Stephen Sondheim were featuring more prominently in Treorchy's concert programmes than Daniel Protheroe and Joseph Parry; or William Mathias.

There was no denying the popular appeal and commercial benefits of this modernised repertoire, and fortunately John Cynan Jones' skilful arrangements, good working relationships with other arrangers like Mike Sammes, and his informed interest in EMI's advanced digital recording technology ensured the maintenance of standards as 'Myfanwy' embraced Freddie Mercury and the choir reached out to new audiences. Morriston, abandoning the competitive stage in 1971, trod the same path and retained, under Alwyn Humphreys (1979–2005), the same high standards of discipline, imagination, commitment and authority. But if the move to the more commercial entertainment end of the repertoire was taken in the partial belief that the interest of younger recruits might be thereby engaged, then the ageing profile of these giants of the choral scene, like most others, suggests the experiment has not been an unqualified success. Understandably, when it comes to a choice between being loved and being admired, choirs will plump for the former. The result is that audiences grow old with the choirs and a vicious circle is created as choirs sing the music they know audiences like since, after all, these audiences are supporting them and the charitable causes they are promoting. We are all martyrs in the cause of conservatism.

What was noteworthy about Treorchy's final competitive appearance in 1967 was the narrowing margin of victory as the young whelps of Pontarddulais snapped at their heels. Compared with the Rhondda choir's decisive victories at Aberystwyth, Ystradgynlais, Aberdare and Ebbw Vale over their traditional rivals Morriston and Pendyrus, the green-blazered gilt-edged tenors of Pontarddulais had been only a mark behind on each of the three pieces at Swansea. At Bala they were only two marks in arrears. Having given Treorchy a good run for their money in 1964 and 1967 and tasted outright victory in 1963 and 1965, Pontarddulais, to their credit, would never retreat from the National stage, and in the years ahead, under Noel Davies (1961–2003) and then Clive Phillips, would shatter the accumulated victories of Morriston and Treorchy combined.

Chapter 9

Life Begins at *Forte*: Pendyrus

Ivor Sims, Arthur Duggan and John Haydn Davies between them dominated the immediate post-war decades, but the 1960s saw a changing of the guard. Duggan was persuaded to stand down in 1960, Sims was still in harness when he died the following year and an ailing John Davies finally relinquished the baton at Treorchy in 1969. A new generation was coming through in north Wales: the young Colin Jones had seized the reins at Rhos in 1957, and Meirion Jones, having decided that the abundant vocal resources of Blaenau Ffestiniog and district could sustain a second male choir to complement Côr Meibion y Moelwyn, formed the Brythoniaid in 1964. In south Wales the new guard was most colourfully personified in 1962 by the appointment of a successor to Arthur Duggan at Pendyrus. Between 1958 and 1960 Glynne Jones had scored a notable hat-trick of National firsts in the second male voice category with the Rhymney Silurian choir. Under dominant personalities like John Price, Dan Owen and Abel Jones, Rhymney had since the 1880s been a cauldron of choralism that frequently boiled over, rivalling neighbouring Dowlais in terms of the fervour and following generated by its mixed and male choirs. Rhymney Silurians were a more recent vintage, born in 1951 during the post-war recovery. Its conductor by the late 1950s was Glynne Jones. Born in 1927 in Dowlais he was a graduate in music and Welsh at University College Cardiff, and his confidence as the first academically qualified musician to take on one of the big choirs emboldened him to bring a new ambition to the Welsh choral scene. He cut his teeth with the Silurians in the second competition in 1958 at Ebbw Vale where he overcame Cwmbach, Morlais and Blaenavon, and the following year defeated the tenacious oil refinery men of Llandarcy who had chalked up six wins since 1950. The N.O.R. had piped their refined sound as far north as Llangefni in 1957, but two years later found that Rhymney Silurian had also made the long trek north, with Treorchy (first) and Pendyrus (third) splitting the two Rhos choirs in the chief competition. The Caernarfon National, with 20,000 on the *maes* and another 9,000 in the Pavilion itself, was a triumph for the choirs of the south Wales valleys.

It was 1960, however, that was the Silurians' *annus mirabilis*. The second competition for choirs of under 80 voices attracted nine entrants with the crack south Wales choirs of BP Llandarcy, Tredegar Orpheus and Morlais (Ferndale) challenged by the pick of north Wales choirs in this category, Froncysyllte, Trelawnyd and Penrhyn. The competition introduced for the first time an own choice to complement the two set pieces by Vaughan Williams and Viadana. Much could hinge on the appropriateness, or otherwise, of the 'own choice'. The Silurians' piece, as the copy proclaims, was actually dedicated to them by William Mathias (1934–1992). This was

Arthur Duggan drives Pendyrus to even greater efforts at the Royal Festival Hall in 1954, with tenor soloist David Galliver.   (*Courtesy of Pendyrus Male Choir*)

his innovative arrangement of the folk song 'Y Pren ar y Bryn' that soon became an eisteddfod and concert favourite among choirs with the agility and ability to master it. On the back of his stunning victory at Cardiff in 1960 where the Silurians won by an overwhelming 16 marks, Glynne Jones was lured from Rhymney to the Rhondda Fach. With his brightly coloured bow tie and flowing cape, self-styled 'Lord Pendyrus' was about to rattle the cage of the Welsh male choral scene. At his first rehearsal in Tylorstown he told his apprehensive choristers that he would give them six months to reach his required standards or he would be off. Chivvied and challenged by the mercurial maestro, they must have met them, as he stayed for 38 years.

In that time he cultivated an endearing showmanship, a wide circle of professional musicians and a stormy petrel image. He feigned to despise the old warhorses, but in truth the tuneful choruses of his fellow-Merthyrian Joseph Parry were his meat and drink, and he recorded, with Pendyrus, a CD consisting entirely of Parry's music. He resurrected the once widely-sung 'Sailors' Chorus' ('Codwn Hwyl'), and the Huntsmen's Chorus (from Parry's opera 'Blodwen' and highly derivative of Weber's chorus of the same name) and breathed new life into 'Iesu o Nazareth' and 'Cytgan y Pererinion' ('Pilgrim's Chorus'), though Arthur Duggan in the 1950s and Eurfryn John with Morriston in the 1960s had also recorded the latter items on vinyl long-playing discs. To the organ recitalist and accompanist Huw Tregelles Williams, former Head of Music at BBC Wales, who enjoyed a 15-year association with Pendyrus and their musical director, Glynne Jones was 'a remarkable pioneer and a breath of fresh air in the repetitive repertoire of Welsh male choral singing.' He recalled pre-concert rehearsals in Tylorstown Infants School where 'surrounded by the smell of damp clothes mixed with coke fumes from the heating stove, discipline, education and humour … were blended seamlessly by an inspirational choral trainer.'

Viewed by many as a visionary and by some as an eccentric, Glynne Jones was determined to widen the repertoire of the choir by introducing new music from both the Baroque period and the contemporary modern Welsh scene. He was helped in achieving this end by the publishing company set up in 1937 by W. S Gwynn Williams (1896–1978), its editor and proprietor. Glynne Jones took advantage of recently issued editions by the Gwynn Publishing Company of motets and madrigals by Palestrina, Viadana, de Victoria and Byrd as well as east European folk songs (arranged by the likes of Kodály, Kjerulf and Lajos Bárdos) and Welsh part-songs to which the Eisteddfod music committee responded with alacrity. T. Hopkin Evans' 'Mordaith Cariad' was published in 1938 and appeared as a test piece at the Denbigh National the following year; Vincent Thomas' 'De Profundis' (1939) and Bryceson Treharne's 'Brain Owain'('The Ravens of Owain', 1940), with their dramatic climaxes depicting death, defiance and revenge, were aimed at the Eisteddfod market and would soon feature regularly as test pieces; those for the second competition at Colwyn Bay in 1947, R. Maldwyn Price's 'Coelcerthi' ('Mountain Fires') and Hopkin Evans' 'Seren Bethlehem' ('Star of Bethlehem'), had been published by Gwynn in 1937 and 1938. Bryceson Treharne's 'Dychwelyd' ('The Return') first appeared in 1938 and took rather longer to catch the committee's eye, but made several appearances from 1956. Gwynn brought out Meirion Williams' 'Di Rosyn, Dos' ('Go, Lovely Rose') in 1938, and when the Eisteddfod finally latched on to it in the mid-1960s, it became a competition favourite, featuring three times in the 1970s.

Many of the motets Glynne Jones performed and recorded with Pendyrus had been published by Gwynn in the post-war decade. Palestrina's 'Adoremus Te' (also taken up by John H. Davies' Treorchy) had been published in 1949, Victoria's 'Domine non sum dignus' in 1948 and 'O Vos Omnes' ('O Chwi Bobloedd') in 1953, and Viadana's 'Ave Verum' in 1949. He wasted little time in including Palestrina's 'Confitemini Deo' and 'Pueri Hebraeorum,' published by Gwynn in 1957 and 1962 respectively, in the Silurians' and then Pendyrus' sophisticated repertoire, before other choirs took them up. Since then, as Gwyn L. Williams reminded the Eisteddfod in 2006, musical scholarship has moved on and W.S. Gwynn Williams' heavy editorial hand had led to over-edited scores with what are now deemed inappropriate tempi and excessive expression markings 'so that Palestrina sounds like an Edwardian church anthem' (Wiltshire, p.322).

Meanwhile at the other end of Glynne Jones' chronological spectrum were the dissonances of Alun Hoddinott, David Wynne and Mervyn Burtch, as well as Carl Orff, Aaron Copland, Max Bruch (his sublime setting of Psalm 23 in particular), Janáček, and Benjamin Britten. When

Pendyrus sang Hoddinott's 'Hymnus ante somnum' in memory of Britten at the Aldeburgh Festival in 1979, the only Welsh choir ever to appear there, Peter Pears was staggered to learn that Pendyrus were an amateur choir. It was after Pears heard them sing a Britten composition at the Cardiff Festival of Contemporary Music that he invited them to Aldeburgh. The work in question has been described as one of the most exacting yet vocally and musically most rewarding works in the male voice repertoire, 'The Ballad of Little Musgrave and Lady Barnard' (1943), which Britten sent to his friend Richard Wood for performance in a German prisoner-of-war camp. According to the historians of the Dunvant choir who, under T. Arwyn Walters, also mastered it, it demands 'a chilly, controlled articulation' to cope with a sword fight and the 'long drawn out guilt-ridden groaning' with which it ends (Mainwaring etc. p.55). This 13th-century Border ballad, viewed from Dunvant as 'shot through with spooky discords and violent eroticism,' became another of Glynne Jones' special Pendyrus deliveries which was to the taste of sophisticates but left Mrs Evans in Ferndale Workmen's Hall wondering what the POWs had done to deserve it. But Glynne Jones was an educator as well as an entertainer, keen to challenge listeners and choristers alike, and he constructed his programmes in such a way as to smuggle in less easy-listening atonal works among Beecham-style 'lollipops' that he knew popular taste demanded. Hence his skilfully designed sacred/secular menus, matched by two equally contrasting outfits from his extensive wardrobe. Simultaneously a big gun and a loose cannon, Glynne Jones' manufactured image of a showman, provocative and outrageous, belied a dedication to his craft, a desire to promote the best of Welsh music and a determination to perform it with conviction and commitment.

It was his Eisteddfod performance of 'Owain ab Urien,' a discordant, bitonal cantata by Hirwaun-born David Wynne (1900–83) that pitched him into a hornet's nest. He had premièred it at the Queen Elizabeth Hall in London in May 1968 in a concert sponsored by the Guild for the Promotion of Welsh Music that also featured the London Gabrieli Brass Ensemble who provided the accompanying septet and percussion required by David Wynne, as well as music by Palestrina, Viadana, Schubert, Mansel Thomas, Ian Parrott, and William Mathias. Glynne Jones then decided on 'Owain ab Urien', with its primitive rhythms, aggressive harmonies and angular melodic lines – for any amateur choir an uncompromising setting of a text by the early sixth-century poet Taliesin – as the choir's own choice of piece by 'a contemporary Welsh composer' as required by the Barry National Eisteddfod of 1968.

Over the years Pendyrus had had little to show for their dogged loyalty to the Eisteddfod which they had maintained even in the depths of the Depression of the 1930s, and had only three firsts, but many second places, as reward for their heroic efforts. Under Arthur Duggan they had produced the most powerful and thrilling sound of any choir in Wales, but at the cost of the musical precision and pure intonation that came from discipline and restraint. Adjudicators remarked on their *fortes* that were 'capable of pulling the house down with sheer exuberance,' but also on their fierce delivery and violent contrasts. This was Glynne Jones' predicament, how to instill restraint and accuracy without compromising Pendyrus' historic sonority and intensity of performance. His helpmate in applying putty to the cracks in the choral edifice was his accompanist Bryan Davies (1934–2011), one of the most brilliant musicians to come out of the Rhondda and associated at one time or another with most male choirs in Wales, for whom he had made widely-sung arrangements of 'Bryn Myrddin', 'Hava Nagila' and 'A Finnish Forest'. Accompanist to the broad-based Côr Meibion De Cymru at the time of his death in 2011, where he was succeeded by his talented daughter Siân, he was intermittently Pendyrus' pianist too, and occupied that role at the time of the Barry National in 1968. Bryan Davies' collaborative piano in assisting Glynne Jones overcome the challenge of 'Owain ab Urien' along with the 'Dies Irae', sung in Latin as it should be, from the Cherubini *Requiem*, and a Renaissance motet, were all factors that would secure for Pendyrus – at least in their conductor's mind – the first prize they had won at Port Talbot two years earlier and he aspired to reclaim.

The aspiration remained in Glynne Jones' mind and got no further. The adjudicators had other ideas. Apart from the fact that Pendyrus did not sing the three pieces in the prescribed order, they were more impressed by Pontarddulais' virile dispatch of 'Y Pren ar y Bryn' whose regular appearance in the Bont's competitive and concert repertoire had virtually made it their calling card. They had eclipsed Pendyrus by a solitary mark in the magnificent Swansea competition of 1964, having decisively trounced them at Llandudno the previous year; in Barry, in what the ajudicators described as 'a thrilling competition … [of] a very high standard,' they were placed two marks ahead of Pendyrus with Dunvant, its glory days still ahead, trailing seventeen marks in the rear. This was sufficient to convince the outspoken Glynne Jones that the adjudicators were fools, and he was not short of saying so. He resolved never to take his choir to the National again, nor did he. It would be over forty years before Pendyrus darkened the premier stage once more, and by then (2010) Glynne Jones was a decade dead. He must nevertheless have derived some quiet satisfaction from one of the letters to the press that the Barry decision prompted. A correspondent from Ebbw Vale (*Western Mail*, 13 August) expressed 'heartfelt thanks' to the Pendyrus Male Choir for 'their superb performance … They succeeded in brilliant fashion in raising Welsh male choral singing to a new high plane rarely achieved on the competition platform … [and] in presenting music which must be comparable with the finest in Britain or on the continent'.

In Pontarddulais they happily acquiesced with the official adjudication, while back in the Rhondda Pendyrus knuckled down to such a tightly packed compensatory schedule of radio and TV appearances that they seemed to be virtually living in the recording studios of the broadcasting companies. By the late 1990s Pendyrus could be said to have suffered from the lack of constructive criticism that eisteddfod adjudications can bring, and Glynne Jones' increasingly impaired hearing was a stimulant to his choir's historically-sanctioned instinct to interpret *p* as 'powerful' and *pp* as 'pretty powerful'. It would take the patient musicianship of his successors John Samuel (2001–09) and Stewart Roberts to restore the tonal integrity that had become a casualty of the final years of the legendary Glynne Jones era of 1962–2000.

It was not the last of 'Owain ab Urien', however. The mantle of promoting contemporary Welsh music was taken up by Martin Hodson and the Risca Male Choir, founded two years after Pendyrus' première of it in 1968. Hodson, who had briefly served as accompanist to Pendyrus in the early 1970s, would make a point of teaching his choristers large scale works by modern Welsh composers, and was not afraid to commission and sing them. One such work was Mervyn Burtch's 'Beowulf and Grendel'. Another was an extended version of 'Owain ab Urien' which they performed in the

Great Hall of Caerphilly Castle in 2000 with the backing of the required brass ensemble and a whole battery of percussion. Risca were not habitual pot-hunters, but when they made an appearance at the National, virtually on home turf in Newport in 1988, they won in the category for under seventy voices, and came a worthy second to Pontarddulais in the newly-introduced (and fortunately short-lived) 'open' competition, again at Newport, in 2004. They performed, in the adjudicators' opinion, 'a difficult and interesting programme with aplomb and refined musicality', and, given the venue in the grounds of Newport's Tredegar House, the enthusiastic audience unsurprisingly made them the unofficial victors. Coping with the Welsh words proving as much of a challenge as the reflected glare of their detergent-white tuxedo jackets, Martin Hodson's own verdict, that 'the experience of working hard for such an event really lifts the standards of the choir and gives it something challenging to aim for', echoed that of Pontarddulais' Noel Davies, and John Davies even earlier, about the value of competition for amateur choirs.

As comfortable donning the motley for grand opera as monkish habits for Renaissance motets, Risca on their extensive travels have made a point of taking works by modern Welsh composers to new audiences, as Pendyrus did in their visit to Pennsylvania and Maryland in 1984. While continental Europe became tentatively explored as the 1960s unfolded – Rhos first visited Germany in 1960, Cwmbach became the first Welsh choir to penetrate the Iron Curtain with a visit to Hungary in 1961, and Treorchy marched through Zürich in miners' helmets and overalls in 1963 – Pendyrus were the first of the large choirs to undertake a transatlantic flight to Western Canada and the USA in 1965, their first of several subsequent visits to North America, and made aviation as well as choral history in 1971 when they boarded the first-ever flight from Cardiff (Rhoose) International Airport to California. They would also claim the unusual double of singing in both the White House and the Kremlin. It was 1973 and 1980, respectively, before their big-gun rivals Treorchy and Morriston reached Canada but they soon made up for lost time. By 2015 Morriston Orpheus had undertaken thirty concert tours abroad, and like their Rhondda rivals had sung at major venues from New York to New Zealand, and joined San Francisco to the Sydney Opera House in landmark bridge-building.

While these 'coyers' get around even more these days, not all take the opportunity to showcase cutting edge music alongside the familiar and often hackneyed show-stoppers which can be guaranteed to get an audience consisting mostly of exiles to its feet in a teary standing ovation. Their concert programmes suggest that some choirs are ambassadors for Wales but hardly for Welsh music, where they are content to be little more than travelling heritage centres, and the more thoughtful resident of New York can be surprised by the readiness of a visiting Welsh choir to sing arrangements of songs from musical theatre when spectacular productions of these very shows can be enjoyed around the block on Broadway.

(Courtesy of Pendyrus Male Choir)

After the blood and thunder of the Duggan era, Glynne Jones urges restraint on his Pendyrus choristers, with Gavin Parry (piano).

Wanderlust was never a south Wales preserve, and Rhosllannerchrugog have been among the lustiest wanderers, visiting Germany twice in the 1960s and returning several times to the USA after their first tour in 1967. The exotic Far East in particular would exert a magnetic attraction to north Wales choirs once they found they had wings, and even smaller choirs had criss-crossed the globe busily by the end of the century, Côr Godre'r Aran flying from Llanuwchllyn on Bala Lake to Buenos Aires, and on to Patagonia in 1977 and again in 2007. No choir, though, has reached the heights quite as stratospherically as Dowlais, who went into orbit in 1998 when a taped recording of their choir was taken into space by Canadian-Welsh astronaut Dafydd Rhys Williams, a member of the 16-day US Columbia space shuttle. Dowlais can thus claim they have circled the globe 256 times and covered 603 million miles. The constant travelling between Dowlais to Liverpool alone had been enough to kill their famous conductor Harry Evans 90 years earlier.

More prosaically, less adventurous, earthbound but not always safer, the extension of the M4 motorway into south Wales, reaching Port Talbot in time for the 1966 National, and the opening of the Severn Bridge that year, facilitated the mobility of south Wales choirs as the A55 had for their north Wales counterparts, who found concert engagements over the border more appealing, and the necessarily meticulous preparation for the Eisteddfod stage correspondingly less attractive. That a busy concert schedule did not necessarily imply renouncing competition was well demonstrated by the Cwmbach choir from the Cynon Valley. Under T.R. James, their musical director for 31 years from his appointment in 1950, Cwmbach combined an impressive reputation on both the concert and competitive platforms, achieving frequent success at the Pontrhydfendigaid and Cardigan semi-nationals when those events in the 1960s and 1970s drew large crowds to rural and coastal Ceredigion, at the Miners' Eisteddfod at Porthcawl, and the National itself, as the choir regularly staged 70 to 80 choristers, widened its repertoire to include Schubert and Bruckner, and took it over the Bridge to the now increasingly accessible Midlands and south of England and to continental Europe.

A readiness to tour could bring troubles in its wake beyond the odd missing suitcase or mislaid chorister. Apartheid-South Africa's constant readiness to circumvent international sanctions as it desperately sought legitimacy for its increasingly isolated regime proved as much a thorn in the side of the Welsh choral body as it did to the Welsh Rugby Union. An invitation to Cwmbach to participate in the Roodepoort International Eisteddfod in a still racially-segregated Johannesburg in October 1981, particularly ironic in view of the honour bestowed on the choir when it had been invited to sing with Paul Robeson at an 'Africa Freedom Day' concert at the Royal Albert Hall in 1960, was eventually declined after mounting disaffection, protests and pickets from a wide spectrum of organisations and unions. A tour of South Africa eventually took place by the ostensibly anonymous 'Jones Choir', composed of members of different Welsh choirs and none, who travelled in a private capacity not as representatives of their own organisations, and were branded as 'mercenaries' on account of their sponsorship by a wealthy Yorkshire businessman with tenuous Welsh connections. Cwmbach later toured there in more settled post-apartheid times and in 1997 were hosted by the black Cenestra Male

Choir, but their earlier experience had revealed how even a recreation as apparently innocuous as male voice choral singing could not, in Wales, be detached from its social environment. Cwmbach, founded during the miners' lockout of 1921, knew better than most that the Welsh choral scene was not immune to the swirling winds that occasionally blew through the wider society with which it was so closely intertwined. It showed too how disruptive white South Africa's subterfuges to attain international respectability could be. On the other side of Maerdy mountain to the west, the Ferndale 'Imps' had been lured there in 1973, while in the neighbouring township of Tylorstown, Pendyrus, still mindful of its 'Little Moscow' associations dating back to the 1920s, threatened any of its members who felt similarly inclined with immediate expulsion.

If the 1960s were years of sweeping success for Cwmbach who in 1966 complemented their National victories of 1966 and, later, 1968 (in Barry, by a staggering margin of 28 marks) by winning at the Miners' Eisteddfod for the fifth time, that year was another milestone in the often interrupted saga of a choir that had been even more closely linked to its industrial past, Dowlais. Once again it experienced re-foundation, this time under the accomplished musician D.T. Davies (1900–83). He had accompanied the Dowlais Penywern choir in the 1920s, as his namesake E.T. had accompanied Dowlais in their victory at London in 1909, when their conductor then, W.J. Watkins, had accompanied Harry Evans' Dowlais in their famous win at Liverpool in 1900. They were all F.R.C.O. and, bar D.T., had succeeded each other at Harry Evans' house, 'Cartrefle' in Merthyr's Upper High Street, where he had installed a three-manual organ and founded the 'Cartrefle dynasty'. D.T. Davies was next in line in this apostolic succession, but it never happened. It was as organist at Zoar Ynysgau Welsh Congregational chapel from 1928 until his death that the self-effacing D.T. achieved competitive success as choral conductor that had eluded his three eminent predecessors: he won National 'firsts' with Dowlais Ladies Choir (in fact, three of them, at Treorchy 1928, Neath, 1934 and Caernarfon 1935), Dowlais United (mixed) choir (at Fishguard 1936), and the Dowlais Male Choir, reconstituted in 1965 to win at Ruthin in 1973. It was a remarkable triple triumph, never achieved before or since. Diffident by nature, one who shunned the limelight, when he stood before his choirs the words used by David Morgans, historian of the musicians

of Merthyr and District to describe the legendary choral conductor Dan
Davies (1858–1930) were equally applicable to D.T.: 'His personality
before the choir was like a great battery of energy, and he had the knack
of communicating this power whenever he wielded the baton' (Morgans,
p.155). As John H. Davies, himself by that time the doyen of Welsh choral
conductors remarked of him when D.T. Davies stepped forward in 1973
to receive the Welsh Guards Cup and the Ivor Sims memorial medal
presented to the winning conductor of the 'chief', *'Dyma'r Tywysog ei hun'*
– 'Here is the Prince himself.' It was a deserved tribute, and Côr Meibion
Dowlais' D.T. Davies Young Musicians Bursary Competition fittingly
perpetuates his name. Such awards, intended to progress the careers of
promising young performers, whether singers or instrumentalists, are
an important aspect of several choirs' contribution, like Flint, Maesteg
Gleemen, Morriston Orpheus, Pontypridd and Treorchy to the wider
musical community.

Another notable feature of the Ruthin National was the appearance
in the 'chief' of Tredegar Orpheus from the heads of the Gwent valleys.
Tredegar had a formidable competition record reaching back to pre-1914
days, their finest hour being when they came second out of 18, and ahead
of all the other Welsh choirs, to the polished Nelson Arion Orpheus Choir
in a monumental contest at Corwen in 1919. After several less successful
entrances in the inter-war years, their re-appearance at Ruthin in 1973,
with the all-Welsh rule now in force, was a heroic recognition of the
special status of the National in the eyes of Welsh male choirs. Tredegar
had by then even fewer than Dowlais' half dozen Welsh speakers, and it
took the intervention of the thoroughly Welsh-speaking Brythoniaid to
divide these two historic choirs whose very names evoked the coal and
iron cradle of the Welsh industrial experience. Gwent, thankfully, like
equally-anglicized east Flintshire in what is effectively Greater Merseyside,
has not turned its back on the National festival, and competing choirs
from Blackwood to Chepstow via Rhymney, Blackwood, Caldicot, Risca,
Beaufort and Blaenavon have since the war all contributed to ensuring
that the Eisteddfod has continued as a truly all-Wales occasion into the
21st century.

Chapter 10

Bridge of Sighs: Pontarddulais

For all the deserved congratulations heaped on Dowlais at Ruthin in
1973, even as experienced a musician as D.T. Davies was unable to
hold the fort against the heavy artillery they faced at Carmarthen the
following year, six competitors headed by Pontarddulais and Rhos who
came first and second with the iron town third. It was the Bont's sixth
success in eleven years. Always well turned out in their crisp white shirts,
green blazers and immediately recognisable breast-pocket badge and
matching tie which, however prestigious the occasion, they have never
abandoned, with a constant membership well in excess of a hundred, a
strikingly youthful appearance for the best part of fifty years (only now
have they started to look older together), and an equally bright, ringing
tenor sound reminiscent of Treorchy in their pomp, they were by 2014
ready for their sixteenth National success, which they secured, to add to
their ten wins at Cardigan (including six in succession 1967–72), two at
Pontrhydfendigaid, six at the Miners' Eisteddfod, and, by then under Noel
Davies' successor Clive Phillips, two at Llangollen.

Shaped by Noel Davies (1928–2003) around a group of young men
who had enjoyed competition at the local youth club which they had
now outgrown – the same youthful energies that made Meirion Bishop's
Pontarddulais the foremost second-class rugby club in Wales in the
early 1960s – it was built on the deep-rooted musical foundations of a
performative Welsh-language chapel culture, and a strong choral tradition
reaching back to the industrial development of the Pontarddulais district
in the late 19th century. A Pontarddulais male choir had competed at the

Merthyr National Eisteddfod in 1901 and came sixth out of seven; later, tables would not only be turned but sent spinning. The modern choir traces its origins to a meeting of those ex-youth club choir members in October 1960, and within a year had acquired over 90 members whose average age was 26 and raised some hackles locally as the illustrious and once thriving Pontarddulais Choral Society suffered such a sharp decline in its men's section that by the mid-1960s it was forced to dissolve. While the new choir were finding their competitive feet, they were soundly beaten by the more experienced Dunvant, who by way of encouragement generously shared their £30 prize with the new kids on the block. Later, as those youngsters matured into a top class prize-winning choir, Dunvant thought of asking for their fifteen pounds back. In 1961 there were twelve choirs at the Miners' Eisteddfod in Porthcawl – in contrast to the two choirs each at the Cardiff and Dyffryn Maelor (Rhos) Nationals of 1960 and 1961 – and the Bont came in third behind Ferndale Imperial and Glynne Jones' Rhymney Silurians. It would not be the last Pontarddulais would see of the flamboyant Glynne. Although membership exceeded a hundred by the time of the 1962 National, the decision was taken to enter the second competition, under eighty voices. Every choir has its own mythology: it is an often repeated chapter in Bont's that there were

Dunvant Male Voice Choir sweeping to National Eisteddfod victory at St David's in 2002 under the baton of Tim Rhys-Evans.   (*Courtesty of Dunvant Male Voice Choir*)

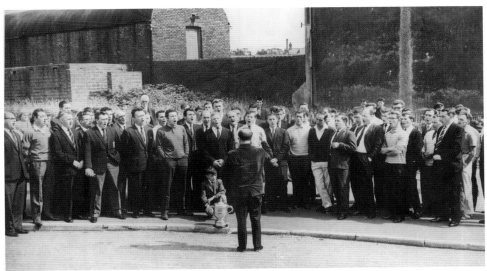

Noel Davies and Pontarddulais with the first of the clean sweep of four cups they won in 1965.

(*Courtesy of Pontarddulais Male Voice Choir*)

thirteen choirs involved in the competition at Llanelli in 1962; in fact there were five, and Bont were runners-up to the in-form Silurian Singers winning for the fourth time in five years.

This was a striking success on the part of the fledgling Bont choir but not as astonishing as the next year's, when for the first time they entered the 'chief' for over eighty voices and inflicted a double-digit drubbing on a Pendyrus struggling to adapt to the idiosyncratic demands of their new conductor and his fondness for silk-lined capes, Jaguar cars, and unwavering commitment to the promotion of modern Welsh music. Glynne Jones, as we have seen, was also equally determined to spice the Welsh male choral repertoire with an array of 16th and 17th-century motets recently made available by the Gwynn publishing company of Llangollen, and he brought them to a new audience. The two test pieces at Llandudno represented both these strands. Haydn Morris' 'Salm Bywyd' ('Psalm of Life') and Jacobus Kerle's 'Agnus Dei', would have been thought tailored to suit 'Lord Pendyrus', who was therefore not best pleased to find himself at the final reckoning 13 points adrift of Noel Davies' young Turks. The following year seemed to indicate that the Bont still constituted a bridge too far for the representatives of the Rhondda Fach, though not for those of the Rhondda Fawr, as Treorchy scored a famous victory, with the Bont in second place one mark ahead of Pendyrus. Treorchy, by now under John Cynan Jones, were again the winners at Bala in 1967, two marks ahead of Bont, but that was the last time to the present day (2015) that Côr Meibion Pontarddulais had failed to take first prize at the National Eisteddfod.

Several features in this remarkable record present themselves. The first is the stark testimony of the figures: unbeaten for 14 National wins since Bala, but never a triple crown in three successive years, for trophies for their own sake exerted little appeal to Noel Davies or his successor since 2003, Clive Phillips, though the choir's record is studded with 'doubles'. And years like 1965 and 1968, when the Welsh Guards' Cup of the National was accompanied by the victors' trophies at Pontrhydfendigaid, Cardigan and the Miners' Eisteddfod, meant there was more silverware in the Bont's display cabinet than in Tiffany's on Fifth Avenue. Over the years they have been drenched in showers of plaudits from the adjudicators. George Guest had nothing but praise for their 'masterful interpretation' of 'Y Pren ar y Bryn' in 1982, 'every note in place, rhythmically secure and disciplined'. Pontarddulais under Clive Phillips lost none of their Midas touch. The experienced adjudicator and composer Brian Hughes at Meifod in 2003 year proclaimed their 'mastery of choral technique secure … their imagination at all times on fire: this is the best male voice choral singing I have heard for many years.' Another Bont competition favourite, Mathias' 'Gloria' was praised, in the judges' shorthand (2006), for its 'powerful rhythmic opening and masterly syncopation. Strong tone on the chords. Excitement and grading of the *crescendi* reflecting technical skills of the highest order. Tension and relaxation co-existing happily', while there was 'enchantment and magic' in their impressionistic presentation of former accompanist (1973–90), now choir president, Eric Jones' beguiling 'Nos o haf ('A summer's evening').

But it was not all plain sailing. Shock waves registered on the Richter scale after the adjudicators' decision at Barry in 1968, where Pendyrus' courageous choice of 'Owain ab Urien' was thought by all except the judges to have outscored Bont's more cautious and familiar 'Y Pren ar y Bryn'. Then, in 1976, Pontarddulais' victory at the Cardigan National was briefly clouded when a formal complaint was lodged by a defeated opponent that one of the adjudicators had worked with the Bont in a professional capacity. Clearly 'cythraul y canu' – the 'devil in the singing' that had soured relationships in years gone by – was alive and well, but the protest was investigated and dismissed, and cordial relations with the aggrieved party soon restored. Nevertheless, it was perhaps a small indicator that the Bont's ever-upward trajectory of unimpeded success was grating on some nerves.

More significant is the fact that Côr Meibion Pontarddulais has kept faith with the National Eisteddfod since the choir's inception in the early 1960s. Other choirs chose to withdraw from the competitive stage in the late 1960s and early 1970s, on various grounds: that lucrative deals with major recording companies demanded constant preparation of new music for a contracted annual LP or CD and that commercial imperatives worked against Eisteddfod test pieces of new Welsh or even classical material; that these commitments precluded the time-consuming attention to detail that competition preparation required; that a record of failure at competitive level did not help publicity or sales (in other words, recording companies did not want Eisteddfod losers so the risk was best avoided); that increasingly regular overseas tours required assembling a wide-ranging eclectic repertoire that takes time and effort to build and a schedule that does not easily accommodate eisteddfodau; that the taste of audiences and choristers themselves was changing; and that new work and leisure patterns ring-fenced August for family holidays not Eisteddfod competition.

In a world of fast-moving technological innovation and changing listening habits, Pontarddulais, Rhos and Risca could make similar claims regarding the pressures of reconciling the popular with the more demanding repertoire and juggling the concert stage, Eisteddfod appearances and overseas tours. But Noel Davies, like Glynne Jones, believed in educating as well as entertaining: 'Our policy ... has always been "something for everyone" and that we try to give as wide a selection of music as possible ... I think also that there should be something ... for choristers themselves and which also interests choristers from other choirs ... We must aim at singing the best and greatest music that is available to male voice choirs'. This did not mean stinting on those pleasurable activities which some choristers exercise their vocal chords expressly to enjoy. Pontarddulais have travelled abroad on at least 15 major overseas

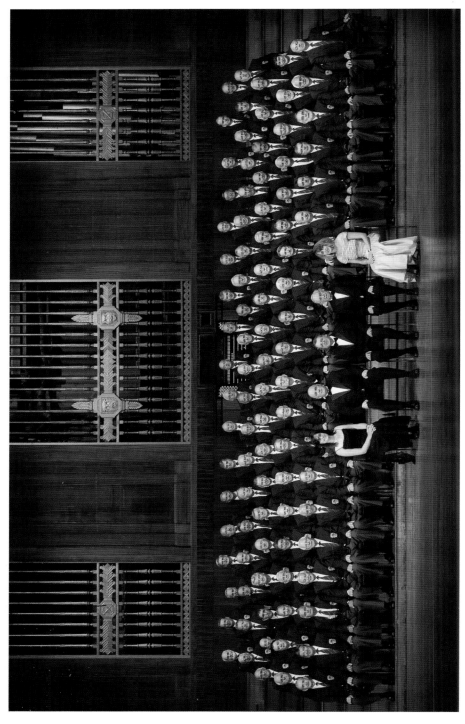

Côr Meibion Pontarddulais in 2010, with Noel Davies' successor Clive Phillips seated between accompanist Rhiannon Williams-Hale (left) and choir president Eric Jones.

(Courtesy of Pontarddulais Male Voice Choir)

tours since their first in 1966 to Sweden (Noel Davies knew how much Welsh choirs have to learn from Scandinavia and east European choirs), recorded regularly (at least 20 discs on vinyl and video), and maintained a busy diary of concert engagements (mostly in Wales, while some choirs virtually have shares in the bridges across the Severn). Bont can still boast consistently over a hundred choristers (they were 109 on stage at the 2014 National at Llanelli), and maintain a regular 90% attendance in three weekly rehearsals. Few choirs can still match their glinting tenors or catholic repertoire where the 'warhorses' rub shoulders with works by Schubert, Bruckner, Gareth Glyn, Brian Hughes and the choir's own prolific Eric Jones, whose setting of Waldo Williams' 'Y Tangnefeddwyr', a plea for peace as the night sky over Swansea reddened during the Blitz of 1941, has become a favourite among Welsh male, mixed and school choirs everywhere.

In contrast, Alwyn Humphreys' Morriston Orpheus between 1979 and 2005 (whereupon soon afterwards the choir split as it had in 1935, its unity eventually salvaged by his wife and accompanist Joy Amman Davies) is a striking example of how a choir's vigorous non-competitive commitment can equally well maintain a performance gold standard. Under Ivor Sims and Eurfryn John's successors Lyn Harry (1969–75), Lesley Ryan (1975–79), Alwyn Humphreys, Sian Pearce (2005–7) and Joy Amman, Morriston have not competed since 1971 but have made 50 bestselling commercial discs, undertaken 30 overseas tours, and have – not unreasonably – been content to settle for the kind of encomium heaped on them by the music critic of the *Hamilton Spectator* (Canada) in 1981 for: 'The subtle shaping of phrases, the sustaining of tones at a whisper, the shaping of even single words with consummately controlled dynamics, the execution of a precise silken attack, the achieving of a rich seamless choral blend and unforced superbly controlled pianissimos.' Who needed an eisteddfod adjudication after such extravagant acclaim?

Another frequently recorded choir, who began life in 1964 in Bynea, made their first National appearance in 1969. Côr Meibion Llanelli have since the late 1960s become the most frequently requested choir on BBC Radio Cymru by virtue of the skilful adaptation for male voices, by their long-serving musical director and tenor soloist D. Eifion Thomas, of modern, popular and patriotic songs by Dafydd Iwan, Ryan Davies,

Huw Chiswell and Tecwyn Ifan like 'Yma o hyd', 'Ti a Dy Ddoniau', 'Pan Fyddo'r Nos yn Hir', 'Y Dref Wen' and 'Yfory'. But Eifion Thomas has also recognised that, in his own words, 'the National stage is no place for "lollipops",' as opponents who too easily dismiss Llanelli as merely an 'easy-listening' choir have discovered to their cost as these choral 'Scarlets' suddenly pull Kodály's peacocks out of the hat, and summon up Heinrich Isaak's 'Innsbruck' and Schubert's 'Nachtgesang im Walde' (backed by the required four French horns) from their substantial classical repertoire. During Eifion Thomas' four decades at the helm, after succeeding founder-conductor Denver Phillips in 1974, Llanelli have been regulars at the National Eisteddfod, and if their five firsts have included three unopposed walkovers, that is hardly their fault. The adjudicators are not under any obligation to award the prize to the sole competitor (they withheld it 1975) and in any case Pontarddulais, Trelawnyd and Rhos have in their time, like Treorchy at the generally well-supported Miners Eisteddfod in 1959, all faced the disappointment of being unopposed.

Llanelli and Pontarddulais are foremost among the few south Wales choirs who perform works by Welsh composers of the last 30 years such as Gareth Glyn, Brian Hughes, Eric Jones, Dilys Elwyn Edwards, Dalwyn Henshall and the more accessible Robat Arwyn, Rhys Jones, and Edward-Rhys Harry. In this respect the record of north Wales choirs is far superior. The language factor is clearly an issue here. While once predominantly Welsh-speaking choirs like Pontarddulais and Morriston are down to 50 and 20 per cent speakers respectively, Gwynedd choirs like Brythoniaid, Caernarfon, Traeth and several smaller ones are composed entirely of Welsh speakers, though further east organizations like Rhosllannerchrugog, Flint and Trelawnyd in Clwyd are far more likely to include a greater proportion of non-Welsh speakers. But competition is in their northern DNA and the desire for 'National' success in their blood.

Chapter 11

Northern Lights: Rhos – and Others

In terms of the number of choirs competing in Wales' premier festival, the golden age was the inter-war period 1918–1939. The average number entering the chief male voice competition, for choirs ever 80, and sometimes over a hundred voices up to 150, was nine in the 1920s, when there were ten choirs or more on eight occasions between 1918 and 1929; the average was even higher for choirs in the second competition (9.4). If the average of the 'chief' was slightly lower in the 1930s (7.6), on only four occasions did it fall below eight contestants, and the relatively low figure of five in 1935 distorts the average for the decade, since on six occasions there were eight or more competing; at Port Talbot in 1932, eleven. These were the years of the fabled encounters between Swansea, Morriston United and Morriston Orpheus, Pendyrus, Rhos, and Powell Dyffryn, with critical interventions, at least when the Eisteddfod was in north Wales, from Hadley (Shropshire), Nelson Arion (Lancs.) and Hebden Briercliffe (Yorks.). The figure for choirs in the second competition in 1930s was higher than for the chief, averaging 9.7 with 13 choirs entering in 1932. When we include dedicated categories for works and factory choirs, and, by the end of the decade, for choirs of the unemployed and the Welsh in exile, the numbers become extraordinary: at Cardiff in 1938 there were 30 male choirs across five categories, from 16–20 voices to not less than a hundred, with depression-hit Brynmawr, Haverfordwest, and several colliery choirs making regular appearances, the Cambrian Colliery of Clydach Vale (Rhondda) recording a notable hat-trick between 1930 and 1932.

Those choirs would put in an appearance in the post-war period too, when overall the fall in the number of entrants is sharp. Three was the consistent decennial average between 1950 and 2000 with some better-attended contests in the 1980s – five each at Machynlleth 1981, Porthmadog 1987 and Llanrwst 1989 – lifting the average to 3.5. It was not a coincidence that the test pieces on those occasions were the popular and accessible 'Y Pysgotwyr' ('The Fishermen'), 'Nidaros' and 'Croesi'r Anial' ('Crossing the Plain'), while the choice of 'Invictus' as the test piece for the chief in Mold in 1991 attracted six choirs. Nor was it an accident, given these northern venues, that most of the entrants too were from north Wales, the exceptions being Pontarddulais, Canoldir (Birmingham) and Llanelli, who took the first three places in 1981, and Swansea, the re-badged Manselton, in 1989. There were ten occasions between 1970 and 2010 when there was only one choir in the chief, a situation rarely encountered in the second competition, though the Ferndale 'Imps', Mynydd Mawr and Whitland were frustrated to find themselves unopposed in 1956, 1984 and 1990 respectively. There were now fewer big choirs of around a hundred voices as the balance tilted in favour of more numerous medium- and small-sized choirs. This was mirrored in the reduction in the required number of voices for the 'chief' as it was gradually reduced from over 100 to over 80, then 70, then over 61, until eventually by 2002 to over 45 voices – a far cry from the 80 to 150 voices requirement of the 1930s.

It is social and economic change rather than the introduction of the all-Welsh rule in 1950 that accounts for the fall-off in competitions, for it is the large choirs of the chief that show the most severe decline: the number of entrants in the second competition has held up, and the introduction of a glee competition from 1966 for choirs of under forty voices would prove enormously popular. The Eisteddfod sought various strategies to retain the allegiance of the big choirs, from permitting an increased element of own choice – until in 2015 a *reductio ad absurdum* was reached with no set test piece at all (and in 2016 no specified number of choristers either) – to increasing the prize money from the then revolutionary £500 introduced at Swansea in 1964, to £750, and for the gimmicky 'open' competition of 2003–07, a thousand pounds. Also downscaled were the demands made of the choirs. At Barry in 1968, for instance, the requirement in the 'chief' was the 'Dies Irae' from the Cherubini *Requiem* to be sung in Latin, and own choices from 1500–1700 and a 20th-century Welsh composer, in a programme of 25 minutes. For the Llanelli National in 2000, when the test piece was again the 'Dies Irae', the required length of programme was 18 minutes and by the time it revisited the Vale of Glamorgan in 2012 it was down to 15 minutes. The second competition as well has, since 1947 when it presented its own Challenge Cup, seen a comparable increase in prize money and a corresponding decrease in the time allowed for the programme, with marks deducted (seldom applied) for exceeding the limit. The average of entrants in the second competition returned to six in the 2000s for the first time since the average of seven in the 1970s.

The number of entries for the 'chief' in 2008 and 2010 was an exceptional seven in each years. Generally the big choirs have declined in number, as glee parties of under 40 voices have mushroomed. Introduced at Port Talbot in 1966, the competition for smaller choirs took the best part of a decade to catch on but by 1974 there were nine choirs in this category, eight the following year, and ten at Cardigan in 1976. It is rare in the extreme for a choir to find itself unopposed in the glee class, though that was the fate of the Eifl after journeying from the foothills of Snowdonia to Swansea in 1982. More common was the eight the following year, and ten at Lampeter in 1984, where Eifl, determined to show that their uncontested prize two years earlier was not a flash in the eisteddfodic pan, properly won. The most populated glee contest ever was at Llanrwst in 1989, when a superb performance by Côr Godre'r Aran, singing second, remained so indelibly imprinted on the adjudicators' mind that they awarded the prize to Eirian Owen's vocally rich party even after hearing another 11 choirs; 13 in all. Godre'r Aran repeated the feat at Aberystwyth three years later when an even more emphatic 15 marks of Bala blue water separated them from their near neighbours Bro Glyndŵr, from the other end of the lake, who came second in a competition among nine choirs.

This part of Wales enjoys a deep-rooted musical and literary history, and its vocal culture is embodied in one of the most assured, technically proficient of any Welsh choir. Godre'r Aran will never match the big choirs for heft, though given its prodigious tonal resources in the lower parts it can well match them for sonority. It was founded in 1949 to compete as a *cerdd dant* (i.e. *penillion*) party at that year's National Eisteddfod in Dolgellau and soon became regarded throughout Wales as the foremost exponents of this unique form of musical expression. In 1970 a new accompanist was appointed in Eirian Owen, a native of Llanuwchllyn, saturated in the competitive ethos but by virtue of her professional qualifications in music, as tutor in voice and piano and as staff accompanist at Chetham's School of Music, was equipped and ready to broaden Godre'r Aran's horizons when in 1975 she succeeded as conductor the influential county councillor, uncrowned king of Merionethshire and *cerdd dant* supremo, Tom Jones, Llanuwchllyn (1910–85). The party's song-list was now increasingly directed towards classical, religious and operatic works, and, tutored and conducted by Eirian Owen from the piano, Godre'r Aran became more recognizably a conventional 'côr meibion' – except there was nothing conventional about the vocal tuition that turned national winners like baritones Tom Evans (Gwanas), Iwan Wyn Parry, Trebor Lloyd Evans and the late *basso profundo* Alun Jones into a thunderous lower section quite capable of giving any Russian chorale a run for its rouble.

The membership was and is entirely Welsh-speaking, mostly employed in agriculture and rural industries, but the restrictions that farming can impose have not prevented Godre'r Aran from being one of the most-widely travelled choirs in Wales, having over the last four decades visited the USA and Canada three times, made eight visits to Australia and most European countries, and driven by their cultural pride and patriotism to visit the Welsh colony in Patagonia in 1977 and again 30 years later. Though never more than a good glee party in number, this qualified them for the National's second competition, winning it four times between 1989 and 1993, and by 2008 as many times again at Llangollen, more than any other Welsh choir, eccentric decisions on the part of the international panel of adjudicators depriving them of the festival's deserved premier choral award on more than one occasion. In the National Eisteddfod, despite having competed over many years, Godre'r Aran holds the unique record of never having been beaten. Given the vocal wealth and musical leadership it enjoys, one might perhaps wish for a more ambitious nod in the direction of continental Europe and works by, say, Kodály, Janáček and Poulenc, but this is more a recognition of Godre'r Aran's quality and achievements than a criticism, and at least they have resisted the wholesale slide into the pleasing but passionless 'easy listening' comfort zone.

Among the several other women who have enjoyed consistent success at the National, in the potentially and sometimes actually mysogynistic world of Welsh male voice choirs, are Bethan Smallwood with Llangwm, Ilid Anne Jones with Hogia'r Ddwylan, and Menai Williams with just about everybody, though none has been as exposed to the unwanted glare of unexpected publicity quite as much as a trained operatic mezzo-soprano from Corwen, Ann Atkinson. Former conductor of the local choir Côr Bro Glyndŵr, she happened to be heading up Côr Meibion Froncysyllte when record executive Daniel Glatman, the former manager of boyband Blue, heard them singing at a celebrity wedding in nearby Trevor Hall, with the result that thanks to some skilfully inserted backing, the 'Fron' choir became an overnight sensation as the oldest boyband in the world. Their 'Voices of the Valley' CD became the best-selling 'classical' album of 2006, irrespective of the fact that they came from nowhere near the coal tips, pit gear and miners' cottages that the 'Valley' cliché was meant to evoke, but the scenic, verdant Vale of Clwyd.

Founded in the shadow of Thomas Telford's famous aqueduct, Froncysyllte was a product of the prevailing post-war youth club culture, and, just as Godre'r Aran were stimulated to compete by the impending Dolgellau National Eisteddfod in 1949, 'Fron' were prodded into action

Eirian Owen and Côr Godre'r Aran share a joke with Rebecca Evans in 2010.

(*Courtesy of Côr Godre'r Aran*)

by the inaugural Llangollen Eisteddfod held on their doorstep in 1947. They achieved considerable success under Lloyd Edwards, then John A. Daniel (1970–91) and Val Jones (1991–2002), by singing a modern repertoire which Daniel Glatman would never have recognised, let alone considered commercially viable. Ann Atkinson was with them the shortest time (2002–09), but in those years 'Fron' signed a major contract with Universal, made four best-selling CDs, an appearance at the Classical Brit Awards and became ubiquitous on television and entertainment shows that had hitherto, in male voice choir terms, been the preserve of the likes of Treorchy and Morriston. It is easy to forget that in their pre-commercial life, Froncysyllte had been formidable National competitors, winning the second competition in 1955, 1961, 1963 and 1977, and when they briefly moved up to the chief category in Newport in 1988, won again.

Hogia'r Ddwylan – literally, 'the boys from both shores' (of the Menai) – began, like Godre'r Aran, as a *cerdd dant* party in 1966 and gradually transformed itself into a male voice choir, first with Menai Williams who was with them from 1968 to 1988, until the baton was passed in 1998, in an unbroken chain of female conductors, to Ilid Anne Jones who, in the best traditions of Welsh Nonconformist precocity, was playing the organ at Capel Seion, Talysarn, at eight years of age. The 'hogiau' won out of seven choirs at Ynys Môn in 1999, out of six in 2001, and in Meifod in 2003, beating their arch rivals Ar Ôl Tri on each occasion, though there were other times when the Cardi boys had the better of them. Ar Ôl Tri ('After Three' – beats rather than beers; perhaps both) were founded in 1985 in the Cardigan and Teifi Valley area by Wyn Lewis, an amateur musician by profession a vet, who formed a group of young men who, now in their forties, have become Eisteddfod regulars, winners more often than not, chalking up four consecutive victories between 2004 and 2007. The closely fought encounters among glee parties in the first years of the 2000s drew rapt and enthusiastic audiences, and with keen rivals Bois y Castell of Llandeilo and the Maesteg Gleemen also in the mix, these hotly contested competitions between the smaller choirs of under forty voices were worthy successors to the clash of choral heavyweights in earlier years.

Bethan Smallwood has been loyal to Côr Meibion Llangwm since the National Eisteddfod of 1973, the choir founded in the Cerrigydrudion-Pentrefoelas area between Bala and Ruthin in 1930. Choirs from a predominantly agricultural background are restricted to relatively few overseas tours, a problem faced by rural choirs from north Powys like Eisteddfod regulars – and winners – Penybont-fawr and Llanfair Caereinion. At home, Llangwm has more than compensated with frequent successes at the glee and second competition level with victories at Fishguard in 1986, Cwm Rhymni (1990), Neath (1994), Llanelli (2000) and the Vale of Glamorgan (2012), and as a diversion from their run of southern successes, in Denbigh in 2013. These firsts were interspersed with several second placings, though there was no disgrace in being runners up to Godre'r Aran and Ar Ôl Tri.

The roll-call of women wielding the wand – figuratively speaking; they leave the baton business to the men and only a few still use it – is remarkable; in north Wales, Eirian Owen at Godre'r Aran, successively Menai Williams, Sioned Webb, and Ilid Anne Jones at Hogia'r Ddwylan, Val Jones followed by Ann Atkinson (now at Trelawnyd) and Leigh Mason at Froncysyllte, Delyth Humphreys at Caernarfon, Linda Gittins at Llanfair Caereinion (1990–2005), Bethan Smallwood at Llangwm, Carol

Conductors of Hogia'r Ddwylan since 1968, rt. to left, Menai Williams, Sioned Webb, Mari Preis and Ilid Anne Jones. Rehearsals are well attended. *(Courtesy of Hogia'r Ddwylan)*

Davies at Aberystwyth (2003-2015), Annette Bryn Parri until recently with Traeth, Sylvia Anne Jones at Blaenau Ffestiniog's Moelwyn, Rhonwen Jones at Penybont-fawr, Angharad Ellis following Mair Selway at Bro Aled (Llansannan) – the list goes on, and that of female accompanists is even longer. Perhaps the masculinist tradition of 'valleys' culture accounts for the fact that south Wales has been slower catching up, but the likes of Joy Amman Davies at Morriston, Darya Brill-Williams (Dowlais), Rhiannon Williams-Hale (Bridgend), Janice Ball (Treorchy, 2007–12), and Elaine Robins (Côr Meibion De Cymru) have transformed the landscape. Among smaller choirs so have Dorothy Connell in Barry, Luned Jones in Builth, Llinos Davies in Treharris, Pauline Carey in Pontnewydd, Jennifer Jones at Ynysowen, Laura Deenik (Caerphilly), Carys Wynne (Mynydd Islwyn), Eira Paskin (Ogmore Vale), Mair Jones (Porthcawl and Port Talbot Cymric), Davinia Harries Davies (Dyffryn Tywi), Mair Lewis (Swansea), Hannah Mitchell at Abercynon, Monica Roblin with Canton RFC, Susan Hopkins with Tonna, Juliet Rossiter at Whitland – that list goes on too. Six of the nine competing choirs at Meifod in 2015 were conducted by women, though we ought not to exaggerate the novelty: three of the five male choirs at the Caio (Carmarthenshire) eisteddfod in 1894 were, too (Y Cerddor 1894, p.23), and Miss Paynter of Amlwch was complimented by the adjudicators at the 1902 National. By contrast, with the exception of Trelanwyd, the big choirs in north Wales – Brythoniaid, Penrhyn, Rhos, Rhos Orpheus and Maelgwn – are all in the hands of men. Menai Williams at Caernarfon, however, achieved one historic feat that seems to have gone unnoticed.

Most of the north Wales choirs (Rhos are the sole exception) have fluctuated in membership, and even the largest among them – Brythoniaid, Traeth, Penrhyn, Trelawnyd – have appeared in the second competition as often as in the 'chief'. Caernarfon is another. It began its modern life – the choral tradition in that part of Wales goes back deep into the 19th century – as the Ferodo Male Voice Choir, founded in 1967 after the tyres and car-parts factory over-looking the Menai Straits which employed most of its members, and under the cellist and choral conductor, Haydn Davies, originally from Pontarddulais (and brother of Helena Braithwaite, conductor of Cardiff's Ardwyn Singers and National adjudicator) achieved striking success and an increased membership to 80 as the Ferodo choir became Côr Meibion Caernarfon in the 1970s. Haydn Davies' successors were Bill Evans and the composer Dalwyn Henshall, while the pianist and harpist Menai Williams, bringing with her a wealth of accumulated experience with Hogia'r Ddwylan and Côr Meibion y Penrhyn, took over in 1993, with Mona Meirion, also a harpist, at the piano. Having poked a toe into the waters of the 'chief' between 1987 and 1992, found the temperature chilly and promptly withdrawn it, Caernarfon began notching up a series of wins in the second competition, meeting the challenging dual tests of Elgar's unaccompanied 'The Reveille' and Morgan Nicholas's fantasia for piano with choral backing, 'Mawr yw yr Arglwydd,' to win at Neath in 1994, an opera chorus by Bellini at Colwyn Bay in 1995, and Gounod's 'Soldiers' Chorus' to make it a hat-trick at Llandeilo in 1996. Their hubristic intention of making it four in a row was punctured at Bala by Côr Meibion Aberystwyth, regular competitors and twice winners in the 1990s under another pianist/harpist, Margaret Maddock whose diminutive frame belied an iron determination, an insistence on restrained singing and a meticulous attention to musical detail, all of which in 1997 commended themselves to the adjudicators over the weightier sound of Caernarfon. Undeterred, the 'Cofis' had the numbers and confidence to make another attempt at the 'chief'. They split more experienced campaigners in that category, Trelawnyd (first) and Rhos (third) on Ynys Môn in 1999, and two years later beat Trelawnyd and Tim Rhys-Evans' Dunvant. While there had been a healthy tradition of winning female conductors in the second competition, Menai Williams in 2001 became the first woman ever to be the recipient of the Ivor Sims memorial medal and hold aloft the Welsh Guards Cup awarded to the winner of the chief male voice competition. And she did it again at Meifod two years later.

Numerically the largest choir in North Wales used to be Rhos but it is now Trelawnyd (until 1954, Newmarket), a village between Dyserth and Holywell in Flintshire, where Geraint Roberts held the reins from 1981 to 2014. Its first conductor in 1933 was William Humphreys, a local headmaster and father of the novelist Emyr Humphreys. His abrupt manner and stern discipline, attributed to his having been gassed in the trenches, intimidated even the hardened farmworkers and Point of Ayr colliery workers who composed most of the choir. When Ann Atkinson, formerly of Froncysyllte, took over in 2015 she was only the sixth to do so in over 80 years, a record marginally better than Morriston's (seven conductors), though inferior to Pendyrus' four over a comparable length of time (Pontewydd in Gwent have had only four since 1904). Some of her predecessors were noted disciplinarians, not only Humphreys (1933–39), but also his successor T. Elford Roberts (1946–55), who 'used to run his fingers through his hair when frustrated by the choir's slowness to pick up a point until it stood up on end like an angry hedgehog'. Neville Owen (1955–69), a stickler for accuracy, on stage 'always seemed to be expecting a bullet between the shoulder blades'. But he built the choir up to 80 voices, and then provided a platform for Goronwy Wynne (1970–81), a botanist and scientist, to increase the membership until Trelawnyd were 115 on stage at Caernarfon in 1979. His podium ritual, in a description that will stand for many (male) conductors in many places, was a mixture of style and nerves:

> Spectacles out of case – pause – case back in top pocket – pause – polish spectacles with handkerchief – pause – place spectacles on nose – pause – shuffle copies on stand so that pages don't stick – pause – hitch up trousers, wipe forehead with handkerchief and return to

Choirs on tour rarely miss an opportunity for an impromptu concert. Trelawnyd in Ontario, 1978.

(*Courtesy of Trelawnyd Male Voice Choir*)

pocket and finally, after what seemed a lengthy fidget – raise baton and off we went.'

(*Côr Meibion Trelawnyd, 1933–1983;* Owen p.206)

Geraint Roberts was appointed in 1981 at 24 years of age and his first two appearances at the National were frustratingly unopposed (1983, 1985), but he savoured two compensating victories over Llanelli and Caernarfon in 1992, Caernarfon and Rhos in 1999, and won the 'open' competition in the teeth of Rhos and Penrhyn at Flint in 2007. Choirs often have a favourite item that they perform often, and often under competitive conditions, with success: they manage the knack of making the familiar sound fresh. For Pontarddulais it is probably Mathias' 'Y Pren ar y Bryn' (they must like those recurrent fourths and open fifths); Côr Meibion Aberystwyth's party piece throughout the 1990s was Gareth Glyn's evocative 'Clychau'r Gog', while Trelawnyd's favourite was Schubert's 'Twenty-third Psalm' ('Duw yw fy Mugail') which they seemed to sing at every conceivable opportunity and was at least preferable to endless repetitions of, say, 'The Rhythm of Life', let alone the more syrupy items preferred by some choirs. The hardened choristers of Rhosllannerchrugog are resistant to syrup. That this remarkably musical village of around ten thousand can produce two big male choirs, Rhos and Rhos Orpheus, is extraordinary enough – Morriston's Orpheus and Rugby Club choirs are their equivalents in south Wales – without also including a luxuriant growth of other blooms like Rhos Light Opera, Rhos Aelwyd Choir, Rhos Aelwyd Amateur Operatic Society and Rhos Ladies Choir in what is by any standard a musical hothouse: the Rhos epiglottis is inexhaustible.

Rhos Orpheus have, in their near sixty years' existence, rarely ventured on to the National stage, though when they have their intervention has been decisive as when they defeated five others representing the cream of north Wales choirs in the chief competition at Mold in 1991. That five, however, did not include Côr Meibion y Rhos. What Côr Godre'r Aran are to the medium-sized choirs of north Wales, especially rich and resonant at the bottom end and superbly marshalled by an outstanding musician, their counterpart among the bigger choirs is undoubtedly Côr Meibion Rhosllannerchrugog. In 1957 22-year-old Colin Jones accepted the invitation to become their musical director. A talented pianist who in his early teens had won the under-16 and open piano competitions at Llangollen, he had opted for nine years underground at the local Hafod colliery and continuing his piano tuition in preference to two years National Service without it. At 26 he came out of the colliery to study under the revered Harold Craxton at Manchester. By then he was already at the helm of Côr Meibion y Rhos, whose accompanist he had been since 1952. In 1959, after less than two years in charge, he took Rhos to the National in Caernarfon and came within a single mark of John H. Davies' Treorchy, then in their prime; even Pontarddulais never came quite that close to unseating the Rhondda champions.

Treorchy's unbeaten run had been inaugurated at Aberystwyth in 1952 and they would remain undefeated until they withdrew from the competitive stage in 1967 – or rather, *almost* unbeaten. The one choir to beat them was Colin Jones' Rhos, who entered the lions' den at Llanelli in 1962, as John Owen Jones' choir had done at Cardiff in 1938, to snatch the prize from under the noses of the best south Wales had to offer: Treorchy, Morriston and Manselton. It was a momentous victory by nine marks, including being awarded 95 on, fittingly, the Rhos composer J. Owen Jones' own 'Chwyth, chwyth aeafol wynt' ('Blow, blow thou winter wind'). The entire population of the village came out to greet the 130-strong heroes of Llanelli the next day. Within five years they were singing at the Opera House in Chicago, where observant concert goers would have marvelled at the conductor's ability to extract an industrial-strength surge of power from his choir with the merest flick of his little finger: Colin Jones' proverbial economy of gesture made Sir Adrian Boult look as histrionic as Leonard Bernstein.

Girded by the strongest bass section in Wales and without the more guttural texture of choirs in the north west, Rhos under Colin Jones never slipped out of the chief male voice class, and went on to further National wins at Flint (1969), Bangor (1971) and Porthmadog (1987) as well as winning the BBC Radio Wales Choir of the Year Competition in 1984 and 1985. After exactly thirty years in charge (1957–87), Porthmadog was Colin Jones' swansong with Rhos, for within a few years he had formed his own North Wales Chorus, fifty beefy hand-picked singers drawn from right across the region, known as Cantorion Colin Jones but not for being eisteddfod competitors. He had learned to be as wary of the capricious nature of adjudicators as his contemporary Glynne Jones at Pendyrus, conceding that occasionally his choir were undeserving winners – though Glynne would never have gone that far – and at other times lost when they should have won, and believed that adjudicating inconsistencies had failed to raise standards. He would have endorsed the memorable phrase of the former Australian rugby union coach Alan Jones: you can be a rooster one day and a feather-duster the next. J. Owen Jones' winning Rhos choir of 1938 came fifth the following year, while the heroes of Llanelli 1962 found themselves sixth and last at Swansea two years later.

Colin Jones was followed by John Tudor Davies (of 'Gwahoddiad' fame), Tudor Jones and the gifted John A. Daniel, all sons of Rhos who remained loyal to the Eisteddfod with only a first at Colwyn Bay in 1995 to show for it. In 2009 another Rhos product, Aled Phillips, was appointed and between 2012 and 2014 brought off the first hat-trick in the 'chief' since Sims' Morriston Orpheus over 60 years before, in the process seeing off his young contemporaries Stewart Roberts leading Pendyrus to a welcome return to the Eisteddfod stage after a 42-year absence, Robert Nicholls

of Côr Meibion Taf (Cardiff), and Trystan Lewis, who had led the Llandudno Junction choir Maelgwn to success in 2005 and 2009; another victim was the experienced Eifion Thomas, who had been keeping the sosban simmering at Llanelli since 1974. Thanks to some innovative programme-building by Aled Phillips, Rhos became addicted to a Swedish piece of funny speech effects – Folke Rabe's 'Rondes' (1964), consisting entirely of non-musical, non-verbal hissing and muttering – to the exasperation of one chorister who leaves the stage in well-rehearsed disgust. Though only half the size they once were, by dint of continuing success

Colin Jones, conductor of Rhos (left), with choir accompanist and arranger of 'Gwahoddiad', John Tudor Davies.
(Courtesy of Rhosllannerchrugog Male Voice Choir)

at National, International (Llangollen) and media (S4C's *Côr Cymru*) level, musically and lingustically versatile with an impressive repertoire covering varieties of genres from Schubert to showstoppers, and with enviable strength at both ends of the register, Côr Meibion y Rhos, along with Côr Meibion Pontarddulais, are today's flagbearers for Welsh male choralism.

Elsewhere in north Wales the old guard was being replaced. Founder-conductor Meirion Jones retired in 2001 from the Brythoniaid choir in favour of tenor soloist John Eifion who had earlier conducted or sung with Côr Meibion Dwyfor, Penrhyn and Caernarfon. Like several north Wales choirs, Brythoniaid had seen a bewildering fluctuation in numbers; numbering 116 at their peak, they became more successful in the second competition where they won in 1969, 1971 and an exceptionally close

Colin Jones prepares his Rhos choristers for their visit to the USA in 1967.

(*Courtesy of Rhosllannerchrugog Male Voice Choir*)

competition at Rhyl in 1985, where only a single mark separated each of Brythoniaid, Traeth, Eifl and Colwyn.

Côr Meibion y Penrhyn of Bethesda who, like Rhos have an illustrious Chicago-tinted history dating back to the early 1890s, and Côr Meibion y Traeth, have also had their moments. Traeth's Anglesey sun shone with particular radiance on those occasions when they seduced a rapt Eisteddfod audience with their involving interpretation of Janáček's meltingly lovely unaccompanied 'Aredig' ('Oráni', 'Ploughing', 1873), which made one wish that other Welsh choirs would tackle more of this composer's choral folk gems (as Glynne Jones did with 'Ach, vojna!' – 'The Soldier's Lot' – in Czech). Traeth moved flexibly between the 'chief' and second competition categories, enjoying several successes in the lower class, though in 1989 Chief Gwyn L. Williams led his Menai Bridge braves across the plain to victory *in* the 'chief' on the ever-popular warhorse 'Croesi'r Anial', with its politically incorrect Wild West caricature of scalp-taking native Americans. Traeth were back on the warpath in 1997 when 22-year-old David Julian Davies, a cathedral organist from Bethesda, claimed the senior scalps of the Rhos Orpheus redskins under John Glyn Williams. Traeth then found their Pocahontas in the experienced pianist and accompanist Annette Bryn Parri whose determined pursuit of a first prize as a musical director was rewarded by achieving it, albeit unopposed, at Flint in 2007.

Ever-popular with audiences everywhere, not least in north America, a concert favourite like 'Crossing the Plain' has only occasionally featured in the National (1900, 1976, 1989), with the unanticipated result that the most frequently heard test piece has been E. T. Davies' unaccompanied 'Y Gwyntoedd' ('The Winds'). First published in 1914, it was given its first National outing at Barry in 1920, then again at Machynlleth in 1937. Curwen re-issued it with Welsh words in 1955 to meet the requirements of the all-Welsh rule, and it was selected as a test piece for the 'chief' in 1956, 1975 and 1992, as well as for the second competition in 1961 and 1967. Other pieces notable for their frequency of selection are T. Hopkin Evans' 'Mordaith Cariad', published with English and Welsh words by Gwynn in time for the Denbigh Eisteddfod in 1939, then variously in the chief and second competitions in 1949, 1959, 1966, 1980, and 1992. D. Vaughan Thomas' 'Prospice', published in 1936, was a regular test piece in mid-century (1937, 1946, 1956, 1962 and 1970) and Meirion Williams' 'Di Rosyn, Dos' six times, 1948, 1965, 1970, 1976, 1979 and 1984. Elgar makes stern demands of amateur choristers, and it is perhaps as surprising as it is gratifying that his 'Reveille' has appeared so often, soon after publication in 1908, then in 1936, 1961 and 1994. William Mathias' 'Y Pren ar y Bryn' is exceptional not so much by reason of its frequent recurrence as a stipulated test piece (1964, 1971, 1982, 1995 and 2005) as because of its undiminished popularity as an own choice in many other years. Given its first airing by Glynne Jones' Silurian Singers over half a century ago, it is likely that, statistically speaking, 'Y Pren ar y Bryn' is the most sung of all National test pieces – not least by Pontarddulais.

The old *canard* that Eisteddfod test pieces have little popular appeal and therefore make unsuitable concert fare does not withstand scrutiny. The excuse was offered in the 1970s, but the merest glance at the post-war pieces disproves the claim; it was the inter-war decades that featured often technically abstruse and unrewarding pieces rarely sung or heard afterwards, the much-favoured Granville Bantock being one of the main culprits. Paradoxically it was in these years, even at the height of the Depression, that crowds of up to 20,000 regularly crowded into the pavilion for the battle of the giants on the last Saturday of the Eisteddfod when upwards of eight choirs entered the lists for the 'chief' competition of choirs of between 80 and 120 voices.

Always popular as concert items even as organised religion loses its appeal and chapels close – often to be acquired and refurbished as choir rehearsal rooms – arrangements of hymn-tunes are generally regarded as not sufficiently challenging at competitive level though 'Deus Salutis' ('Llef', in 1958), 'Tydi a Roddaist' (1973), 'Y Delyn Aur' (1974), 'Christus Redemptor' ('Hyfrydol', 1975) and 'Arwelfa' (1994) have featured for smaller choirs, and a memorably full-blooded rendition of Mansel Thomas' robust arrangement of 'Llanfair' contributed to Llanelli's win in the 'chief' at Llandeilo in 1996.

Given its reputation as a standard bearer of the male voice repertoire, it is difficult to credit that 'Martyrs of the Arena' has never in fact been a test piece since Liverpool in 1884; neither has Joseph Parry's 'Iesu o Nazareth' since Ammanford in 1922. However, nearly a hundred years separate the two appearances of Parry's 'Pilgrim's Chorus' ('Y Pererinion') at Swansea in 1891 and Lampeter in 1984, while other concert favourites that have appeared at both ends of the 20th century include 'Invictus' (1919, 1991), 'Y Pysgotwyr' (1894, 1981, 1988), Dard Janin's 'King of Worlds' (1907, 1982) and Daniel Protheroe's masterpiece 'Nidaros' (1907, 1954, 1961, 1987).

Among other major choruses, Protheroe's 'The Crusaders' has never featured and, now, is unlikely to do so. Gounod's 'By Babylon's Wave', composed in the 1850s, arranged for TTBB by Percy Fletcher in 1908 and provided with Welsh words in *Y Cerddor* in 1912, made the cut solely in 1985. Christmas Williams's pulsating depiction of 'The Charge of the Light Brigade' (1910) never made the National stage at all, to the mortification of Arthur Duggan's Pendyrus. If the admirable Duggan had more often forsaken the blood and thunder of the battle of Balaclava for the more disciplined approach favoured by his successors John Samuel and Stewart Roberts, or the controlled muscularity of Rhosllannerchrugog, he might have reaped better dividends. The continuing success of Rhos, Godre'r Aran and Trelawnyd, and the expertise over several decades of such musicians as Colin Jones, John Daniel, Eirian Owen and Menai Williams have been a salutary reminder that the choirs of 'y sowth' (the south) have never had it all their own way, by any means.

Chapter 12

Yma o Hyd

There are still over a hundred male voice choirs in Wales today, though their demise has been regularly forecast since the 1950s. In truth, their obituary has been as premature as Mark Twain's.

The social and musical landscape of those choirs has of course seen far-reaching changes since the emergence of the fully-fledged *côr meibion* from the glee environment of the mid-19th century. It would be odd indeed if that were not the case: there never was a time before change began. The age profile of most choirs is older as men, in appearance and lifestyle, get relatively younger, and the young members in their 20s and 30s that stocked the choirs between 1945 and 1960 have grown old, and died, together. Few of the traditional choirs which began life 70 to 80 years ago, organically linked to their community, nowadays have young men in the 16–25 age group. On the other hand, relatively new Cardiff-based choirs, composed almost entirely of Welsh-speakers in the professions like Bechgyn Bro Taf and Côr Meibion Taf; in west Wales, thanks to a seamless policy of natural wastage and regular recruitment, the apparently ageless Ar Ôl Tri and the young cubs of Islwyn Evans's Teifi-side academy Ysgol Gerdd Ceredigion, as well as in mid Wales the young voices in the recently formed Côr Meibion Machynlleth, include few or none of the retirees who dominate choir membership elsewhere.

The repertoire, though, has changed significantly over the last 40 years, even if little in the last 20. Due in large part to the greater availability of published works for male choirs set to English and Welsh words, a wider range of classical music entered the male choral repertoire from the 1950s which enterprising conductors like John H. Davies and Glynne Jones were quick to exploit. The better-qualified musicians on the podium were also prolific arrangers for TTBB; John Davies and his successor at Treorchy John Cynan Jones were prominent in this regard, Morriston's Alwyn Humphreys has made over 200 frequently-sung arrangements, and brilliant executants like the late Bryan Davies and more recently conductor-pianists John Samuel, Eric Jones, Eirian Owen, Jeffrey Howard and Stewart Roberts have enjoyed making arrangements that keep accompanists fully occupied. Easy-listening adaptations for male voices from musical theatre, film and pop songs please modern audiences, but if the move to update in the direction of a light entertainment repertoire has been made in order to attract younger members, it has rarely worked. Young men who do join will often express a preference for the gripping chordal opening of 'Martyrs' to more transient chart-toppers. The old favourites are still being called on to redress the balance of the new.

Some things do not change. Treorchy make no concession to age or infirmity and remain standing throughout every practice as they have done since their re-formation in 1946. Their annual subscription has not stood still though: what was once three old pence a week, or twelve shillings a year (roughly 60p.) has become an annual forty pounds, which is what Rhos also pay for the privilege of singing together. Choristers elsewhere would regard them as getting off lightly: Rhymney's Silurians pay a pound a week while Pontarddulais' annual subscription is more than twice the hundred pounds a year paid by Penrhyn, Pendyrus and Pontypridd, and four times London Welsh's sixty pounds. Running a choir is an expensive business and the financial secretary vies in the stress stakes with the much put-upon transport manager. Moreover, a changing social and political climate has dictated that where rehearsal and concert space was once freely made available, now ever-increasing charges are imposed for rent, heating and lighting, and the response of many choirs has been to acquire a recently abandoned chapel – a social change in itself with significant implications for singing style and musicality – and make it their headquarters.

Choristers are no longer, in a post-industrial Wales, composed of miners, quarrymen and steelworkers, but in fact many choirs never were, though they too were occupationally-based. The Barry Male Voice

Choir of a hundred years ago was mostly made up of railwaymen and dock-workers. Côr Meibion Aberystwyth began life in the 1960s among post office employees, and learned to tolerate jokes about being a 'mail' choir. Côr Meibion Caernarfon were originally Ferodo, and Côr Meibion Penybont-ar-Ogwr were until 1987 the Bridgend Police Choir. In west and north Wales, the backbone of choirs like Caron, Ardudwy, Godre'r Aran, Llangwm and Penybont-fawr has always been in agriculture and forestry.

The popular massed male choir of any size upwards of two hundred voices is hardly a recently concept either, not even at the Albert Hall. The charismatic Caradog conducted 500 male voices at the Albert Hall, Swansea, in November 1895, comprising eight choirs from Neath to Carmarthen, and they sang 'Comrades', 'Martyrs', and the 'Soldiers' Chorus'; earlier in the year he had conducted nine combined choirs of 700 voices, a band and an orchestra, in a testimonial concert for Joseph Parry in Cardiff. Wales was not the first in the field of course: massed concerts by – surely unwieldy – five to fifteen thousand *orpheonistes* were common in France from the 1860s. Caradog's Welsh concept was revived when, to great acclaim, a massed choir of 500 voices choirs sang at the opening concert of the Swansea National Eisteddfod in 1964; they sang 'Martyrs' then, too, as well as 'Pererinion' and 'Nidaros', which suggests

Côr Meibion Aberystwyth conducted by Margaret Maddock, regular National competitors and twice winners in the second competition (under 61 voices) in the 1990s. (*Courtesy of Côr Meibion Aberystwyth*)

that massed concerts, however enjoyable, encourage in repertoire terms a hardening of the arteries. But the Welsh choral scene has always, generally speaking, been more of a social phenomenon than a musically progressive one, with no further ambition than to fulfil and entertain. The popular 'Thousand Male Voices' event at London's Royal Albert Hall was inaugurated to celebrate the investiture of Prince Charles in 1969, and still flourishes under the alternate auspices of the London Welsh Choir and the Welsh Association of Male Choirs; and under, too, a veritable 'who's who' of well-known musicians like the high-energy Dr Haydn James whose enthusiastic baton whips up the on-field choirs and a 70,000 crowd on international days at the Millennium Stadium. Numbers alone of course can be self-defeating. The centenary of the Welsh Rugby Union in 1980–81 was fittingly celebrated by a concert given by 2,000 male choristers at the then National Stadium, but was later followed up by a pointless and ill-fated attempt in 1993 to transport 8,000 choristers, who had sung at the ground the previous year, to Atlanta, Georgia.

Welsh choirs have been visiting the USA since the 1880s, and in the decade before the outbreak of war in 1914 the North Atlantic was awash with Welsh singers. Between the wars their acquaintance with world geography languished, like most things in Wales except the dole queues, but from 1960 there was not a continent safe from the arrival of singing Welshmen, whether South America, South East Asia, South Australia or the south island of New Zealand, and most European countries including Scandinavia, as well as the Soviet Union, the Arab Emirates and China have had to grin and bear it. The 'ex-pat' network comes in useful here and goes far to explain why Welsh male choirs travel twice as much as their English counterparts, who tend to confine their visits to northern Europe. When the Welsh do, they will often take with them a promising soloist in the early stages of a professional career, like the young Bryn Terfel who accompanied Caernarfon in 1982 and Dunvant in 1985 on their North American tours. Similarly when that promise has been more than realised, these now internationally-acclaimed stars of the opera and concert stage always welcome the opportunity to appear with Wales' leading choirs in gala events to express their appreciation, gratitude and indebtedness to those modest communities from which they emerged and who take such pride in their achievements. Like other choirs of similar standing

Near-invincible in their category in the National since 1997, Cardigan's Ar Ôl Tri under Wyn Lewis, at Llangollen in 2004 came second to Pontarddulais.

(Courtesy of Ar Ôl Tri)

Pendyrus, for example, shared the stage with the likes of Geraint Evans, Janet Price, Stuart Burrows, Margaret Price, Gwyneth Jones and Dennis O'Neill; even earlier, in 1937, these Rhondda Fach Little Muscovites sang with the great Russian bass Fyodor Chaliapine in the Capitol Cinema in Cardiff. In recent years Pendyrus has seen its annual concert enhanced by Rebecca Evans, Rhys Meirion, Gwawr Edwards, Shan Cothi and Lesley Garrett, as well by box-office stars like Katherine Jenkins, John Owen-Jones and Rhydian Roberts. Other major choirs will tell the same story.

For Welsh male choirs are nothing if not versatile. They will as happily provide backing to rock bands as welcome Royal and Papal visitors; when Pope John kissed the tarmac at Cardiff International airport in 1982 he was greeted by a hurriedly-assembled male choir under the quick-thinking Alwyn Humphreys. They will sing in school halls, sports centres, on cruise liners, in cinemas and inside and outside department stores. They will perform at venues as disparate as acoustically awesome cathedrals and at corporate junkets at less reverential hotels, while many choirs' existence depends on the income they earn as purveyors of occasional music at weddings and funerals. It is by now a civic commonplace that no major commemorative, celebratory or ceremonial event can take place anywhere in Wales without a male choir – and soldiers – in attendance. While there is clearly a danger that unambitious choirs can thus be shunted into a siding down which they are complacently content to steam, these occasions should not be underestimated, for hymn-singing by a male choir provides a warm, comforting sound, and they are often opportunities for smaller, non-competitive choirs to boost their self-esteem and assert their local identity. Nor is that identity undermined by linguistic versatility. Under the tuition of their polyglot musical director John Asquith, Rhondda's Côr Meibion Morlais, in addition to singing in the familiar languages of western Europe, have performed in Russian, Finnish, Estonian, Hungarian, Czech and Greek, an impressive multi-lingualism that shrinks the 'difficulty' of the National Eisteddfod's all-Welsh rule to near-invisibility.

Singing with others in combined choir concerts also provides less linguistically confident choirs than Morlais with opportunities to become acquainted with new, perhaps unfamiliar music, and especially Welsh items. Male choirs even, or especially, those the bulk of whose members are not Welsh-speaking feel a desire and an obligation to include Welsh-language music in their repertoire and master new Welsh songs, for they know this is expected of them, not least when they perform outside Wales. For this reason choirs from Haverfordwest to Chepstow are anxious to badge themselves as Côr Meibion Hwlffordd and Côr Meibion Cas-gwent, as also in Gwent are Côr Meibion Caldicot, Côr Meibion Blaenafon and Côr Meibion Glyn Ebwy. It is not only exiles in Calgary and Hong Kong who express their Welsh identity through the male voice choir.

Large occasions also provide opportunities welcomed by smaller choirs to perform, in combination with others, bigger works beyond their own individual resources of 30 or fewer choristers – unless, that is, they are Only Men Aloud, formed in 2000, who astonished a UK television audience unfamiliar with the Welsh choral eisteddfodic tradition by winning BBC TV's *Last Choir Standing* competition in 2008. When in 2013 their charismatic conductor Tim Rhys-Evans, who had cut his teeth with the touring Black Mountain choir and with Dunvant, decided to reduce his 18 professionally-trained singers to a hand-picked octet, he was doing what William Thomas had done over a century earlier when he radically restructured the 80-strong Treorchy choir to the 20 Royal Welsh choristers who proceeded to globetrot with all the enthusiasm but less of the comfort – or choreography – of Only Men Aloud.

Gareth Malone, chorus master to the LSO's youth and community choirs and resourceful populariser of choral singing, has been rightly recognised for developing choirs from scratch in socially deprived areas of the UK. There are no more socially deprived areas than the south Wales valleys, but Tim Rhys-Evans had an historic base to build on when, for the same reason, he founded Only Boys Aloud, who received a rapturous reception at the National Eisteddfod in Ebbw Vale in 2010, went on to beat off thousands of other entrants to come third in television's *Britain's Got Talent* competition later in the year, and saw their version of 'Calon Lân' go viral as that favourite Welsh hymn reached a worldwide audience. This involvement of a younger generation reflects a healthy awareness of the perils of stagnation and a determination to rejuvenate an ageing tradition. More widely, the enterprising Tim Rhys-Evans and Only Men Aloud see themselves as a parent body keen to encourage in their 'offspring' self-confidence and social skills, not unlike the post-war youth club movement from which, as we have seen, choirs like Treorchy, Froncysyllte and Pontarddulais emerged.

The convivial side of the male choir is well established and well known, but there is an important social dimension also. All Welsh male choirs are dedicated to raising money for benevolent causes. In the course of providing choristers with the sociability and recreation that most people – especially it would appear, men of pensionable age – crave, and in addition to bringing inordinate pleasure to millions in performances at home and abroad and on disc, DVD and via the internet, these choirs as registered charities raise hundreds of thousands of pounds annually for local causes and national foundations. A hundred years ago it was for church and chapel restoration; today it is to help repair tears in the fabric of a more secular and individualistic society.

At the same time, the apparent homogeneity of today's choirs can be deceptive. Where most of their members were once mostly church and chapel adherents, if only nominally, few are now; they are of all or no religions. Politically they represent every colour in the spectrum. Given Wales' increasing cultural diversity, however, there are regrettably few non-white faces in their ranks, though choirs sing far more pieces from

Only Men Aloud, telegenic, co-ordinated and sonorous, have reached parts that more traditional male voice choirs have failed to reach. *(Emyr Young)*

a wider range of national and ethnic traditions than they once did, just as they are less homophobic than when they were predominantly based in the masculine heavy industries. The 40 members of the Cardiff-based South Wales Gay Men's choir, founded in 2008, sing all types of music from plainsong to pop classics, though the barbershop harmonies which they favour do not wholly commend themselves to lovers of the traditional Welsh male choir and its addiction to the 'big amen'.

For these choirs have never been impervious to wider social developments. Deeply rooted in their communities as many have been, they have a record of activity on the side of protest and the righting of industrial wrongs. There is a connecting thread that runs from the quarrymen choirs of Bethesda that travelled the UK to help beleaguered families during the Penrhyn lockout of 1900–3 and the pre-1914 choirs that participated in coalfield 'white-shirting' rituals designed to shame strike-breakers and other social transgressors, through the unemployed songsters who tramped the streets of London in the 1930s, to the South

Wales Striking Miners' Choir which drew on the Dulais valley choristers of Onllwyn, Creunant, Glynneath, Resolven and Gyrlais (Ysradgynlais) during the anguished coalfield strike of 1984–5.

Far more traumatic, beyond anguish and even beyond words, was the unspeakable horror of the disaster which killed 116 children and 28 adults at Aberfan on 21 October 1966. A natural urge and tribal instinct persuaded the numbed menfolk of that grieving village that one of the ways they might collectively come to terms with their potentially unhinging bereavement would be to form a choir from the members of the (all-male) coal tip removal committee. In this way too they could thank all who had contributed to the disaster fund, and themselves contribute to a broad range of charities. Thus the Ynysowen Male Choir came into existence in Aberfan and, with a membership drawn also from the neighbouring villages of Merthyr Vale, Troedyrhiw, Abercanaid and Pentre-bach, has since 1992 been conducted by the experienced Jennifer Jones, pianist, harpist and former accompanist to Treorchy, the agreeable personification of today's well-qualified musical directors. Down to the 1960s the positions of conductor and accompanist were often held by those who held similar posts in their churches and chapels, but well before the end of the century these same functions were being performed by semi-professional and professional musicians, mostly employed in education. The long day of the well-meaning and generally capable amateur conductor has closed, with rare exceptions like the musically highly-capable professional veterinary surgeon Wyn Lewis of Cardigan, whose success with the thirty-odd men of Ar Ôl Tri – eleven 'National' wins and five second places in seventeen attempts between 1995–2014, including four consecutive firsts from 2004 to 2007 – is as inspiring as it is astonishing.

Like its neighbouring choirs of Treharris, Abercynon, and Ystrad Mynach, Ynysowen is not competitive for, even in eisteddfod-geared Wales, competition is neither the rationale nor the explanation for the continuing vigour and enduring hold on the collective Welsh consciousness of its male voice choirs. In any case, there have been competitions, festivals and eisteddfodau patronised by choirs who have never darkened the pavilion of the National but prefer to test themselves outside Wales: at the Cornish International Male Voice Choral Festival, for instance, which is still regularly supported by Welsh choirs. Nor within Wales is the National the only eisteddfod. Just as the 'semi-nationals' of Bridgend, Mountain Ash, Ferndale, Porth and Abergavenny in south Wales ('semi-national' was the favoured south Wales name for them, eisteddfodau 'taleithiol' – regional – in the north), and Caernarfon, Porthmadog, Ffestiniog and Dolgellau attracted large numbers before 1914, since 1945 so have the Miners' Eisteddfod at Porthcawl (1948–2001) and the Pantyfedwen Eisteddfodau of Cardigan and Pontrhydfendigaid. Founded in the 1960s by the London Welsh businessman and philanthropist Sir David James (1897–1967), they were viewed as an opportunity to compete at an intermediate level between local eisteddfodau and the National event. But Sir David had the wider ambition of eclipsing the National. He put up larger money prizes and, as a further inducement, removed any all-Welsh requirement. The heyday of the Pantyfedwen Eisteddfodau was the 1960s and 1970s when they drew enormous crowds to the depths of rural Cardiganshire. North Wales choirs came down to test these stepping stones to the National which was held a few months later, as they did not to the Miners' in October, while on their home patch, where they had once flocked to the New Brighton and Morecambe festivals before 1914, from the 1950s they transferred their rivalries to the keenly contested eisteddfodau at Butlins Pwllheli, the Stena/B&I Eisteddfod at Llandudno, Eisteddfod Powys, and the Pan-Celtic Festival at Irish venues like Killarney and Cork.

But nothing, not even success at Llangollen, has matched the fame, kudos and cachet of being a 'National winner'. It is a badge of honour still proudly referred to in programme notes and websites by choirs who last won, or even appeared there, over half a century ago. The eisteddfod, and the National Eisteddfod in particular, is woven into the cultural life of Wales and its male voice choirs have constituted a central strand in it since the late 19th century. The purist and the sophisticate will dwell on the narrow range of the male choir's vocal compass, which in comparison with a mixed choir let alone an orchestra or band is self-evidently true. And without question there are technically more assured, vocally better equipped amateur choirs elsewhere, in Sweden, eastern Europe, Russia, even England. But none carries that compelling emotional charge of a Welsh male choir at its best, in the purring pianissimos or the surging climaxes of the great choruses, like the 'Christ is eternal' finale to 'Nidaros' that reaches out to seize the listener by the throat.

Alwyn Humphreys, the best known of today's conductors, formerly of the Morriston Orpheus (1979–2005), recalls how his father, an ardent top tenor in the Bodffordd Male Voice Choir on Anglesey, 'would get up at dawn, spread his sol-fa music copies over the kitchen table and lose himself in them'. Such devotion would be rare to find among even the most dedicated chorister today, but the commitment is still there in the twice weekly practice and the frequent weekend engagement, and Alwyn Humphreys, speaking from a wealth of experience, is surely right to conclude that male voice choral singing 'has concentrated the minds and talents of innumerable men over the years, helped people to face unimaginable hardship and lifted them on to a higher and better plane ... ordinary dedicated people who made music as if their lives depended on it. In many ways they did.' (Owen, 2009, pp. 8-9)

And still do. The long day has not yet closed on the Welsh male choir. As the blazered choristers at the Millennium Stadium defiantly proclaim: 'Ry'n ni yma o hyd' – 'We are still here'. The Welsh male voice choir is not going gentle into that good night any time soon.

Pontarddulais at the Millennium Stadium in 2011, with Dr Haydn James on the rostrum.
(*Courtesy of Pontarddulais Male Voice Choir*)

Part Two

MYFANWY (ARABELLA)

FOUR-PART SONG,

For Male Voices.

English Words by the late "Ouhelyn."
Welsh Words by Mynyddog.

Music by Joseph Parry (*Mus. Bac. Cantab*).

Trailblazers

Part One began and ended with men in blazers. Part Two is also about blazers: trailblazers, the handful of pathfinders who blazed the trail of the male voice tradition in Wales before the first settlers arrived. If later generations saw further it was because they were able to stand on the shoulders of these pioneer choir-founders, composers and conductors who by 1914 had placed a nation in their debt. First up has to be Dr Joseph Parry, 'y doctor mawr'.

JOSEPH PARRY (1841–1903)

Few Welsh composers had written specifically for Welsh male choirs by 1870, though by 1900 no self-respecting Welsh composer neglected to do so, if only for commercial reasons. The person mainly responsible for this development was Joseph Parry. The finest exponents of the genre like Daniel Protheroe (composer of 'Nidaros', 'Laudamus' and 'The Crusaders'), Maldwyn Price ('Crossing the Plain' and 'Y Pysgotwyr') and D. Christmas Williams ('The Charge of the Light Brigade') had all been students of Parry's and inherited the tripartite formula of narrative, prayer and climax with which he structured his larger choruses.

Joseph Parry was born to a poor, Nonconformist, working-class family in Chapel Row, Merthyr Tydfil, and became one of the best known musicians Wales has ever produced. The major musical influences on him were the chapel which the family attended before emigrating to Pennsylvania when he was 13, the strains of Italian opera, notably Bellini and Donizetti, played by the Cyfarthfa Band, and his Welsh-born music

Joseph Parry

(*National Library Wales*)

teachers in America, John Abel Jones and John M. Price, from Merthyr and Rhymney respectively. These instilled in him the principles of harmony as he sweated in the Danville rolling mills, and encouraged him to immerse himself in the competitive atmosphere of the eisteddfod to which he submitted glees, motets and anthems on both sides of the Atlantic. He studied at the Royal Academy of Music in London between 1868 and 1871, where his teacher, Sterndale Bennett, was a pupil of Mendelssohn's. It was a pity that he never had the opportunity to study on the continent, which might have helped him develop a more original voice. He was appointed Wales's first professor of music at the newly-opened University College at Aberystwyth in 1874 from which he was forced to resign in 1880 because of his frequent absences conducting, performing and adjudicating the length and breadth of Wales. He set up his own school of music in Swansea in the 1880s, until he moved to revive his academic career at University College, Cardiff, where he lectured until his death.

He composed tirelessly, too much and uncritically, over 300 hymn-tunes (few of which are still sung today, 'Aberystwyth' the best known), and innumerable anthems, cantatas, glees, choruses and large-scale choral works, including oratorios and operas. During his period at Aberystwyth his popularity was at its zenith and his muse at its most prolific in the form of male choruses for conspirators, colliers, sailors and druids. There he composed not only the hymn-tune which bears its name – in the minor key of which he was too fond; in becoming a classic, 'Aberystwyth' immovably fixed the minor-key hymn-tune as a Welsh speciality – the opera *Blodwen*, and the celebrated love-story 'Myfanwy' which was first published by Isaac Jones of Treherbert in 1875. It is a frequent source of amusement to those Welsh choristers who actually look at the score to see the subtitle 'Arabella' which they take to be a somewhat gormless

136

translation of Myfanwy. In fact, Parry wrote it to English words first. Mynyddog's more familiar 'Paham mae dicter, O Myfanwy?' being a translation of Cuhelyn's clumsy 'Why shoots wrath's lightning, Arabella, from those jet eyes? What clouds thy brow?'

We will never know what audiences made of 'Myfanwy' during the first 50 years of its existence and it seems to have been little sung (although there is record of it from 1914 by an anonymous 'Welsh Choir') until two classic recordings confirmed its popularity, one by Ivor Sims' Morriston Orpheus for Columbia in 1950, and another by Pendyrus under Glynne Jones on the Sain label in the late 1980s. Parry's large-scale compositions among his 25-odd works for male choirs include his 'Cytgan y Pererinion' ('Pilgrims' Chorus', known in the male voice lexicon as simply 'Pererinion'), which dates from c. 1886, and 'Iesu o Nazareth', first published in 1898, commissioned as a test piece for the Cardiff National Eisteddfod the following year, a competition won by the then equally recent Barry Male Voice Party. It never found favour outside Wales, except among Welsh exiles: one English critic in the 1920s dismissed it with the remark that 'only Welshmen could listen to it for more than a minute'. There are post-war recordings of it by Morriston under Eurfryn John in the 1960s, and Pendyrus in the 1950s (Arthur Duggan, on Qualiton) and 1980s (Glynne Jones, on Sain). 'Iesu o Nazareth' is never heard today. 'Pererinion's dramatic climax is still given the occasional outing, the entire work rarely, though it was a test piece at Lampeter in 1984 in a competition won by Llanelli under Eifion Thomas.

Parry learned from the German *Männerchöre* he heard in America and the French *orphéoniste* style he encountered in Wales. Industrious, prolific, conceited, emotional, Parry, in the words of a fellow native of Merthyr was 'a genius – but something was wrong with the balance' (Morgans, p.103). Despite the many legitimate criticisms levelled against him, he wrote with a technical assurance and melodic accessibility for the Welsh male choir that only Daniel Protheroe and Maldwyn Price could rival. Unlike his English contemporaries C.H.H. Parry, C.V. Stanford and the early Elgar, he wrote for the musically-uneducated ordinary people, *y werin bobl* of Wales, among whom he was born, who he understood and who reciprocated with affection and adulation. An audience's sigh of satisfaction can still be heard when it is announced that 'Myfanwy,' preferably unaccompanied and in Parry's original key of D flat, will be sung as an encore. The appeal of this warm and soothing love-song remains curiously undimmed. For all his detractors – and there were, and are, many – Joseph Parry's music brought him fame in his lifetime and wrote his name on the wall of Welsh history.

CARADOG (GRIFFITH RHYS JONES, 1834–1897)

Griffith Rhys Jones was the dominant musical personality in late Victorian Wales: with his chunky frame and charismatic personality his fame rivalled that of Joseph Parry. While he will always be associated with the double triumph of the South Wales Choral Union (*Y Côr Mawr*) at the Crystal Palace in 1872–3, his contribution to the development of Welsh male voice choral singing is also significant. The Côr Mawr drew on men and women from across the entire south Wales coalfield from Brynmawr to Llanelli; it was a mixed choir. Caradog, a name derived from the *nom de plume* Caradog ap Brân he adopted for himself at a time when it was common practice to do so, was truly a 'harmonious blacksmith' who believed that his musical ear was derived from the clanging of the

hammer and always sought to give the men of the mixed choirs he conducted from a young age opportunities to perform as an independent choral body. He did this, for instance, with the men of the Aberdare Choral Union, which he conducted in the 1860s, and of the Treorchy Choral Society, when he moved to the Rhondda in 1870.

The group of men who sang at the public house where Caradog was the licensee, the Treorchy Hotel, can with justification be regarded as the forerunner of the later Treorchy Male Choir. Disbanding and re-formed, they were singing at the Red Cow when in 1885 the temperance advocate William Thomas took them over, on

Caradog
(*National Library Wales*)

138

condition they quit the public house for a schoolroom in Glyncoli Road. Temperance was a cause for which Caradog, born in the Crown, Trecynon, had less enthusiasm – he was landlord of the Fothergill Arms in Cwmbach before taking over the Treorchy Hotel, and by the time of his death had acquired considerable wealth from the drinking establishments he owned and the directorships of several brewing and bottling companies. The physical embodiment of the link between male choristers and their proverbial thirst, Caradog, 'whose memorable performance nearly a quarter of a century ago at the Crystal Palace is still fresh in the memory of the people of Wales' (*South Wales Daily News*, 1 July, 1895), was also the pioneer of the massed male voices concert, in that year conducting between 600 and 800 choristers in Cardiff and another 500 in Swansea in the evergreen 'Comrades in Arms' (Adam), 'Soldiers' Chorus' (Gounod), de Rillé's 'Martyrs', and Parry's 'Pererinion'.

TOM STEPHENS (1856-1906)

Although he would always be associated with the Rhondda Glee Society, popularly known as the Gleemen, Tom Stephens was born in Brynaman on the borders of Glamorgan and Carmarthenshire. His family moved to Aberdare when he was 18 months old. In his teens he sang in Caradog's South Wales Choral Union, the Côr Mawr, and aged 20 became deputy to Rhys Evans, conductor of the Aberdare Choral Union. A competent viola player, he played an active part in the musical life of the Cynon valley, conducting the Aberdare String Band as well as the town's Glee Society.

He moved to the Rhondda in 1877 when he became landlord of the Blacksmith's Arms, Treherbert, and *codwr canu* (precentor) at Bethesda chapel, Ton Pentre. The Rhondda Glee Society, based in Ystrad and drawing members from neighbouring Ton, had been recently formed by Rhys Jones, a local schoolmaster, but Tom Stephens' fame had preceded him and he was invited to take up the baton. He built up the number from the 30 he inherited to around 50 and entered the competitive arena. They won first prize out of 17 choirs at the Cardiff National Eisteddfod in 1883, and in 1887 shared it with John North's prestigious Huddersfield choir. Two years later they toured the Welsh settlements in Pennsylvania, singing an extraordinary 140 concerts.

Tom Stephens   (*National Library Wales*)

After winning at the Pontypridd National in 1893, they sailed to compete at the World's Fair Eisteddfod, which was the contribution of the 12,000 Chicago Welsh to the Columbian Exposition held in their city in September that year. A hauliers' strike had brought the coalfield to standstill and a thousand soldiers were sent to south Wales with a detachment of the Devonshires stationed at Pentre. The strike enabled Tom Stephens to rehearse his choir twice daily. Each practice lasted an hour, and in that time no-one was to speak except Tom Stephens. The Chicago test pieces were Parry's 'Pilgrims' Chorus' ('Y Pererinion') and 'Cambria's Song of Freedom' by the Welsh-American composer T.J. Davies. There were seven competing choirs, the Gleemen and Penrhyn from the quarries of Bethesda, north Wales, plus choirs from Pittsburgh, Edwardsville and Wilkes-barre in Pennsylvania, Iowa, and Salt Lake City. The Rhondda Gleemen won the greatest choral victory since Caradog's at the Crystal Palace, and Caradog was there to witness the momentous event in person; when his bulky frame presented itself at the entrance to the auditorium the audience of over 2,000 went wild – 'Dacw Caradog!' ('There's Caradog!'). He somehow got home ahead of the choir in time to welcome them back at Pontypridd station. He wrote to Tom Stephens: 'My dear friend, it is with feelings of joy and pride that I congratulate you on your victory. I have been amply repaid for a long and tedious journey across the Atlantic in witnessing this triumph … Caradog is growing old but … as long as Tom Stephens lives Wales will not be without a leader to guide her … to victory'.

The Gleemen did not compete again, though in February 1898 they sang in front of the Queen at Windsor. There was some disappointment that more of the Royal Family were not present; with exquisite timing the Duke and Duchess of York, who had been staying there, had left a few hours earlier, and therefore were unable to hear Tom Stephens conduct his 58-strong miners' choir in items like Joseph Parry's latest composition 'Annabelle Lee', the Frenchman Dard Janin's hunting song 'Night and Day', a version of 'Men of Harlech', Gounod's 'Soldier's Chorus', Richard Genée's 'Italian Salad' and the Gleemen's signature song, Ambroise Thomas' graphic 'The Tyrol'. The audience expressed regret that six of the ten works were by French and German composers for it is a feature of concerts to the present day that audiences outside Wales like to hear Welsh choirs sing Welsh music. The royal organist Sir Walter Parratt said that the Welsh sang even English music 'better than the English themselves'.

Eos Dâr (John Evans), himself a choral conductor and *penillion* singer who sang solo on that royal occasion, conducted the several hundred mourners assembled at the graveside when Tom Stephens died in Llantwit Fardre, near Pontypridd, in January 1906, his funeral attended by every notable musician across south Wales. His Glee Party died with him, but according to one tribute, 'the present popularity of male voice choral singing in Wales is traceable to Tom Stephens,' and his was the first Welsh choir to make a commercial recording in Wales in September 1899, the nine items including Parry's 'Cytgan y Morwyr,' Thomas' 'The Tyrol,' and Gwilym Gwent's 'Yr Haf'.

WILLIAM THOMAS (1851–1920)

Musical life in the Rhondda, and indeed most of south Wales, was dominated in the late 19th century by the intense rivalry between Tom Stephens' Rhondda Gleemen, based on Ton Pentre and Ystrad, and William Thomas' Treorchy from Treorchy and Pentre, all neighbouring coalmining townships. On one occasion the Gleemen attacked the Treorchy choir as they were leaving a Mabon's Day eisteddfod at Porth in 1890. Behaviour of this kind would have prepared William Thomas for his later experiences as an adjudicator. In 1897 he and the nationally-known musician J.T. Rees withheld the prize in the male voice choir competition in an eisteddfod at Llandybïe and were chased to the train station and railroaded out of town by an abusive crowd of disappointed choristers and their frustrated followers.

William Thomas was born in Mountain Ash, where he conducted a choir at the age of ten. Like several of the Welsh musicians who came

William Thomas   *(National Library Wales)*

to prominence in the late Victorian era he had been a member of Caradog's Côr Mawr, winners at the Crystal Palace in 1872 and 1873. In that latter year he moved to Treorchy, where he became choirmaster at Noddfa Baptist chapel, a school board attendance officer, and manager of the local co-operative store. A zealous temperance reformer, he agreed to the request of a group of young men who had since 1883 been meeting to sing informally at the Treorchy Arms, the Red Cow and other venues, to become their conductor, if they in turn agreed to exchange the public house for a schoolroom. This in 1885 they did, and the Treorchy saga began. As an informal group they had won their first prize of a pound singing 'Myfanwy' at an eisteddfod in the Red Cow in 1883. Two years later, now more formally constituted under the authoritarian baton of William Thomas, the same young men won first prize at a Whitsun eisteddfod in St Fagan's, on 'Comrades in Arms', when the adjudicator was none other than Caradog. They soon established themselves as National contenders, winning at Brecon in 1889, where they faced their Gleemen rivals for the first time, and pushed them into second place, though they themselves came second in two memorable tussles in 1891 and 1893. In 1891 the male voice competition was of epic proportions as the choirs took five hours to attack de Rillé's 'Destruction of Gaza', and Joseph Parry's 'Pilgrim's Chorus' ('Y Pererinion'), the eventual winners proving to be Glyndwr Richards' Pontycymer choir.

Treorchy came off second best in 1893 too to the Gleemen, but returned to winning ways at Llanelli in 1895 when, from a small field and in the absence of the Gleemen, they were awarded an unprecedented 100 marks out of 100 by the judges Joseph Parry, David Jenkins, R.C. Jenkins and Joseph Barnby. Barnby, formerly director of music at Eton and now of the Royal Choral Society, reckoned Treorchy's performance to be 'the finest specimen of singing he had ever heard,' but that 70-strong Treorchy choir would not compete again. More than any other choral organisation they were embraced by the Glamorgan gentry, and the patronage of the Earl and Countess of Dunraven Castle near Southerndown on the Glamorganshire coast secured a royal invitation to sing at Windsor Castle in 1895, the Dunraven connection covering their expenses. William Thomas had a choir of 77 at his command, Queen Victoria an entourage of 60 under hers, comprising several minor royals, assorted aristocrats, her Welsh-speaking gardener Owen Thomas, and – a wise precaution given the warlike fare on offer – the royal physician, Sir James Reid. The meeting of a Rhondda school attendance officer and the Queen Empress attracted much comment back home, but William Thomas confessed later than an audience with William Jenkins of Ystradfechan, director and general manager of the Ocean Coal Company, was far more terrifying.

With his choir now entitled to style themselves the Royal Treorchy Welsh choir, William Thomas eyed an extended overseas tour to cash in on their fame, and set about a ruthless cull of his choristers to a logistically more manageable maximum of 20, who performed 66 concerts in the course of a 64-day visit to the Welsh settlements in the USA in 1906–7, and in 1908–9 embarked on a 50,000-kilometre world tour, consisting of 310 engagements. The audiences that turned out to hear them from Durban to Dunedin numbered nearly half a million and included hundreds of choirs.

William Thomas, after 30 punishing years, relinquished the baton in 1916 and lived just long enough to hear his daughter Cissie win the soprano solo at the Neath National in 1918. Meanwhile, the unhappy rump of discarded Treorchy choristers disbanded in 1897 and did not re-form until 1917, first under John Pugh and then Gwilym Jones who proceeded to revive old resentments by dividing his time between the Treorchy and Royal Welsh choirs. While Gwilym built Treorchy's strength up to 140, he did so by bringing in some of his Royal Welsh singers, placing them in the front two rows and paying them, a tactic which led to his enforced resignation in 1927. Another three conductors picked up the baton before the choir disbanded again in 1943. Meantime the Royal Welsh soldiered on, enjoying much success under John Samuel until it eventually expired in the early 1990s, nearly a century after its creation by William Thomas.

Harry Evans

(*National Library Wales*)

HARRY EVANS (1873–1914)

Merthyr Tydfil with adjoining Dowlais was the oldest industrial town in Wales. It could also claim to be the most musical, with choirs and bands dating back to the 1840s. Harry Evans belonged to the generation of professionally qualified musicians that emerged in Wales from the turn of the century, and was the first of a local succession of distinguished conductors, composers and organists like W. J. Watkins, Alaw Morlais (Evan Thomas), E. T. Davies and D. T. Davies, all of whom in turn would be associated with the Dowlais Male Choir for most of the 20th century.

Organist from the age of ten at Gwernllwyn chapel, Dowlais, then at Bethania which could seat over 1300, he took the ARCO in 1893 and the FRCO four years later. He gave organ recitals and taught privately at his home in High Street, Merthyr, where he installed a three-manual organ. His father John Evans (Eos Myrddin), a rollerman in the ironworks, was a self-taught musician who is said to have conducted the first 'Messiah' ever heard in Dowlais and it was as a choral conductor that Harry Evans became known. He achieved competitive success with the Dowlais Philharmonic, the Dowlais Male Choir, Dowlais and Merthyr combined Choral Society, and from 1902 to his death with the Liverpool Welsh Choral Union, drawn from the 100,000 Welsh population of Merseyside and with whom he performed the most taxing classical and contemporary works, from Bach to Bantock.

During his brief period with the Dowlais male choir he brought a new technical accomplishment to the Welsh choral scene. Influenced by regularly attending the major English festivals, he learned how to harness the emotion of Welsh singing without compromising its natural fire. He concentrated on voice production, secure intonation and purity of tone and got his Dowlais choristers to sing scales *pianissimo* three times up

144

and down in the same breath. The thirds are notoriously flat among Welsh amateur male choirs but Evans claimed that 'all our practices were unaccompanied so we did not flatten'. He taught his top tenors to use the head voice, not the favoured contraction of the Welsh throat, so that all his first tenors could sing an effortless B flat, a tradition inherited by Alaw Morlais' Dowlais Penywern choir whose fame prompted even Dylan Thomas to get one of Captain Cat's shipmates to ask, 'How's the tenors in Dowlais?'

The answer was provided by Harry Evans' striking success at the Liverpool National Eisteddfod in 1900. All the main choral prizes had been snatched by English choirs, until the last day when, in front of an audience of 19,000 and against ten other choirs including the renowned Manchester Orpheus and Nelson Arion choirs, Harry Evans' Dowlais won a famous victory. The *Merthyr Express* proclaimed that Dowlais had 'saved Wales from utter obliteration.' Some of Harry Evans' arrangements for male choirs are still sung, like 'Ar Hyd y Nos' and 'Rhyfelgyrch Gwŷr Harlech'. Sir Edward Elgar considered Harry Evans to be 'a great conductor', while the English critic Gerald Cumberland, who despised the music of Joseph Parry, recognised that Parry's fellow-citizen 'possessed a cultured and distinguished mind, an ear of abnormal sensitiveness, and a temperament that is at once glowing and responsive' (*The Times*, 29 July, 1914). Conductor of Dowlais for only a few years, his life cut short from a brain tumour aged 41, Harry Evans is perhaps the greatest of all Welsh choral conductors.

DANIEL PROTHEROE (1866–1934)

Daniel Protheroe's male voice choruses have lasted better than Joseph Parry's and several are still sung with enthusiasm today. He had lost both parents before he was eight, but was soon noted for his precocious musical talent in the neighbouring villages where he was born (Cwmgiedd) and raised (Ystradgynlais), a highly musical area where Ivander's Swansea Valley Temperance Choral Union had recruited strongly in mid-century. At 18 he was conducting the Ystradgynlais choir, before emigrating to Scranton, Pennsylvania, in 1886. The ample vocal resources among the Welsh migrants there enabled him to found his subsequently famous

Daniel Protheroe
(*National Library Wales*)

Scranton Cymmrodorion choir which within six months performed the first oratorio ever heard in the city, Handel's 'Alexander's Feast'. In 1894 he moved to Milwaukee, where his tireless musical activities attracted the attention of the Central Church of Chicago who in 1904 engaged him as Director of Music, a position he held for almost thirty years. In 1926 in front of an audience of 10,000 in Philadelphia in a concert broadcast across North America, he conducted the 3,000 male voices of the United Choir of Associated Glee Clubs, whose nucleus was his Côr Meibion Cymraeg Chicago, founded earlier that year.

Like Joseph Parry, Protheroe probably composed too much too uncritically, and the copyrights of more than a thousand of his compositions are held in the Library of Congress, Washington D.C., as well as the complete collection of his works at the National Library in Aberystwyth. He was much sought after on both sides of the Atlantic and was a regular visitor to conduct at Welsh festivals and sit in judgement at the National Eisteddfod, the last time in 1933.

Some of his compositions have survived better than others, like his children's hymn tune 'Blodau'r Iesu', the small-scale anthem 'Y Mae Afon', and his hymn-tunes 'Hiraeth', 'Price' and 'Milwaukee'. His part-song for male voices, 'O Mor Bêr yn y Man' ('In the Sweet by and by'), recorded by the Morriston Orpheus Choir in the 1960s, has lost the popularity as a concert and test piece it once enjoyed. Yet Protheroe more than any other Welsh composer for this medium consciously wrote with an awareness of the strengths, weaknesses and idiosyncrasies of Welsh and Welsh American choirs, and what vowel sounds, for instance, fell most naturally in each part of the voice.

Though he composed in various genres, from instrumental works to children's pieces, it is as an incomparable writer of dramatic men's choruses that his name lives on. Chief among these are 'The Crusaders'

('Milwyr y Groes') which first appeared as an attachment to the monthly journal *Y Cerddor* ('The Musician') in 1891, 'Castilla', 'Invictus', 'Nidaros' and 'Drontheim' ('King Olaf's Christmas'), written in the style of de Rillé's 'Martyrs of the Arena' and a test piece at Port Talbot in 1932 but rarely if ever heard since. Like the ever-popular 'Nidaros' which famously opens 'in the convent of Drontheim' with the excitable 'Astrid the abbess alone in her chamber', it was first published by Rohlfing Sons Music Co., Milwaukee in 1902. Still widely sung, and more within the scope of smaller choirs who cannot manage the demands of 'Nidaros,' is Protheroe's splendid arrangement of William Owen of Prysgol's hymn tune, 'Bryn Calfaria' (*'Gwaed y groes sy'n codi fyny'*) which he dedicated 'to the Sherman Park Lutheran choirs of Milwaukee, Wis.' – or to 'the Associated Glee Clubs of America', according to which edition is used – and called 'Laudamus'. An early published version of it c.1930 situates it in the somewhat remote key of B flat minor. Fortunately for the several generations of choir accompanists who have played it since, Protheroe was happy to see it raised it a semitone to B minor with the climax 'Nac aed hwnnw byth o'm cof' slamming it into the major on the last chord. Not even Parry could compose a climax like Daniel Protheroe, as any chorister who has sung the 'Christ is eternal' finale to 'Nidaros' will readily attest.

"NIDAROS"

Chorus for Male Voices and Orchestra.
Cydgan i Leisiau Meibion a Cherddorfa.

Words by LONGFELLOW.
Y GEIRIAU CYMRAEG gan G. ap LLEISION.

DANIEL PROTHEROE, Mus. Doc. Op. 63.

Pendyrus Male Choir

Tenors.

Basses.

Moderato.

PIANO.

Yn un-igrwydd Nid-ar-os, Yn llei-an-dy Dront-heim, Ym-grym — ai'r ddwys
In the con-vent of Drontheim, A-lone in her chamber, Knelt As trid the

As — trid, Ryw hwyr i a-ddol-i, Ac ym-bil mewn gweddi A'r y
ab — bess. At mid-night, a-dor-ing, Be-seeching, en-treating The

Price:

Published by SNELL & SONS, 68 West Cross Lane, West Cross, Swansea SA3 5LU

Part Three

The Male Voice Choir Competitions at the National Eisteddfod 1881–2015

Welshmen are very competitive whether it be on the rugby field or in choral competitions. Competing is good for choral discipline – it gives a choir something to aim for. Having to learn a new or unknown work is a challenge both to the choir and to the musical director. Whether you are able to use the work again in concert is not important. You decide whether you compete or not. Winning the chief male choir competition at the National Eisteddfod is a goal for every large choir. It means it has arrived and is a means of maintaining standards.

Noel Davies, conductor Côr Meibion Pontarddulais 1961–2002

The conductors of each choir wait like matadors about to enter the bull ring, except for the blood, heat and sand we could substitute rain, cold and mud – good honest Welsh mud of a variety which comes to exist only on the National field. The effect that a National has on competitors is remarkable. Normally solid people find their legs turn to jelly. Some men revel in the atmosphere, suggesting that perhaps their ancestors were related to the noble Roman gladiators who delighted in death and glory before Great Caesar. Others are so obviously nervous that I am sure they utter not a single note for fear of making a mistake. However, the majority seem look upon competition as a great spur and tremendous challenge.

John Cynan Jones, conductor Treorchy Male Choir 1969–91

(The) adjudicators are fools

Glynne Jones, conductor Pendyrus Male Choir 1962–2000

These are the results of the male voice choir competitions at the National Eisteddfod of Wales, in an unbroken sequence, excepting the war years, from 1881 to 2015. Self-styled 'national' eisteddfodau were intermittently held from the 1860s, but it was only after the National Eisteddfod Association was established in 1880 to regulate its affairs that the event settled down to the recognisably modern pattern of an annual National Eisteddfod held alternately in north and south Wales. The sequence begins properly and annually in 1881.

I have recorded each Eisteddfod year by year. In each case I have sought to provide the following details: the number of choristers permitted in each class, the number of choirs competing, the test pieces and their composers, the adjudicators and, of course, the result. The information on the early years is uneven, but as male choirs proliferated, as the popularity of the event intensified and the eisteddfod tent – the Pavilion – became, we are told, 'uncomfortably filled' or 'full to suffocation' with audiences of between of ten and twenty thousand listeners, the desirability for more competitions was recognised to cater for choirs of different sizes. By the 1930s the main competition popularly known as the 'chief' was for choirs in excess of a hundred voices. By today the choirs that can meet that requirement are few and far between: maybe Côr Meibion Pontarddulais who regularly stage over a hundred, and the non-competitive, broadly-based Côr Meibion De Cymru. But choirs like Pendyrus, Treorchy, Morriston, Rhosllannerchrugog, Trelawnyd, Dunvant and Llanelli have managed this in the past, and where the numbers are striking, like Pendyrus' 138 in 1934, Treorchy's 153 in 1950, or Rhosllannerchrugog's 130 in 1962, I have noted them. Not all choirs could or were ever likely to match these figures. In rural areas where the population was thinner, and also in the townships where smaller, social club choirs flourished, there were far more choirs in the 40–80 voices range and these could not realistically compete for sonority and vocal weight – musicality was a different matter – with three-digit juggernauts. It therefore became necessary from 1921 to provide a second competition, and from 1966, with a belated nod to the origins of the movement a century earlier, a third competition for 'glee choirs' of under 40 voices.

This development had been anticipated from another direction with the introduction in the 1930s of competitions for 'works' or 'factory' choirs. That depressing decade saw those works frequently closing down though their choirs (e.g. Cambrian Colliery of Clydach Vale in the Rhondda) continued in the hope that conditions of fuller employment might return. The Cardiff

National of 1938 tells its own story: as well as the 'chief' competition for choirs of not under a 100 voices, and the second for 50–75 voices, there was a third (glee) competition for 30–40 voices, another for choirs for the unemployed, and, equally significantly, a competition for choirs of Welshmen in exile, and there was no shortage of those as choirs from Hammersmith, Oxford, Coventry, Welwyn Garden City and Luton all testified. Part Three therefore is not merely a factual accumulation of detail for its own sake, nor even merely a statistical directory to supplement the narrative in Part One, but a lens through which the social and industrial history of Wales over the last 130 years may be viewed.

At the risk of information overload I have occasionally, where I have been able to find them, provided the marks. These are sagas in themselves: the extraordinary tight marking (e.g. in the 'chief' at Ammanford 1922 and Caernarfon 1959, and the second competition at Rhyl in 1985), the dog fight for second and third places, like the single mark over three pieces separating the two big Morriston choirs, the United and the Orpheus, at Denbigh in 1939. There have been exceedingly close contests among the smaller choirs too. I have highlighted the names of conductors (who, with no diminution of conducted electricity, we now call musical directors) who have become iconic figures in the history of competitive Welsh choralism – Ivor Sims, John H. Davies, Colin Jones, D.T. Davies, Glynne Jones, Noel Davies and Eirian Owen, as well as earlier titans like William Thomas, Tom Stephens, Glyndwr Richards, Cadwaladr Roberts and Elgar's 'great conductor,' Harry Evans. I have noted the prize money, too, where it has suddenly lurched upwards, either the better to reward the effort and dedication involved, or to lure more gladiators into the arena. The modest five pounds offered at Merthyr in 1881 had increased ten-fold by the London festival six years later, and crept steadily upwards until it reached fifty pounds and stayed there until the First World War. By the time the Eisteddfod convened in 1920 at Barry (always a leader) it was decided to double it to £100 where it remained until after the Second World War when it doubled again at Ystradgynlais in 1954. The big breakthrough came lower down the valley when an unprecedented £500 was offered ten years later, and provided a competition worthy of it: see the epic contest at Swansea, 1964. As can also be seen, it increased again to £750 and briefly to a prize of a thousand pounds in an experimental 'open' competition for choirs of any number, introduced in 2002 and abandoned five years later.

In 1947 challenge cups were introduced for the winners in the 'chief' and second male voice competitions, the Welsh Guards Cup for the larger choirs and the Royal Welsh Fusiliers Cup for the second competition. In 1979 the Welsh Association of Male Choirs presented a cup to the Eisteddfod to be awarded to the winners of the glee competition, under 40 voices. The Ivor E. Sims Memorial medal, presented to the winning conductor of the 'chief,' was introduced at Swansea in 1964.

Finally, I have scattered throughout this choral 'Wisden' additional comments where I have thought they might be of interest. It seemed worth noting, for instance, that the famous 'Martyrs of the Arena' has only once ever been a test piece at the National Eisteddfod; I leave it to the diligent reader to find out when that was. I discuss the introduction of the 'all-Welsh rule' at Caerphilly in 1950, where it was introduced. I provide examples of the views, alternating between the acerbic and the astounded, of visiting critics, who were sometimes intimidated by the 'almost terrifying' atmosphere that often prevailed, of tense competitions that could sometimes last up to five hours (e.g. Swansea 1891, or Abergavenny 1913 where there were 18 choirs in the competition for 60–80 voices, or Port Talbot 1932), and note the first and – regrettably – last appearances to date of some of the historic choirs of Wales that once raised the pavilion 'full to suffocation' to its feet.

I have begun in the beginning, in 1881.

THE RESULTS

1881 Merthyr

Over 25 voices

Prize: 5 guineas & 25 vols of Curwen's *Standard Course*
Test piece: 'Cytgan y Chwarelwyr'/ 'Quarrymen's Chorus' (D. Jenkins)
Adjudicators: Joseph Parry, J. S. Curwen, Ivander (W. Ivander Griffiths)
6 choirs
Result: 1. Morriston (David Francis)

Glee parties up to 25 voices

Prize: as above
Test piece: 'The Tyrol' (Ambroise Thomas)
Adjudicators: as above
2 choirs
Result: Joint-winners – Taibach/Aberavon, and Maesteg

1882 Dolgellau

Prize: £15

Test piece: 'Cytgan y Medelwyr'/ 'The Reapers' Chorus' (D.Jenkins)

Adjudicators: Owain Alaw, Tanymarian (Edward Stephen), David Jenkins

4 choirs

Result: 1. Arvonia, Llanberis (R. Phillips)

1883 Cardiff

Prize: £10

Test piece: own choice

Adjudicators: Joseph Bennett, Brinley Richards

7 choirs

Result: 1. Rhondda Gleemen (T. Stephens), 2. Excelsior, Swansea, 3. Brynmawr

The adjudicators expressed 'surprise and delight' at the high standard of the singing which 'afforded ample proof of the continued progress of choral music in Wales' (*South Wales Daily News*, 8 August), but thought it 'best for the future that a test piece be agreed on in order that the adjudicators can more easily arrive at a decision'.

1884 Liverpool

30-35 voices

Prize: 30 guineas & gold baton

Test pieces: 'Martyrs of the Arena' (Laurent de Rillé), 'Ymdaith y Mwngcod' / 'Monks' War March' (Joseph Parry)

Adjudicators: George Macfarren, John Thomas (Pencerdd Gwalia), Joseph Parry

12 Choirs

Result: 1. Preston Harmonic Society

This is the only occasion on which the famous 'Martyrs of the Arena' has been a designated test piece at the National Eisteddfod, though Ar Ôl Tri of Cardigan sang it in Welsh ('*Y Merthyron*') as an 'own choice' in the competition for under 40 voices at the Denbigh National in 2001. The winning conductor in 1884, Dr Roland Rogers (1847–1927), organist at Bangor Cathedral, was born in West Bromwich, and communicated with his monoglot Welsh-speaking quarrymen through an interpreter.

1885 Aberdare

20–25 voices

Prize: £20

Test pieces: 'Nyni yw'r Meibion Cerddgar' (Gwilym Gwent) 'Bedd y Dyn Tlawd' (D. Emlyn Evans)

Adjudicators: Dr E. H. Turpin, Caradog, Dr W. Frost

5 choirs

Result: Joint winners – Aberdare and Rhymney

1886 Caernarfon

40–60 voices

Prize: £25

Test pieces: 'Oh with me' (Seyfried), 'Y Gof'/ 'The Blacksmith' (D. Jenkins)

Adjudicators: David Jenkins, Ebenezer Prout, John Thomas (Pencerdd Gwalia), J. H. Roberts

3 choirs

Result: 1. Glantawe, 2. Cynon Glee Society

1887 London

50–70 voices

Prize: £50

Test pieces: 'Where is He?' (Beethoven), 'The Beleaguered' (Arthur Sullivan), 'Valiant Warriors' (David Jenkins)

Adjudicators: George Macfarren, John Thomas, Signor Alberto Randegger, Joseph Bennett, D. Emlyn Evans, D. Jenkins.

10 choirs

Result: Joint winners – Rhondda Gleemen (T. Stephens) and Huddersfield (John North)

                Other competitors included Tredegar Orpheus, Dowlais, Port Talbot and Brynaman.

1888 Wrexham

30–50 voices

Prize: £20

Test pieces: 'Greek War Song' (J.C. Bridge), 'The Long Day Closes' (Sullivan)

Adjudicators: John Thomas (Pencerdd Gwalia). C. F. Lloyd, D. Emlyn Evans, A. J. Caldicott

3 choirs

Result: 1. Clwydian, Ruthin (E. Harris Jones), 2. Arvonia, Llanberis, 3. Cynon Harmonic, Mountain Ash

1889 Brecon

30–40 voices

Prize: £25

Test pieces: 'The Young Musicians' (F.W. Kücken), 'Y Seren Hwyrol'/ 'The Evening Star' (Tom Price)

Adjudicators: Dr E. H. Turpin, A. J. Caldicott, D. Jenkins

2 choirs

Result: 1. Treorchy (William Thomas), 2. Ton Orpheus (Alaw Cynon) There were five entrants originally but Cynon, Llangeitho and Newtown withdrew.

1890 Bangor

30–40 voices

Prize: £20

Test pieces: 'The Wind' (J.T. Pritchard), 'Hushed in Death' (Henry Hiles)

Adjudicators: D. Emlyn Evans, John Thomas (Pencerdd Gwalia), William Davies.

Only 1 choir entered

Result: 1. Nantlle

1891 Swansea

60–80 voices

Test pieces: 'Destruction of Gaza' (de Rillé), 'Cytgan y Pererinion' / 'Pilgrims' Chorus' (Joseph Parry)

Adjudicators: Alberto Randegger, Dr Joseph Parry, David Jenkins, John Thomas (Pencerdd Gwalia)

10 choirs

Result: 1. Pontycymer (T. Glyndwr Richards), 2. Treorchy (William Thomas)

Twenty thousand squeezed into the pavilion to hear a titanic five-hour contest. Laurent de Rillé was already well known in Wales as the composer of the popular and dramatic 'Martyrs of the Arena', the test piece at Liverpool in 1884. Dr Parry composed the 'Pilgrims' during his period in Swansea where he ran a private academy between 1881 and 1888. He claimed that the voice he had in mind when writing the baritone solo in it was that of Gwilym Thomas, one of the heroes of the rescue party at the Tynewydd disaster in the Rhondda in 1877 when five miners were saved after being trapped underground for ten days by flood waters. The conductor of the winning choir, T. Glyndwr Richards (1859–

1935), made his name with Pontycymer before moving on to Resolven (winners in 1905 and 1907) and then Mountain Ash, who he took to the USA in 1908 to sing in the White House for President and Mrs Roosevelt. We wonder how Pontycymer would have fared had they travelled to the World's Fair Eisteddfod in Chicago in 1893 when the 'Pilgrims' was the test piece and the competition was won by Tom Stephens' Rhondda Gleemen. It was also sung at Parry's funeral at Penarth in 1903. Treorchy, who came second in 1891, were in their pomp. They had won at Brecon 1889 and would do so again at Llanelli in 1895; that year they were summoned to Windsor Castle for a command performance in front of Queen Victoria. One of the adjudicators in 1891, Signor Randegger, Italian-born professor of singing at the Royal Academy of Music, reckoned that the Treorchy tenors at Swansea were superior to anything he had ever heard in England or on the continent. But it was the 'grand, passionate, inspiring' performance of Pontycymer that carried the day. The unplaced Brynaman choir was perhaps noticed for its accompanist, 18-year-old David (Vaughan) Thomas, later to become one of Wales's foremost composers, and father of broadcaster and war correspondent Wynford Vaughan Thomas (1908-87).

1892 Rhyl

30–40 voices

Prize:	£25
Test pieces:	'Meibion y Don'/ 'Sons of the Wave' (D. Jenkins), 'On the Ramparts' (de Saintis)
Adjudicators:	Joseph Parry, D. Emlyn Evans, David Jenkins, C.F. Lloyd, John Thomas
8 choirs	
Result:	1. Caernarfon, 2. Middlesbrough
	Also competing were Penrhyn, Ebbw Vale, Cefn Mawr, Machynlleth, Treorchy and Walton (Liverpool).

1893 Pontypridd

Prize:	£50
Test pieces:	'The Tyrol' (Ambroise Thomas), 'The Warhorse'/ 'Y Rhyfelfarch' (D. Jenkins)
Adjudicators:	Caradog, Samuel Coleridge Taylor, Alexander Mackenzie, John Thomas, C. F. Lloyd, J. T. Rees, George Risely.
6 choirs	
Result:	Rhondda Gleemen (T. Stephens), Treorchy (W. Thomas)

This was a timely victory for the Gleemen as they had already declared their intention of competing at the World's Fair Eisteddfod in Chicago in September. They could now travel to the USA as Welsh champions and took first prize there in the competition for male voice choirs (50–60 voices). The Pontycymer choir, winners in 1891, also intended competing at Chicago but failed to raise enough money. They heard that Tom Stephens' Gleemen had already raised £500 whereas they themselves had so far managed only £370. The Gleemen paid an American agent 'a large sum on account', and used the thousand dollar first prize and income from concerts in the U.S. to pay it off. In second place in Chicago were the Penrhyn quarrymen of Bethesda, Caernarfonshire, who were partly funded by a contribution of £300 from quarry owner Lord Penrhyn, their own efforts, and the second prize of five hundred dollars. They beat five other Welsh-American choirs from Pittsburgh, Wilkes-barre, Salt Lake City, Iowa and Edwardsdale, Pa. The test pieces were Joseph Parry's 'Pererinion' ('Pilgrim's Chorus'), and T. J. Davies' 'Cambria's Song of Freedom'.

1894 Caernarfon

40–50 voices

Prize:	£40
Test pieces:	'Y Pysgotwyr' (T. Maldwyn Price), 'Dewi Bydd Wych'/ 'Hail, Dewi, Hail' (*Dewi Sant*, David Jenkins)
Adjudicators:	A. J. Caldicott, John Thomas (Pencerdd Gwalia), D. Emlyn Evans, J. H. Roberts, C. F. Lloyd
7 choirs	
Result:	1. Penrhyn (Edward Broome) 2. Pontycymer (Glyndwr Richards)

1895 Llanelli

60–80 voices

Prize:	£60
Test pieces:	'The Druids' (Joseph Parry), 'Safe in Port' (Jean Limnander)
Adjudicators:	Joseph Barnby, Joseph Parry, D. Jenkins, R. C. Jenkins, J. O. Shepherd.
4 choirs	
Result:	1. Treorchy
	Also competing were Pontycymer (Glyndwr Richards), Aberaman (Dewi Mabon), and Porth and Cymmer (Rees Evans). Swansea Cymmrodorion and Blaina withdrew.

While the choirs sang, reported the *South Wales Daily News* (3 August) 'the audience appeared to be in ecstasies. Every eye was fixed on the singers; every ear was strained; throughout the whole of that immense assembly not a movement was detected; a solid mass of humanity was spellbound.' Sir Joseph Barnby, Principal of the Guildhall School of Music, thought it 'the finest specimen of music I have ever heard', that 'the four [choirs] were of the finest description;' and that 'it had not been the privilege of any being on the face of the globe to listen to better.' It was 'the one unique experience of his life to have heard it. They in England know nothing of all this. Welshmen did not let them know, but the time would come when they *would* know.' Afterwards, the winning conductor William Thomas was carried shoulder high out of the pavilion and through the streets.

1896 Llandudno

Prize:	40 guineas (£42)
Test pieces:	'Dwynwen' (Joseph Parry), 'Drinking Song' (H. Goetz)
Adjudicators:	Frederick Cowen, Joseph Bennett, J. H. Roberts, D. Jenkins
8 choirs	
Result:	Joint winners – Porth (Tal Hopkins) and Moelwyn (Cadwaladr Roberts)

1897 Newport

60-80 voices

Prize:	£70
Test pieces:	'Ah, were I on yonder plain' (Mendelssohn), 'Llywelyn ein Llyw Olaf' (Tom Price)
Adjudicators:	Sir Alexander Mackenzie, Dr Walter Macfarren, David Jenkins
10 choirs	
Result:	1. Swansea Cymmrodorion (J.D. Thomas) 2. Mountain Ash (T. Glyndwr Richards)

Glee competition (25-30 voices)

Prize:	£15
Test piece:	'The Bells'/ 'Y Clychau' (Gwilym Gwent)
3 parties	
Result:	1. Glamorgan Choristers, Pontypridd

1898 Ffestiniog

50-60 voices

Prize: 30 guineas

Test pieces: 'Gyrrwch Wyntoedd' / 'Storm Winds Driving' (D. Jenkins), 'Teyrnged Cariad' / 'Love's Tribute' (D. Pughe Evans)

Adjudicators: Joseph Bennett, D. Jenkins, William Davies

Result: 1. Rhosllannerchrugog (Wilfrid Jones), 2. Port Talbot (Alderman John Phillips)

Joseph Bennett compared the singing of the Rhos choir, mostly miners, to 'the delicacy of a Damascus blade, and strength and energy of a Nasmyth steamhammer'.

1899 Cardiff

60-80 voices

Prize: £70; £10

Test pieces: 'Iesu o Nazareth'/'Jesus of Nazareth' (Joseph Parry), 'Hushed in Death' (Henry Hiles)

Adjudicators: Sir Frederick Bridge, Dr Joseph Parry, Dr Roland Rogers, D. Emlyn Evans, T.E. Aylward

5 choirs

Result: 1. Barry (David Farr), 2. Mountain Ash (Glyndwr Richards), 3. Port Talbot (Alderman John Phillips, Mayor of Aberavon)

Sir Frederick Bridge urged choirs to avoid exaggeration, and ensure that *marcato* passages did not descend into a series of 'barkato' yelps. After announcing 'The first prize goes to no. 4 [Barry],' he 'then rushed pell-mell off the platform' before 'every Barry man rushed pell-mell shouting, yelling, screaming, cheering, crying' onto it. The once rural hamlet of Barry (population 500 in 1881) had suddenly become a busy railhead and coal shipping port of 27,000 people. Its male voice choir is believed to have numbered 85 on stage at Cardiff in 1899, its sole National Eisteddfod win. It disbanded soon afterwards but re-formed in 1903 under D.J. Thomas, since when it has enjoyed an unbroken history and last competed at the National in Cardiff in 1978. In 1900 Barry combined with Tom Stephens' Rhondda Gleemen at the Paris Exhibition to sing 'The Destruction of Gaza', 'Martyrs of the Arena', Parry's 'Pilgrims' Chorus' and Welsh airs. French critics like Saint-Saëns were not impressed, though they greatly admired the singing of Madame Clara Novello Davies' Welsh Ladies Choir.

Glee competition (25–30 voices)

Prize:	£10 for each piece
Test piece:	'O snatch me swift' (Calcott) plus a sight-reading competition
Adjudicators:	Sir Frederick Bridge, Dr Roland Rogers, D. Emlyn Evans
Result:	1. Mid Rhondda Glee Society, 2. Ebenezer Glee Society (Swansea)

Dr Roland Rogers urged choirs 'to cultivate glee singing as much as possible as it would lead to more delicate singing in all branches'.

1900 Liverpool

not to exceed 60 voices

Prize:	60 guineas & gold medal
Test pieces:	'Crossing the Plain' (T. Maldwyn Price), 'Cyrus in Babylon' (Boulanger)
Adjudicators:	Joseph Parry, Signor Randegger, Dr Varley Roberts, C. Francis Lloyd, Daniel Protheroe
11 choirs	
Result:	1. Dowlais (Harry Evans, accomp. W.J.Watkins) [82 marks], 2. Joint – Port Talbot and Swansea [75], 4. Manchester Orpheus [70], 5. Rhymney [65], 6. Moelwyn [60]
	Also competing were Nelson Arion, Porth and Cymmer, Aberaeron, Bangor and Ebbw Vale.

Pressure of time meant that only the Boulanger was sung, though after the adjudication Dowlais mounted the stage to sing 'Crossing the Plain'. The size of the audience (19,000) confirmed the opinion of the adjudicators that 'in the eyes of the musical public it [the male voice choir competition] overshadows the chief choral contest', where there were four entrants as compared to 11 male choirs. It was a personal triumph for the young Harry Evans who had assembled his Dowlais choir nine months earlier in order to bid for the National prize. According to the *Merthyr Express*, whose readers would have been aware that all the major choral prizes in Liverpool earlier in the week had been snatched by English choirs, 'Dowlais saved Wales from utter obliteration.' After leading Merthyr and Dowlais United mixed choir to victory in the chief choral at Llanelli in 1903, Harry Evans renounced competition and took up the directorship of the Liverpool Welsh Choral Union, where Sir Edward Elgar hailed him as 'a great conductor'. He died at 41 years of age in 1914.

1901 Merthyr

> *70–90 voices*
>
> Test pieces: 'Soldiers of Gideon' (Saint-Saëns), 'Ar Lan Iorddonen Ddofn' (Bryceson Treharne)
>
> Adjudicators: Joseph Parry, Henry Coward, David Jenkins, C. F. Lloyd, Daniel Protheroe
>
> 7 choirs
> Result: 1. Rhymney (Dan Owen), 2. Port Talbot, 3. Porth and Cymmer

In view of later developments, it is interesting to note that a 'Pontarddulais male choir' came last but one in 1901. Times would change! There was also a competition for glee parties of 30–40 voices, the test consisting of three pieces, one of which was a glee to be sung at first sight. The only entrant, Ebenezer Glee Party (Swansea), was adjudged fully worthy of the prize.

1902 Bangor

> *40–50 voices*
>
> Prize: £50
>
> Test pieces: 'The Word went Forth' (Mendelssohn), 'The Long Day Closes' (Sullivan)
>
> Adjudicators: Joseph Parry, D. Emlyn Evans, Henry Coward, T. Westlake Morgan, Lieutenant Miller
>
> 15 choirs
> Result: 1. Manchester Orpheus, 2. Cardiff, 3. Southport, 4. Port Talbot

There were six choirs from south Wales, four from north Wales, and five from England. A further three English choirs failed to show: Runcorn missed their train; another was actually present but 'lost heart at the last moment and declined to sing.' The *Musical Times* (1, October) observed: 'The [Welsh] national pride, justified in the past by splendid exhibitions of capacity for choral performance, has been dealt a serious blow. It is not that the standard of Welsh choir singing has deteriorated, but rather that English choirs ... are generally more highly trained and better led. Meantime, Welsh choirs generally have remained where they were years ago and have been almost impervious to criticism. No one will deny that Welsh singers have great capacity: their inspiration and enthusiasm are often extraordinary and electrifying. But the potter who shapes this magnificent clay needs more art and a wider knowledge of what has been accomplished elsewhere.'

This was not an opinion shared by the *Western Mail* (11 September): 'it was a tame, flat and deadly dull day as English choirs ruled the roost. Even the male voice competition failed to realise its wonted excitement and the audience sat with a stoical coldness and a wearying silence to listen to one choir after another until the fifteenth had finished its task.' There was some dissatisfaction that a choir that had failed to keep in tune (Manchester) should have been rewarded over a choir that was perfect in its intonation (Cardiff, conducted by Roderick Williams). During the Sullivan, Manchester, it was claimed, had gone down half a tone. The competition included several choirs from north-west Wales like Llanrwst and Trefriw, Moelwyn, Padarn and Amlwch. The adjudicators especially commended 'the courage of the young lady' (Miss Paynter), who conducted the Amlwch choir.

1903 Llanelli

60–80 voices

Prize:	£80
Test pieces:	'Caractacus' (Joseph Parry), 'The Destruction of Pompeii' (D. C. Williams)
Adjudicators:	W. Shakespeare, Dr W.G. McNaught, R.C. Jenkins
7 choirs	
Result:	1. Port Talbot [56], 2. Pentre [54], 3. Rhymney [53], 4. London Welsh [49], 5. Mid Rhondda [47], 6. Ebbw Vale [45], 7. Tawe [44]

The audience was quick to react when any choir went sharp or flat. 'Among so many musicians', noted one correspondent, 'it was unnecessary to wait for the verdict of the adjudicators on such obvious points.' (*Western Mail*, 8 August)

1904 Rhyl

Test pieces:	'King of Worlds' (Dard Janin), 'Y Dwyfol Fab' / 'Son of God' (D. Jenkins)
Adjudicators:	W. A. Cummings, C. Francis Lloyd, David Jenkins, D. Emlyn Evans
7 choirs	
Result:	1. Cardiff, 2. Manchester Orpheus

1905 Mountain Ash

60–80 voices

Prize:	£50; £10
Test piece:	'Homeward Bound' (D. Christmas Williams)

Adjudicators: Sir Walter Parratt, Edward German, David Evans

7 choirs

Result: Joint-winners – Resolven (T.J. Williams) £30, and Rhymney (Dan Owen) £30

Glee competition (24-30 voices, male or mixed)

Prize: £10

Test piece: 'O Lovely May' (Edward German)

3 choirs

Result: 1. Mid Rhondda

1906 Caernarfon

Test pieces: 'The Rising Storm' (Neumann), 'The Village Blacksmith' (Parry)

Adjudicators: Dr W. McNaught, John Thomas, D. Emlyn Evans, W. Greenish, David Evans

4 choirs

Result: 1. Cynon (W.J.Evans), 2. Swansea and District (Llew Bowen)

1907 Swansea

60–80 voices

Prize: £50

Test pieces: 'Nidaros' (D. Protheroe), 'Teyrnged Cariad'/ 'Lovely Maiden' (D. Pughe Evans)

Adjudicators: Dr F. Cowen, Dr H. Walford Davies, Dr Daniel Protheroe, Harry Evans, Emlyn Evans

10 choirs

Result: 1. Resolven (T.Glyndwr Richards), 2. Port Talbot (John Phillips), 3. Morriston (L.C. Evans)

Only 'Nidaros' was sung. If the twelve choirs that entered had turned up, and all sung both pieces, the competition would have lasted six hours.

1908 Llangollen

50–70 voices

Prize: £50

Test pieces: 'Trysorau'r Dyfnder' / 'Treasures of the Deep' (J. H. Roberts), 'Meibion Gwalia' / 'Sons of Gwalia' (D. Jenkins)

Adjudicators: S. Coleridge Taylor, J.T. Rees, D. Emlyn Evans, Harry Evans, David Jenkins

Result: 1. Manchester Orpheus (W. S. Nesbitt), 2. Bargoed Teifi (Tom Luke), 3.Moelwyn (Cadwaladr Roberts)

The Bargoed Teifi choir consisted 'chiefly of working men, many being employed in the woollen factories of Felindre and Dre-fach.' See also 1911.

1909 London

75–100 voices

Test pieces: (a) 'Fair Semele's Highborn Son' (Mendelssohn), (b) 'O Peaceful Night' (Edward German), (c) 'The Reveille' (Edward Elgar)

Adjudicators: Sir C.V. Stanford, Dr W.G. McNaught, D. Emlyn Evans, Harry Evans, Dan Price

8 choirs

Result:

	(a)	(b)	(c)	
1. Dowlais (W.J. Watkins, accomp. E.T. Davies)	90	+ 94	+ 95	= 279
2. Swansea and District (Llew Bowen)	80	+ 86	+ 90	= 256
3. Newcastle	85	+ 80	+ 80	= 245
4. Bargoed Teifi	85	+ 76	+ 65	= 226
5. Mid Rhondda				222
6. Ebenezer Mission, Swansea				220
7. Llanelli				195
8. Maesteg				182

1910 Colwyn Bay

Test pieces: 'The Rider's Song' (Peter Cornelius), 'Sorrow's Tears' (Cornelius) 'Battle of the Baltic'/ 'Brwydr y Baltig' (T. Osborne Roberts)

Adjudicators: Dr H. Coward, Dr Roland Rogers, Professor David Evans, David Jenkins

4 choirs

Result: 1. Manchester Orpheus (W. Nesbitt), 2. Swansea (Ll. Bowen)

Also competing were Garw Valley and Warrington.

1911 Carmarthen

60–80 voices

Prize: £50

Test pieces: 'Walpurga' (F. Hegar), 'Gosteg Fôr'/ 'Peace, be still' (D. Jenkins)

Adjudicators: Dr H. Walford Davies, Dr D. Protheroe, Dr D. Vaughan Thomas, S. Coleridge Taylor, D. Emlyn Evans

10 choirs

Result: 1. Bargoed Teifi (Daniel Jenkins), 2. Ebenezer Mission, Swansea (Turner Thomas)

For the circumstances explaining Bargoed Teifi's dramatic appearance on the male choral scene, see chapter 4 in Part One.

1912 Wrexham

Test pieces: 'The Glories of our Blood and State' (Granville Bantock), 'Deep Jordan's Banks' (Cyril Jenkins), 'Y Gariad Gollwyd'/ 'The Lost Love' (D. Vaughan Thomas)

Adjudicators: Granville Bantock, J. Owen Jones, Harry Evans, Dr H. Walford Davies

7 choirs

Result: 1. Swansea and District (Llew Bowen, accomp.Ivor Owen) [283 marks, including 99 for 'The Lost Love'], 2. Ebenezer Mission, Swansea (Turner Thomas) [270], 3. Dowlais Penywern (Alaw Morlais) [261]

1913 Abergavenny

60–80 voices

Test pieces: 'Fallen Heroes' (Cyril Jenkins), 'Oleuni Claer' (Daniel Protheroe)

Adjudicators: Dr Walford Davies, Dr D. Vaughan Thomas, Dr Roland Rogers, Dr D.C. Williams, David Jenkins, Harry Evans

18 choirs

Result: 1. Ebenezer Mission (Turner Thomas), 2. Cleveland Harmonic, Middlesbrough, 3. Williamstown

Among the other choirs competing were Barry, Dowlais Penywern, Bargoed Teifi, London Welsh, Bargoed, Plymouth and Abercarn.

1914 No eisteddfod

1915 Bangor

Prize: £15

Test pieces: 'Dance of the Gnomes' (E. MacDowell), 'Y Derwyddon'/ 'The Druids' (Joseph Parry), 'The Phantom Host' (F. Hegar)

The competition was cancelled at first, owing to a 'lack of cheap excursions' (rather than the war), but in the face of public disappointment the committee relented and decided to 'extemporise' a competition, for choirs of around 30 voices singing their own choice of music:

Result: 1. 16th Batt., Royal Welsh Fusiliers (Pte T. Tucker, Skewen)

There were two choirs in khaki competing, both in training at Llandudno. After the contest they combined on the stage to sing 'Comrades in Arms', to great applause. Dr D. Vaughan Thomas in his adjudication made a plea for the avoidance of such 'barbaric pieces as "Martyrs of the Arena"' and urged the adoption of tests more in accord with the Eisteddfodic standard of culture. 'They should sing songs of Augustus' Rome rather than those of Nero's Rome.'

1916 Aberystwyth No competition

1917 Birkenhead No competition

1918 Neath

50–80 voices	
Prize:	£30; £5
Test pieces:	(both unaccompanied) 'Here's to Admiral Death' (D. Vaughan Thomas), 'Cares Hinon' (David Jenkins) – not sung
Adjudicators:	Dr Granville Bantock, Dr D. Vaughan Thomas, E.T. Davies, Dr David Evans, Dr Caradog Roberts
14 choirs	
Result:	1. Williamstown, Rhondda (Ted Lewis) [92], 2. Welsh Guards [82], 3. Maesteg [80], 4. Swansea [78]
	There were five Rhondda choirs in this competition: Williamstown, Blaenclydach, Wattstown, Cwmparc, Tonyrefail

1919 Corwen

Choirs over 40 voices	
First prize:	£50
Test pieces:	(a) 'Y Gariad Gollwyd' / 'The Lost Love' (D. Vaughan Thomas), (b) 'Invictus' (Daniel Protheroe)
Adjudicators:	Dr David Evans, Dr D.C. Williams, Dr Caradog Roberts, E.T. Davies
18 choirs	
Result:	1. Nelson Arion (Lawson Berry) 95 + 93 = 188
	2. Tredegar Orpheus (J.D. Evans) 93 + 92 = 185
	3. Williamstown (Ted Lewis) 92 + 90 = 182

The choirs, seven of them from England, varied greatly in size from 60 to 130, and the atmosphere was described by the *Musical Times* as 'almost terrifying.' Rhondda's Williamstown had brought off a famous victory out of 14 choirs at Neath the previous year. They would win again at Barry in 1920 but the premier Welsh choir on this occasion was the Tredegar Orpheus, who having just absorbed three rival local choirs, were able to stage 108 in Corwen. But it was Nelson Arion, twenty fewer in number, which won. Established in 1884 among the Lancashire cotton mills, their history was similar to many of the Welsh choirs they defeated. They were upholding the pre-war tradition set by Manchester Orpheus of being an English thorn in the Welsh side. This dominance, by socially more diverse, emotionally more restrained and musically better disciplined English choirs, prevailed throughout the 1920s, though they competed only in north Wales.

With the government becoming paranoid about the spread of communist ideas among the industrial working class following the 1917 revolution in Russia, the *Musical Times* thought that male choral singing had a useful role to play:

> The male voice contest [at Corwen] took place in an atmosphere of tense excitement that occasionally flamed up into a threat of disorder … Both [test] pieces left a good deal to be desired as music. The first ['The Lost Love'] almost entirely failed to express the poignant personal feeling of the poem, and the second ['Invictus'], in spite of some dramatic moments, was spoilt by the conventional character of the means employed for emotional purposes … The strife was long – nearly three and a half hours. With few exceptions the choirs displayed beautiful tone and blend, the best of them, in breadth and sonority, suggesting organ-tone. The chief failing was in regard to intonation, few ending the unaccompanied song ['The Lost Love'] without a slight loss of pitch … the best of the singing was wonderfully good. The amount of discipline that must have gone to the production of such ensemble made one wonder why our none too economical Government does not spend a few thousand pounds on male voice choralism as an antidote to Bolshevism. It would be difficult to imagine anything less suggestive of industrial unrest than the sight of these men – nearly two thousand of them altogether and many of them from South Wales collieries – singing difficult music from memory, absorbed in their task, obedient to every sign from their conductor … Nobody stopped to demand a soviet and there was no talk of downing voices.

Second competition, choirs not over 25 voices

Test piece: 'Alawon Cymraeg' ('Welsh Melodies') arr. Harry Evans

7 choirs

Result: 1. Gwalia, Nantyglo [176], 2. Glynclydach Singers, Blaenclydach, Rhondda [174]

1920 Barry

 60–80 voices

 Prize: £100; £20

 Test pieces: (a) 'Ballade' (Granville Bantock), (b) 'The Winds'/ 'Y Gwyntoedd'
      (E.T. Davies), (c) 'The Drummer' (F.G. Bennett) – not sung

 Adjudicators: Dr H. Walford Davies, Dr Ralph Vaughan Williams, Dr David
      Evans

 12 choirs

 Result: 1. Williamstown (Ted Lewis) 91 + 97 = 188

      2. Dowlais Penywern 96 + 87 = 183

      3. Tredegar Orpheus 92 + 89 = 181

      4. Abertillery Orpheus

      5. Rhymney

The pavilion, with 12,000 seated, was packed to its 20,000 capacity and its sides had to be lowered to allow the audience to breathe and so that those outside could have a chance of seeing the choirs. While volume of tone and careful expression distinguished most of the choirs, 'the higher conception and thrilling interpretation of the leaders were magnificently impressive' and much appreciated by the large audience. Summing up his impressions of the week, Ralph Vaughan Williams hoped he would 'have the pleasure and honour of coming to one of these festivals again' so that he 'would hear again those beautiful male voice choirs'. Ted Lewis (Williamstown), he thought, had 'refined gold under his baton and … welded it into a jewel of the highest lustre.'

1921 Caernarfon

 Over 60 voices

 Prize: £100, £20

 Test pieces: 'The Phantom Host' (Hegar), 'O Peaceful Night' (Edward
      German)

 Adjudicators: Dr Henry Coward, Dr D. Vaughan Thomas, Dr Caradog
      Roberts, Dr D. de Lloyd, J. Owen Jones

 12 choirs (6 from England)

 Result: 1. Holme Valley, Huddersfield (Irving Silverwood) [198], 2.
      Nelson Arion [192], 3. Llanrwst [189]

The adjudication took forty minutes: the competition took five hours. The performance by the winning choir of *The Phantom Host* 'stunned people into breathlessness.' In Dr Coward's view the singing was 'on a wonderfully high level'. Dr Vaughan Thomas thought that 'the pronunciation of the English words by one of the choirs was music itself and naturally it was an English choir. They recited the words "O Peaceful Night, so calm and still" beautifully. They knew the music of their own tongue and appreciated it.' Welsh choirs were at a disadvantage singing in English. For all that, Vaughan Thomas reckoned he had never listened to such magnificent singing in a male voice contest. The 1921 lockout in the coalfield had prevented south Wales choirs from appearing.

Dr Henry Coward (1849–1944) was a renowned chorus-master and enthusiastic advocate of the sol-fa. His father had been a pub landlord and a black-face minstrel. Given the origins of many Welsh male voice choirs in the glee tradition of sociability and blacking up, these facts, if known, would have endeared Dr Coward to them. He was knighted in 1926.

Second competition, over 30 voices

Test pieces: 'Lament for Prince Llywelyn' (Cyril Jenkins), 'Nos Gân'/ 'Serenade' (Joseph Parry)

Adjudicators: Cyril Jenkins, D. Vaughan Thomas, J. Owen Jones

7 choirs

Result: 1. Caernarfon, 2. Elidir, Llanberis

Competition for ex-servicemen's choirs, not under 20 voices

Test piece: 'O Dad y gwroniaid'/ 'Father of heroes' (Robert Bryan)

5 choirs

Result: 1. Llanberis Comrades

1922 Ammanford

60–100 voices

Test pieces: (a) 'Sea Fever' (Cyril Jenkins), (b) 'Iesu o Nazareth' (Joseph Parry), (c) 'Y Deryn Pur' (arr. E.T. Davies) – not sung

Adjudicators: Henry Coward, E.T. Davies, T. Hopkin Evans, Cyril Jenkins

13 choirs (the competition lasted six hours)

Result: 1. Dowlais (Alaw Morlais, accomp. D. T. Davies) 88 + 95 = 183

                    2. Swansea (Llew Bowen)   89 + 93 = 182

                    3. Barclays Bank, London   94 + 87 = 181

                    4. Rhymney   84 + 96 = 180

As can be seen from the marks awarded in this exceptionally tight contest, it was fourth-placed Rhymney that scored highest in 'Iesu o Nazareth' (96), and Barclays Bank the highest in 'Sea Fever' (94), whose composer, Cyril Jenkins, was one of the adjudicators.

There had never been a keener competition, though perhaps there was a hint of mixed blessing in the *Western Mail's* headline: 'Battle of Giants at the Eisteddfod: six hours of Joseph Parry and Cyril Jenkins'. It was an ironic juxtaposition given Jenkins' recent much-publicised onslaught on the reputation of Joseph Parry, all of whose music, he believed, had 'the stamp of an inferior mind', most of it smeared in a 'disagreeable emotionalism ... at its very best Parry's work is only second rate; at its worst it is beneath contempt' (*The Sackbut*, November 1921, pp. 19-22).

1923 Mold

> *not under 60 voices*
> Prize: £75
> Test pieces: 'Kubla Khan' (Bantock), 'Nidaros' (Daniel Protheroe)
> Adjudicators: R. Vaughan Williams, E.T. Davies, D. Vaughan Thomas, Wilfrid
>   Jones, J. Chas. McLean
> 7 choirs
> Result: 1. Hadley and District, Staffs.   95 + 97 = 192
>   2. Crossley Motors, Manchester   95 + 92 = 187
>   3. Manchester Orpheus   86 + 87 = 173

E.T. Davies, adjudicating, thought the Bantock technically abstruse and unrewarding for singers and listeners. However, R. Vaughan Williams, in his remarks, quoted Thomas Carlyle to the effect that 'if you search deep enough there is music everywhere'. Ouch!

> *Second competition, not under 30 voices*
> Test pieces: 'O tyr'd i fyw' (R. Bryan), 'Up-hill' (D. Vaughan Thomas)
> Adjudicators: Caradog Roberts, E. T. Davies, Wilfrid Jones
> 6 choirs
> Result: 1. Orpheus Male Voice Choir, Cleveland, Ohio 86 + 84 = 170
>   2. Leeswood (Flints)   89 + 80 = 168
>   3. Cymric, Pontlottyn   89 + 69 = 158

The Cleveland choir wore blue flannel jackets and cream flannel trousers. It is unlikely that any of the Welsh choirs did.

1924 Pontypool

70–120 voices

Prize: £100

Test pieces: 'Hereward the Wake' (S.E. Lovatt), 'Dominus Illuminatio Mea' (Walford Davies)

Adjudicators: Sir Richard Terry, T. Hopkin Evans, D. Vaughan Thomas, David Evans

8 choirs

Result: Joint winners – Swansea and Dowlais:

Swansea (Llew Bowen)	94 + 97 = 191
Dowlais (Alaw Morlais)	98 + 93 = 191
3. Cardiff	94 + 90 = 184
4. Fishguard and Goodwick	89 + 91 = 180

Second competition, 40–60 voices

Test pieces: 'Y Deryn Pur' (E. T. Davies), 'Castilla' (Daniel Protheroe)

Adjudicators: E.T. Davies, H. Walford Davies, D. Vaughan Thomas, David Evans

6 choirs

Result:

1. Brynmawr	89 + 93 = 182
2. Glanffrwd, Abersychan	89 + 89 = 178

1925 Pwllheli

60–90 voices

Test pieces: 'Cry from the Twilight' (Leigh Henry), 'Storm Joy' (Henry Walford Davies)

Adjudicators: H. Walford Davies, D. Vaughan Thomas, David Evans, Caradog Roberts, T. Hopkin Evans

4 choirs

Result: 1. Hadley and District [180], 2. Crossley Motors [174], 3. Fishguard [159], 3. Welsh Guards [143]

Second competition, 40–60 voices

Test pieces: 'Plant y Cedyrn'/ 'Sons of the Mighty' (W.T. David), 'Ar Hyd y Nos' (arr. Harry Evans)

Adjudicators: as above

5 choirs

Result: 1. Llithfaen [181], 2. Trefor [179], 3. Port Talbot [171]

1926 Swansea

> *not under 60 voices*

Prize: £100

Test pieces: 'The Twilight Tombs of Ancient Kings' (Bantock), 'The Wanderer' (Elgar) 'Chwyth, Chwyth Aeafol Wynt'/ 'Blow, Blow Thou Winter Wind' (J. Owen Jones) – all unaccompanied

Adjudicators: Granville Bantock, Daniel Protheroe, T. Hopkin Evans, E.T. Davies, Arthur Davies, D. Vaughan Thomas

11 choirs

Result: 1. Cleveland Orpheus, Ohio (Charles P. Dawe) [279], 2. Dowlais (Alaw Morlais) [264], 3. Burry Port (William Lewis) [260], 4. Cardiff [256], 5. Wattstown [251]

'National' adjudicators, despite frequent assertions to the contrary, were no respecters of reputation. Here, previous winners came badly unstuck: Hadley were placed eighth (234), Williamstown tenth (230) and Swansea eleventh (221). Making their first appearance were Morriston United, conducted by Ivor E. Sims.

'If Sir Edward Elgar had been at Swansea', remarked an English critic, 'he would have thought twice and thrice before he ever again indicated *staccato* for men's choirs. The sense of this piece ['The Wanderer'] was very generally missed. The poem – an extraordinary anonymous lyric of the seventeenth century, a piece of inspired ecstatic verse and as someone said, no doubt the best poem of the whole Eisteddfod – apparently conveyed nothing to the singers.' The winning conductor, Charles Dawe, had migrated to the U.S.A. from Port Talbot in 1912.

> *Second competition, 40– 60 voices*

Prize: £40

Test pieces: 'Fierce Raged the Tempest' (Ioan Willliams), 'Yr Hufen Melyn'/ 'The Yellow Cream' (arr. Osborne Roberts), 'Men of Eric' (James Lyon)

Adjudicators: Sir Richard Terry, Arthur Davies, E.T. Davies, D. Vaughan Thomas

5 choirs

Result: 1. Beaufort Celtic (Randall Williams) [173], 2. Excelsior Haverfordwest (Eddie Jones) [171], 3. Glanffrwd, Abersychan (W.R.Lewis) [167]

1927 Holyhead

Not more than 100 voices

Prize: £100

Test pieces: 'He who comes here' (Thomas Morley), 'Treasures of the Deep'/
                'Trysorau'r Dyfnder' (J. H. Roberts), 'War Song of the Saracens'
                (Bantock)

Adjudicators: Granville Bantock, Daniel Protheroe, David Evans, E.T. Davies,
                T. Hopkin Evans

3 choirs

Result: 1. Manchester C.W.S. [275], 2. Scunthorpe [267], 3. Caernarfon
                [232]

Second Competition, not more than 60 Voices

No entrants

1928 Treorchy

not under 100 voices

Prize: £100

Test pieces: 'Song of the Spirits over the Waters' (Schubert), 'Cân i'r Eos'/
                'Ode to the Nightingale' (John Owen Jones)

Adjudicators: Sir Henry Coward, Dr T. Hopkin Evans, Dr David Evans, Dr
                David de Lloyd, Dr Daniel Protheroe

10 choirs

Result:

1. Swansea (Llew Bowen)	97+95 = 192	
2. joint – Morriston United (Ivor Sims)	92+93 = 185	
Dowlais (Alaw Morlais)	92+93 = 185	
4. Rhymney (Abel Jones)	89+87 = 176	
5. joint – Pendyrus (Arthur Duggan)	85+88 = 173	
Garw (John Butler)	89+84 = 173	
7. Tredegar Orpheus (J. D. Evans)	163	
8. Beaufort (Randall Williams)	160	
9. Cardiff (Ted Lewis)	158	
10. Ogmore Valley (Theo. Beynon)	153	

This was Pendyrus' first National appearance, led by their 34-year-old founder-conductor Arthur Duggan. Massive crowds attended the Treorchy National with a hundred trains arriving daily. This was Wales on the cusp of the Depression and most of the 3,000 miners employed at the local Parc & Dare and Abergorki pits chose to listen to the competition from the hillside above rather than pay the price of admission.

Second competition, not under 60 voices

Test pieces: 'Bells of Aberdovey' (Daniel Protheroe), 'Hyfryd Nos' / 'Beloved Night' (Dan Jones)

Adjudicators: Sir Henry Coward, Dr T. Hopkin Evans, Dr David Evans, Dr David de Lloyd

9 choirs

Result: 1. Anthracite Male Chorus of Scranton USA (Luther Bassett) [173], 2. Cwmbach United (Herbert Davies) [167], 3. Haverfordwest Excelsior (Eddie Jones) [166], plus Treboeth [164], Porth [158], Llanharan and Welsh Guards [both 150], Cambrian, Clydach Vale [147]

Over 2,000 male choristers sang in the two competitions. The *Musical Opinion* (September 1928) was unimpressed by the test pieces: 'The average man, it would seem, not only supports the National Eisteddfod by his attendance but is allowed a voice in the selection of the music to be heard at it.' The choir from Scranton, Pa., where the largest number of Welsh immigrants in the USA was concentrated, were 62 on stage, their white check trousers and blue serge jackets a startling contrast to the sombre dark suits of their opponents. They sang, too, in the words of the *Musical Times*, 'with excessive contrasts and explosive effects. They had apparently not a thought for what they were singing about.' The decision in their favour was followed by 'promiscuous kissing of each other and any young girls in sight,' to the evident distaste of some home-grown observers: 'Decent manners it would appear, are not to be picked up in the United States.' Their conductor, Kidwelly-born Dr Luther Bassett, took his 150-strong mixed Scranton Choral Union to the Liverpool National the following year and won again.

1929 Liverpool

80–100 voices

Test pieces: 'The Herald' (Elgar), 'Y Rhaeadr'/ 'The Cataract' (T. Hopkin Evans)

'Moab', no. 3 of *Seven Burdens* (G. Bantock)

Adjudicators: Dr Granville Bantock, E.T. Davies, Dr David Evans, Dr David de Lloyd, Dr Daniel Protheroe, Dr Caradog Roberts

10 choirs (5 from England)

Result: 1. Nelson Arion and Colne Orpheus Choir (Luther Greenwood) [280] 2. Swansea and District (Llew Bowen) [273], 3. Morriston

United (Ivor E. Sims) [271], 4. Hadley and District (Raymond Lewis) [263], 5. Duffryn (Tudor C. Jones) [258], 6. CWS Manchester (Alfred Higson) [256], 7. Joint – Manchester Orpheus (J. Albert Hill) and Llanellli (D.H. Lewis) [250] 9. Treorchy (John Isaac Jones) [244], 10. Chester (J. Weadall) [240]

Whether due to the distance involved or the onset of the Depression, it was reported that 'the attendance did not flatter such a doughty contest of the champions' and a noticeable feature was the absence of the followers of the individual choirs. 'There was generally applause but little of the electricity in the air which a big male choral contest creates'. Granville Bantock, composer of one of the test pieces and adjudicator, warned that mass, weight and volume of tone, 'even shouting at times, is not singing, much less music'. Welsh choirs were slow to heed this warning.

Second competition, under 80 voices

Test pieces: 'Myfanwy' (Harry Evans), 'The Strength of the Hills' (Rhys Herbert), 'Tra Bo Dau' and 'Cyfri'r Geifr' (arr. Caradog Roberts)

Adjudicators: as above

6 choirs

Result: 1. Gwent Glee Singers, Nantyglo [173], 2. Warrington [160], 3. Sandbach [158], 4. Cwmbach [157], 5. Hiraddug, Dyserth [151, 6. Gelli [147]

Most of the winning Nantyglo choir were unemployed. The prize was £50, the cost of travelling to the Eisteddfod £70. Members of Cwmbach working the morning shift in the early hours of Saturday went straight from the colliery to Liverpool. Hiraddug were conducted by William Humphreys, who in 1933 founded Côr Meibion Trelawnyd. He was the father of the novelist Emyr Humphreys.

1930 Llanelli

80–120 voices

Test pieces: 'The Arsenal at Springfield' (J. Owen Jones), 'Cymru Rhydd' (David de Lloyd)

Adjudicators: D. de Lloyd, J. Owen Jones, Caradog Roberts, W. S. Gwynn Williams, Julius Harrison, J. Frederick Staton

8 choirs

Result: 1. Morriston United (Ivor Sims) [182], 2. Swansea and District [174], 3. Powell Dyffryn, Llanharan [167], Pontypridd [155], Pendyrus [154]

Second competition, 40–60 voices
Test pieces: 'The Fugitive' (D. Tawe Jones), 'The Rider's Song' (P. Cornelius)
Adjudicators: as above
4 choirs
Result: 1. Carmarthen [161], 2. Haverfordwest Excelsior [155], 3. Cwmbach [140]

Works choirs, 30–40 voices
Test pieces: 'The Wintry Winds are Blowing' (J. Muller), 'Lovely Maiden' (D. Pughe Evans)
Adjudicators: Caradog Roberts, J. Owen Jones
24 entered, 7 staged
Result: 1. Cambrian Colliery, Clydach Vale [175], 2. Cwm Cynon, Mountain Ash [172] 3. Joint – Pentremawr Colliery, Pontyberem, and Hafod Colliery, Wrexham [163]

All the choirs in the 'Works' competition were composed of colliery, foundry, railway and tinplate workers. The seven that reached the stage were colliery choirs.

Dr Caradog Roberts inadvertently revealed a variety of prejudices when he said that 'as adjudicators they had experienced rough voices and crude ideas, but to their amazement and enjoyment the competition revealed excellent vocal material and splendid interpretation and imaginative powers. He was very delighted to find such exceptional talent among the workers, and the harmony and comradeship which they revealed was a vindication of what was wanted in industry today (*Applause*).' One wonders what he thought the social composition of the choirs was in the other two competitions.

1931 Bangor

75– 100 voices
Test pieces: 'Sing out ye Nymphs' (S. Bennett), 'Zut! Zut! Zut!' (Elgar), 'Môr-gân Gavran'/ 'The Sea-song of Gavran' (Tawe Jones) – all unaccompanied
Adjudicators: Dr T. Hopkin Evans, Granville Bantock, Dr Thomas Keighley, Dr David Evans, Owen M. Price
5 choirs

Result: 1. Swansea (Ivor Owen) [278], 2. Morriston United [276], 3. Powell Dyffryn, Llanharan [260]

Second competition, 40–60 voices

Test pieces: 'Come live with me and be my love' (Iorwerth Prosser), 'Gwcw Fach'/ 'Cuckoo Dear' (arr. E.T. Davies)

Adjudicators: Caradog Roberts, Granville Bantock, David Evans, T. Hopkin Evans, David de Lloyd

10 choirs

Result: 1. Cambrian Colliery, Clydach Vale   91 + 93 = 184

       2. Haverfordwest   90 + 90 = 180

       3. Llanerchymedd, Anglesey   88 + 90 = 178

       4. Abertillery Orpheus   84 + 86 = 170

1932 Port Talbot

80–120 voices

Prize: £100

Test pieces: 'Bid me to Live' (Iorwerth Prosser), 'Jean Richepin's Song' (J. Holbrooke) 'Drontheim' (Daniel Protheroe)

Adjudicators: Drs J. Morgan Lloyd, Caradog Roberts, T. Hopkin Evans, Daniel Protheroe, David Evans, David de Lloyd

11 choirs

Result: 1. Morriston United (Ivor Sims) [283], 2. Pendyrus (Arthur Duggan) [274], 3. Swansea (Ivor Owen) [259]

Caradog Roberts, adjudicating this five-hour competition, wished for 'more culture, more finish' which the test pieces did not encourage. He deplored the excess of 'trick singing – the whisper and shout of pseudo-dramatic singing, the pauses, the broken bits of piano exercises', and urged choral conductors to 'realise that successful singing was not a bag of Eisteddfod prize-winning tricks but a natural and soulful expression'. The Welsh-American Iorwerth Prosser's 'Bid me to live' was dismissed by the *News Chronicle* as 'more a declaration of war than of love,' and Daniel Protheroe's 'Drontheim' as 'the kind of thing turned out on demand by the the Chicago machine.' Neither work appeared again as a National test piece.

Works choirs, 30–40 voices

Test pieces: 'Cities of the Plains' (Dan Jones), 'The Lee Shore' (Coleridge Taylor)

Adjudicators: as above

13 choirs

Result: 1. Cambrian Colliery, Clydach Vale [183], 2. Newlands Colliery, Pyle [181], 3. Powell Dyffryn, Llanharan [171], 4. Morlais, Ferndale [170], 5. Wyndham Colliery, Ogmore Vale [164]

1933 Wrexham

not under 80 voices

Test pieces: 'In Summertime on Bredon' (H. Roberton), 'Chwyth, chwyth aeafol wynt'/ 'Blow, blow, thou winter wind' (J. Owen Jones), 'The Fighting Temeraire' (Bantock)

Adjudicators: Sir Granville Bantock, J. Owen Jones, Sir Hugh Roberton, Dr J. Morgan Lloyd, John Hughes

8 choirs

Result: 1. Hadley and District Orpheus, Salop, 2. Hebden Briercliffe, Yorks, 3. Pendyrus

Second competition, not under 50 voices

Test pieces: 'Two Celtic Songs' (Caradog Roberts), 'Feasting I Watch' (Elgar)

10 choirs

Result: 1. Talk o' the Hill, Staffs. [270], 2. Rhos British Legion [264], 3. Cwm-yr-hebog, Tonypandy [262]

The distinguished founder-conductor of the Glasgow Orpheus Choir from 1906 to 1951 Sir Hugh Roberton (1874–1952), remarked of this competition, 'When you people of Wales go out in search of your aristocracy, you will find it among your singers of songs and tellers of tales. Coming from Scotland, I envy you very much your capacity to fill a place like this [the 12,000 capacity Eisteddfod Pavilion) and put before your public such a wonderful display'.

Works choirs, 30– 40 voices

Prize: £20

Test pieces: 'Mwynder y Meusydd'/ 'Song of the Woodcutters' (Daniel Protheroe) 'Eldorado' (Roland Rogers)

Adjudicators: J. Owen Jones, Dr J. Morgan Lloyd, John Hughes

6 choirs

Result: 1. Cambrian Colliery, Clydach Vale, 2. D. Davies & Sons, Ferndale

1934 Neath

80–120 voices

Prize: £100

Test pieces: 'Apollo and the Seaman' (J. Holbrooke), 'Crossing the Bar' (Caradog Roberts) 'Meibion yr Anial'/ 'Sons of the Desert' (T. Hopkin Evans)

Adjudicators: Caradog Roberts, T. Hopkin Evans, J. Morgan Lloyd, Vincent Thomas

8 choirs

Result:
1. Swansea (Ivor Owen)	95 + 91 + 94 = 280
2. Pendyrus* (Arthur Duggan)	93 + 89 + 95 = 277
3. Morriston United (David Rees)	90 + 89 + 87 = 266

* 138 choristers on stage

Second competition, 40–70 voices

Prize: £25

Test pieces: 'Alawon Cartref' (W.T. David), 'Music when soft voices die' (D. de Lloyd)

11 choirs

Result: 1. Tabernacle, Skewen, 2. Pontardawe, 3. Aberbaiden Colliery

1935 Caernarfon

80–100 voices

Test pieces: 'Rise Red Sun' (Mussorgsky), 'Cleddyf yr Ysbryd' (Caradog Roberts)

Adjudicators: J.F. Staton, David Evans, T. Hopkin Evans, David de Lloyd, W. Matthews Williams

5 choirs

Result: 1. Pendyrus [182], 2. Morriston United [172], 3. Ffynnongroyw [169]

Second competition, not under 40 voices

Test Pieces: Nos. 2 and 4 of *Rig Veda Hymns* (Holst), 'Inchcape Bell' (J. Owen Jones)

Adjudicators: as above

8 choirs

Result: 1. Penrhyn, 2. Joint – Deeside, and Cambrian Colliery, Clydach Vale

1936 Fishguard

80–150 voices

Test pieces: 'The Reveille' (Elgar), 'The Wanderer's Song' (Delius), 'Desideria' (Tawe Jones)

Adjudicators: Dr Harvey Grace, Dr T. Hopkin Evans, Sir Richard Terry, William Rees, Tawe Jones, Dr Sydney Northcote

7 choirs

Result:

1. Swansea (Ivor Owen)	95 + 88 + 96 = 279
2. Rhosllannerchrugog (Ben Evans)	87 + 88 + 89 = 264
3. Pendyrus (Arthur Duggan)	87 + 82 + 84 = 253
4. Morriston Orpheus and Treorchy (joint)	244
5. Morriston United	241
6. Pontypridd	235

Second competition, 50– 80 voices

Test pieces: 'The Lee Shore' (Cyril Jenkins) 'Tra Bo Dau' / 'Two Fond Hearts' (arr. Caradog Roberts)

Adjudicators: as above

12 choirs

Result: 1. Ystalyfera [164], 2. Cynon, Mountain Ash [162], 3. Tabernacle, Skewen [156]

1937 Machynlleth

80– 120 voices

Prize: £100

Test pieces: 'Prospice' (D. Vaughan Thomas), 'The Winds' (E.T. Davies), 'The Fond Lover' (G.Bantock) – all unaccompanied

Adjudicators: C. Armstrong Gibbs, Dr David de Lloyd, Dr J. Morgan Lloyd, Sir Ernest Macmillan, Dr J. Frederick Staton

8 choirs

Result:

1. Morriston Orpheus (Ivor Sims)	90 + 91 + 93 = 274
2. Morriston United (Idris Evans)	90 + 89 + 88 = 267
3. Powell Dyffryn, Pontypridd (Frank Temple Evans)	87 + 86 + 89 = 262
4. Rhollannerchrugog (J. Owen Jones)	86 + 83 + 90 = 259
5. Tredegar Orpheus (Abel Jones)	84 + 86 + 82 = 252
6. Treorchy (W. D. Evans)	85 + 82 + 81 = 248
7. Pontypridd (Gwilym T. Jones)	78 + 83 + 83 = 244
8. Pendyrus (Arthur Duggan)	78 + 80 + 75 = 233

Second competition, 60– 80 voices

Test pieces: 'Sound an Alarm' (Handel), 'Y Bugail' (arr. E.T. Davies), 'The tide rises, the tide falls'/ 'Fe ddaw llanw, fe ddaw trai' (E.J. Hughes)

Adjudicators: as above

9 choirs

Result: 1. Mountain Ash [273], 2. Western Tinplate Works, Llanelli [259], 3. Penrhyn [257], 4. Tabernacle, Skewen [255], 5. London Welsh [253]

1938 Cardiff

not under 100 voices

Test pieces: 'A Festal Psalm' (W. G. Whittaker), 'Lucifer in Starlight' (Granville Bantock), 'Hei Ho' (Haydn Morris)

Adjudicators: Sir Hugh Allen, E.T. Davies, Dr Charles Dawe, Dr T.Hopkin Evans, J. Morgan Nicholas, Bryceson Treharne

7 choirs

Result: 1. Rhosllannerchrugog (J. Owen Jones) [285], 2. Morriston United (Idris Evans) [284], 3. Morriston Orpheus (Ivor E.Sims) [268], 4. Pontypridd (Gwilym T. Jones) [259], 5. Pendyrus (Arthur Duggan) [245], 6. Powell Duffryn (George James) [238], 7. Tredegar Orpheus (Abel Jones) [234]

The Treisdorf Berlin choir had entered this competition and the Berlin Philharmonic had entered the Chief Choral (mixed), but neither turned up. The year was 1938.

Second competition, 50– 75 voices

Test pieces: 'Come Away Death' (T. Dunhill), 'A Clear Midnight' (Charles Wood), 'Si Hei Lwli Mabi' (arr. E.T. Davies)

Adjudicators: as above

8 choirs

Result: 1. Machynlleth [261], 2. Cwmbach United [259], 3. Cwm Cynon [258], 4. Tredegar [251]

Glee competition for male choirs of the unemployed, 16–20 voices

Prize: £12

Test piece: 'Hey Robin, Jolly Robin' (Geoffrey Shaw) plus an unaccompanied own choice

Adjudicators: as above
5 choirs
Result: 1. Nantyglo Social Service Club, 2. Garth (Maesteg), 3. Williamstown Gleemen

Glee confined to Welsh choirs outside Wales, 30–40 voices
Test piece: 'Y Delyn Aur' (arr. D. Pughe Evans)
Adjudicators: as above
Result: 1. Hammersmith Welsh, 2. Oxford Welsh, 3. Welwyn Garden City, 4. Coventry Welsh Gleemen, 5. Luton Cambrian Male Choir

Glee for male voices, 30–40 voices
Prize: £5
Test pieces: 'Hail O Moon' (Sibelius) or 'The Constant Lover' (Vincent Thomas). 'Hawddamor i Ti'/ 'Farewell my Love' (Robert Jones). None sang the Sibelius.
5 choirs
Result: 1. Breconia, Brynmawr (W. Bevan) [171], 2. Morgannwg Gleemen, Ton Pentre (D.Lukey) [170], 3. Pontardawe [165], 4. Morlais, Ferndale [159], 5. Cardiff G.W.R. [157]

Under the headline 'Death of a Glee Party', the *Rhondda Leader* (17 January, 1959) reported the termination of the famous (in Mid-Rhondda) Morgannwg Glee Singers. Dai Lukey had been connected with them for over 26 years. With his budgie, Joey, sitting on his shoulders, Dai told how it had been 'practically his life.' They had sung under his baton at innumerable eisteddfodau all over Wales and England. In 1912 he was the conductor of a glee party attached to Bethania Chapel, Ton Pentre, where he had been caretaker, organist and conductor for many years. The number of the myriad glee parties like these, pre-1914 and in in the inter-war period when they were connected to labour and workingmen's clubs and chapels across Wales, is unknown and ultimately unknowable, but no account of the 'land of song' is complete without them. Their nearest equivalent were the German workmen's singing clubs of the Ruhr (Dowe, 1978).

1939 Denbigh

> *80–120 voices*
>
> Test pieces: 'Paty O'Toole' (Charles Wood), 'Siege of Kazan' (Tawe Jones), 'Mordaith Cariad' / 'Love's Voyage' (T. Hopkin Evans)
>
> Adjudicators: Charles Dawe, E.T. Davies, David Evans, Dr A. W. Wilcock, W. Matthews Williams
>
> 8 choirs

Result:		
1. Nelson Arion (George Altham)	93 + 94 + 91 = 278
2. Morriston United (Idris Evans	84 + 90 + 89 = 263
3. Morriston Orpheus (Ivor Sims)	86 + 87 + 89 = 262
4. Warrington (Alfred Higson)	86 + 85 + 90 = 261
5. Rhosllannerchrugog (J.Owen Jones)	83 + 86 + 90 = 259
6. Swansea (Ivor Owen)	82 + 84 + 90 = 256

This victory signalled a remarkable triple triumph for Nelson Arion who won in 1919, 1929, and 1939.

> *Second competition, 40–80 voices*
>
> Prize: £40; £10
>
> 9 choirs

1. Breconian, Brynmawr (W. Bevan)	93 + 94 + 92 = 279
2. Penrhyn (W. Ffrancon Thomas)	90 + 93 + 88 = 271
3. Western Tinplate, Llanelli	85 + 88 + 92 = 265

Virtually all the Brynmawr choir were unemployed, including the conductor. Formed in 1934, they had achieved 42 firsts in 46 competitions across Wales. In the previous two years, despite coming from one of the most severely depressed areas in the country, they had raised a thousand pounds for charitable causes.

1940 Radio Eisteddfod (5–10 August, broadcast from the B.B.C. Welsh Region)

> *not under 80 voices*
>
> Test pieces: 'De Profundis' (Vincent Thomas), 'Full Fathom Five' (T. Dunhill)
>
> Adjudicator: Dr David Evans
>
> Result: 1. Morriston United (Idris Evans) [89]; 2. Pendyrus [86], 3. Bargoed [83]

Idris Evans, who was 38 in 1940, had been conducting choirs since his teens. Before becoming conductor of Morriston United in 1937 he had for 14 years been conductor of Ystalyfera men's choir, leading them to victory out of 12 choirs in the second competition at Fishguard in 1936.

1941 Old Colwyn   no competition

1942 Cardigan   no competition

1943 Bangor   no competition

1944 Llandybïe   no competition

1945 Rhosllannerchrugog
25–30 voices
Prize: £15
Test pieces: 'Gobaith' (Ieuan Rees-Davies), 'Cân i'r Eos' (J. Owen Jones)
Adjudicators: John Hughes, J. Morgan Nicholas, D.E. Parry-Williams
2 choirs
Result: 1. Pontyberem Glee Party, 2. Mond Glee Party, Clydach

1946 Mountain Ash
Prize: £70; £40; £20
Test pieces: 'Prospice' (D. Vaughan Thomas), 'Y Carwr Ffyddlon'/ 'The Faithful Lover' (Vincent Thomas)
Adjudicators: David de Lloyd, David Evans, E.T. Davies, W. Matthews Williams
3 choirs
Result: 1. Morriston Orpheus [186], 2. Pendyrus [165], 3. Morriston United [158]

Second competition
Test pieces: 'Cân Buddugoliaeth'/'The Triumph Song' (Mansel Thomas), 'Ar Hyd y Nos' and 'Llwyn Onn' (arr. David Evans)
Adjudicators: E.T. Davies, Dan Jones, J. Charles McLean
Result: Breconian, Brynmawr

Factory and Works choirs, 30–40 voices (male or mixed)
Own choice
Result: 1. Chwarelwyr Llithfaen (Quarrymen) sang 'Deus Salutis' ('Llef') arr. Mansel Thomas, 2. Mond Glee Singers

1947 Colwyn Bay

not under 60 voices

Prize: £100 & Welsh Guards Challenge Cup

Test pieces: 'Angladd y Marchog'/ 'The Knight's Burial' (W. Matthews Williams) 'Cadlef y Weriniaeth'/ 'Our God is Marching On' (Haydn Morris)

Adjudicators: E.T. Davies, David Evans, W. Matthews Williams, Haydn Morris, J. Chas. McLean

6 choirs

Result: 1. Morriston Orpheus [186], 2. Rhymney [183], 3. Dinorwic [174]

While the slate quarrying districts of north-west Wales continued to produce several smaller choirs like Llithfaen, Deiniolen and Elidir, as well as countless mixed choral societies, the choirs of Dinorwic, Penrhyn, Moelwyn and, later, the Brythoniaid, consisting mostly of quarrymen, were larger organisations comparable to those of south and north-east Wales.

Second competition, under 60 voices

Prize: £40 & Royal Welsh Fusiliers Challenge Cup

Test pieces: 'Coelcerthi'/ 'Mountain Fires' (R.Maldwyn Price), 'Seren Bethlehem' (T. Hopkin Evans)

Adjudicators: E.T. Davies, David Evans, J. Morgan Lloyd, D.E. Parry-Willliams, W. Matthews Williams

6 choirs

Result: 1. Penrhyn, 2. Hammersmith Welsh

Male Voice Parties, not over 30 voices

Test pieces: 'Pan fwyf mewn bedd' (Oliver Edwards), 'Tra bo dau' (arr. Caradog Roberts)

Adjudicators: J. Chas. McLean, D.E. Parry-Williams

Result: 1. Gwalia, Old Colwyn, 2. Crosville, Llanberis

1948 Bridgend

not under 80 voices

Test pieces: 'Storm Joy' (H. Walford Davies), 'Where shall the lover rest' (Hugh Hughes)

Adjudicators: Hugh Roberton, Haydn Morris, Charles Dawe, Sidney Northcote, David de Lloyd

5 choirs

Result: 1. Morriston Orpheus [186], 2. Rhymney [178], 3. Manselton [171], 4. Pendyrus [154]

Sir Hugh Roberton, former conductor of the Glasgow Orpheus Choir, was loudly cheered when he criticised the Eisteddfod committee for its choice of test pieces, telling the choirs, 'I wish to God you were singing something better.' But he was still overwhelmed by their performance of them.

Second competition, under 80 voices
Test pieces: 'After many a dusty mile' (Elgar), 'Di Rosyn, Dos'/ 'Go, Lovely Rose' (Meirion Williams)
Adjudicators: as above
12 choirs
Result: Penrhyn [166], 2. Morlais, Ferndale [165], 3. Breconian, Brynmawr [162]

The winners, Penrhyn, were the first of the 12 choirs to sing. Wishing they could sing 'something sweeter and more delicious,' Sir Hugh Roberton, again criticised the selection of test pieces and the tendency of Welsh choirs to dramatize them. 'You Welsh choirs can't indulge in this constant dramatization without suffering. Some of the sensitive members of today's choirs must have suffered agonies.'

Glee, confined to Welsh exile choirs
Test pieces: 'Hey Nonny No!' (Bryceson Treharne), 'Cwsg, Filwr, Cwsg' (John Price)
Adjudicators: E.T. Davies, J. Morgan Lloyd
2 choirs
Result: 1. Hammersmith Welsh, 2. Binley and Coombe, Coventry Welsh

1949 Dolgellau

not under 80 voices
Test pieces: 'Mordaith Cariad'/ 'Love's Voyage' (T. Hopkin Evans), 'Full Fathom Five' (T.Dunhill), 'Tiger, Tiger' (C. Armstrong Gibbs)
Adjudicators: W. Matthews Williams, E.T. Davies, Haydn Morris, Dan Jones, John Clements
6 choirs

Result: 1. Morriston Orpheus (Ivor E. Sims) [281], 2. Treorchy (John H. Davies) [273], 3. Dinorwic (Peleg Williams) [264], 4. Manselton (Emrys Jones) [255], 5. Rhymney (Vernon Lawrence) [243]

On the eve of the competition Rhymney faced the predicament all choirs dread when their conductor, Victor Lewis, was rushed to hospital the night before travelling. The 140-strong choir's accompanist, Vernon Lawrence, deputized.

Second competition, not under 50 voices

Test pieces: 'Fy Mreuddwyd' (Albert Williams), 'Yr Arddwr Llawen'/ 'The Merry Ploughman' (John Brydson)

Adjudicators: Haydn Morris, J. Morgan Nicholas, J.C. McLean

4 choirs

Result: 1. Penrhyn [170], 2. Kidwelly [167], 3. Breconian [165], 4. Llanegryn (Mer.) [159]

Both pieces took only four minutes to sing between them. The adjudicators were particularly unhappy at the selection of 'The Merry Ploughman', which 'seemed too trivial to be a test piece and hardly worth bringing the choirs to the Eisteddfod for it'. The winners, Penrhyn, who achieved a notable hat-trick, were greeted by a jubilant crowd of 2,000 on their arrival home in Bethesda.

1950 Caerphilly

not under 80 voices

Test pieces: 'Baich Damascus' (G. Bantock), 'Deryn y Bwn' (arr. E.T. Davies), 'Cysga Di Fy Mhlentyn Tlws' (arr. E.T. Davies)

Adjudicators: E.T. Davies, J. Morgan Lloyd, D.E. Parry-Williams, Leslie Woodgate, Herbert Bardgett

5 choirs

Result: 1. Manselton [277], 2. Treorchy* [272], 3. Rhymney [252], 4. Pendyrus [248], 5. Rhosllannerchrugog [246]

*153 choristers on stage

Second competition, 40–60 voices

Test pieces: 'Arglwydd Da, nid wyf deilwng' ('Domine non sum dignus', T.L. de Victoria), 'Y Gariad Gollwyd' (D. Vaughan Thomas)

Result: 1. N.O.R. (National Oil Refinery), Llandarcy [173], 2. Morlais, Ferndale [169], Kidwelly [167]

Industrial choirs

Test pieces:	'O Ddistaw Nos' ('O Peaceful Night', Edward German), Ble ti'n mynd (E.T. Davies)
Adjudicators:	E.T. Davies, J. Morgan Lloyd, Herbert Bardgett
5 choirs	
Result:	1. N.O.R., Llandarcy, 2. Gwaun-Cae-Gurwen Collieries

The all-Welsh rule came into force this year. Before, choirs could sing in either English or Welsh, if those words were on the published copy. From 1950 all pieces would have to be sung in Welsh, though occasionally Latin was permitted. This has not deterred choirs from e.g. Monmouthshire (Gwent), like Rhymney, Beaufort, Blaenavon, Caldicot, Tredegar, Risca, Mynydd Islwyn (Blackwood) and Chepstow, and from beyond, Aldershot, Cornwall, and Melbourne, from competing; nor non-Welsh speaking adjudicators from officiating.

1951 Llanrwst

not under 80 voices

Test pieces:	'Dana Dana' (Lajos Bárdos), 'Chwyth, chwyth aeafol wynt' (J. Owen Jones), 'Matona fy Anwylyd' (di Lasso)
Adjudicators:	W. Matthews Williams, E.T. Davies, J. Morgan Lloyd, Maurice Jacobson, D.E. Parry-Williams
2 choirs	
Result:	1. Manselton [266], 2. Dinorwic [249]

Second competition, under 80 voices

Test pieces:	'Yr Alwad Adre' ('Crossing the Bar', Caradog Roberts), 'Y Bugail' (E.T. Davies)
Adjudicators:	as above
5 choirs	
Result:	1. Abergele [174], 2. Point of Ayr [168], 3. Joint – Penrhyn and Trelawnyd [167]

Industrial choirs, under 40 voices

Test pieces:	'Yr Hufen Melyn' (arr. T. Osborne Roberts), 'Sul y Blodau' (Owen Williams)
3 choirs	
Result:	1. Côr y Clarion, Rhos, 2. Côr Meibion Iâl (Wrexham)

1952 Aberystwyth

not under 80 voices

Prize: £50

Test pieces: 'Sieryd Pres '('Money Talks', Ian Parrott), 'Y Llynges Wen' (' The Silver Fleet', Charles Clements), 'Salm 23' (Schubert)

Adjudicators: W. Matthews Williams, Idris Griffiths, J. Morgan Lloyd, Dan Jones, Oliver Edwards, A. C. Tysoe

5 choirs

Result:

Treorchy	90 + 89 + 96 = 275	
Manselton	82 + 91 + 92 = 265	
Ystradgynlais	85 + 85 + 89 = 259	
Penrhyn	80 + 83 + 85 = 248	

Schubert's 'Psalm 23' ('Duw yw fy Mugail'), with German, Welsh and English words, had been published by W.S. Gwynn Williams the previous year. Commenting on Treorchy's perilous strategy of interpreting literally the *adagio* marking on the copy so that it took over six minutes to perform, W. Matthews Williams remarked that, 'It is only once in a century one hears such marvellous singing. If there is singing like this in heaven I can't wait to get there'. This was the first of John Haydn Davies' seven National victories.

Second competition, 60–80 voices

Test pieces: 'Traeth Cil-y-Gwynt' ('The Lee Shore', Coleridge Taylor), 'Robin Ddiog' (arr. E. T. Davies)

Adjudicators: John Hughes, Dan Jones, D. E. Parry-Williams, A. C. Tysoe, Oliver Edwards

6 choirs

Result: 1. N.O.R. Skewen [175], 2. Point of Ayr [167]

N.O.R., founded in 1946, were conducted by Gwyn Thomas who had led Skewen and District Choral Society to victory in the Chief Choral (mixed) earlier in the week.

1953 Rhyl

not under 80 voices

Test pieces: 'Meibion yr Anial' ('Sons of the Desert', T. Hopkin Evans), 'Ti a Addolwn' ('Adoremus Te', Palestrina)

Adjudicators: E.T. Davies, W. Matthews Williams, John Hughes, J. Morgan Nicholas, W.S. Gwynn Williams

3 choirs

Result: 1. Pendyrus [174], 2. Manselton [171], 3. Ystradgynlais [161]

Second competition

Test pieces: 'De Profundis' (Vincent Thomas), 'Gwcw Fach' (Haydn Morris)
6 choirs

Result: 1. N.O.R. Skewen [172], 2. Penrhyn [164], 3. Point of Ayr [161]

1954 Ystradgynlais

not under 80 voices

Prize: £200

Test pieces: 'Nidaros' (Daniel Protheroe), 'Henffych Gorff Diymwad'
(Viadana), 'Salm Bywyd' (Haydn Morris)

Adjudicators: W. Matthews Williams, Haydn Morris, J. Morgan Nicholas
2 choirs

Result: 1. Treorchy   89 + 92 + 85 = 266
2. Pendyrus   84 + 90 + 87 = 261

Second competition, under 80 voices

Test pieces: 'Dinistr Senacherib' (Lewys Thomas), 'Pan fwyf mewn bedd'
(Oliver Edwards)

Adjudicators: Elfed Morgan, John Hughes, Arthur E. Davies
5 choirs

Result: 1. N.O.R. Skewen [180], 2. Cambrian (Clydach Vale) [168],
3. Ferndale Imperial [155]

1955 Pwllheli

not under 80 voices

Test pieces: 'Paracelsus' (Granville Bantock), 'Ust! y llon fugeiliaid '('Ha! the
jolly shepherds', T. Morley), 'Un o fy mrodyr a yrrodd i mi' (J.
Lloyd Williams)

Adjudicators: John Edwards, Idris Griffiths, Ceridwen Ll. Davies
1 choir

Result 1.Morriston Orpheus

Second competition

Test pieces: 'Ffarwel y Bardd' (T. Osborne Roberts), 'Cytgan yr Helwyr'
('Huntsmen's Chorus', Weber)

Adjudicators: Llifon Hughes Jones, Arwel Hughes, Hubert Davies
3 choirs

Result: 1. Froncysyllte [172], 2. Penrhyn [169]

1956 Aberdare

not under 80 voices

Prize:	£175
Test pieces:	'Y Gwyntoedd' (E. T. Davies), 'Mawr yw yr Arglwydd' (J. Morgan Nicholas), 'Dydd Da fy Mherl' ('Bonjour mon coeur', di Lasso)
Adjudicators:	E.T. Davies, J. M. Nicholas, Redvers Llewellyn, Mansel Thomas

3 choirs

Result		
	1. Treorchy	90 + 91 + 93 = 274
	2. Morriston Orpheus	87 + 89 + 92 = 268
	3. Pendyrus	80 + 88 + 90 = 258

Second competition

Test pieces:	'Prospice' (D. Vaughan Thomas), 'Dychwelyd' (Bryceson Treharne), plus any folk song

1 choir

Result:	1. Ferndale Imperial

1957 Llangefni

no entries for the chief male voice competition

Second competition, under 60 voices

Test pieces:	'Tra Bo Dau' (arr. Caradog Roberts), 'Nos-gân' (Borodin)
Adjudicators:	D.E.Parry-Williams, W. Matthews Williams, Llifon Hughes Jones, Meirion Williams, John Hughes

9 choirs

Result:	1. B.P. Llandarcy, 2. Penrhyn

1958 Ebbw Vale

not under 60 voices

Test pieces:	'Y Rhaeadr' (Haydn Morris), 'Angladd y Marchog' (W. Matthews Williams)
Adjudicators:	Arwel Hughes, W. Matthews Williams, Haydn Morris

3 choirs

Result:		
	1. Treorchy (John H. Davies)	95 + 94 = 189
	2. Pendyrus (Arthur Duggan)	90 + 90 = 180
	3. Beaufort (Alcwyn Savage)	89 + 87 = 176

Second competition, under 60 voices

Test pieces: 'Deus Salutis' ('Llef', arr. Mansel Thomas), 'Ble Caiff y Carwr Fedd' (Hugh Hughes)

Adjudicators: Mansel Thomas, John Hughes, J. Morgan Nicholas

6 choirs

Result:
1. Rhymney Silurian (Glynne Jones)   88 + 91 = 179
2. Cwmbach (T.R. James)   87 + 86 = 173
3. Joint: Morlais   82 + 87
          Blaenavon   87 + 82 = 169

1959 Caernarfon

not under 60 voices

Prize: £200

Test pieces: 'Matona fy Anwylyd' (di Lasso), 'Cadlef y Weriniaeth' (Haydn Morris)

Adjudicators: Arwel Hughes, John Hughes, Meirion Williams

4 choirs

Result:
1. Treorchy   90 + 88 = 178
2. Rhosllannerchrugog   90 + 87 = 177
3. Pendyrus   173
4. Rhos Orpheus   171

This was the closest that any choir came to defeating Treorchy in their heyday, without actually beating them – which Rhos would do three years later at Llanelli. 'The hesitant almost uncertain note in the adjudicator's announcement,' it was reported, 'indicated that there was even a smaller margin between the choirs than the one mark. And when the result was finally announced it was greeted by a hum of comment instead of the customary cheering.' Caernarfon was Côr Meibion Rhosllannerchrugog's first National appearance under the former coalminer and brilliant pianist Colin Jones, who had been appointed conductor at the age of 22 years in 1957 and who would lead them to several victories before standing down in 1987. His accompanist throughout those thirty years was John Tudor Davies (1930–2015) whose arrangement of Lewis Hartsough's hymn-tune 'Gwahoddiad' must by now be the most-sung male voice favourite of all time. The intense musicality of the mining village of Rhos (population under 10,000), situated only a few miles from the English border, is reflected in the fact that it could boast two large male voice choirs as well as several other choirs, youth and ladies. When the male choir was at a low ebb, Rhos Orpheus was founded in 1957 under J. Raymond Williams with Brian Hughes, soon to become a renowned composer, as accompanist, just as the international piano recitalist Llŷr Williams for a time accompanied later Côr Meibion y Rhos. Rhos Orpheus won in 1991 under John Glyn Williams (1966-2003). Caernarfon was their first National appearance. The Rhos choirs took nearly a thousand supporters with them to Caernarfon in 1959.

Another notable feature of this competition came at the very end. As the 'chief' was the final competitive event of the Eisteddfod, it had become customary for the conductor of the winning choir to lead the pavilion audience in singing 'Hen Wlad fy Nhadau.' With typical generosity, John Haydn Davies of Treorchy handed the baton to his Rhondda friend and rival Arthur Duggan of Pendyrus, while John Haydn himself joined his own choristers in the ranks. Later that evening Treorchy and Pendyrus combined in the Eisteddfod's closing concert. A thousand people welcomed Treorchy back to the Stag Square on Sunday night. The choir sang 'Llef' then joined the crowd to sing the national anthem.
Treorchy were without a quarter of their usual number; thanks to sickness and holidays 37 choristers were missing. They still staged well over a hundred. They were greeted by 'terrific crowds' on their arrival back home. 'As Treorchy's three coaches entered the valley on Sunday evening, with the cup prominently displayed in the leading coach,' reported the *Rhondda Leader* (15 Aug, 1959), 'cheering people lined the streets or waved from their door step,' and while dignitaries and the local MP Iorwerth Thomas expressed public congratulations, John Davies paid tribute to the singing of the other choirs in the competition.

Second competition, not over 60 voices

Test pieces: 'Mordaith Cariad' (T. Hopkin Evans), 'Mintai Briodas' (H. Kjerulf)

Adjudicators: J.M. Nicholas, Llifon Hughes Jones, Ivor Owen

8 choirs

Result: 1. Rhymney Silurian (Glynne Jones), 2. B.P. Llandarcy, 3. Penrhyn

Since the Blue Riband was won by Stuart Burrows of Cilfynydd near Pontypridd, at that time a school teacher in Bargoed, Caernarfon was a good eisteddfod for the south Wales valleys.

1960 Cardiff

not under 80 voices

Test pieces: 'Cân yr Ysbrydion dros y Dyfroedd' ('Song of the Spirits over the Waters', Schubert), plus own choice

Adjudicators: W. Matthews Williams, W. S. Gwynn Williams, D. T. Davies

2 choirs

Result: 1. Morriston Orpheus (Ivor Sims) [180], 2. Rhosllannerchrugog (Colin Jones) [173]

Second Competition, under 80 voices

Test pieces: 'Can yr Yfwr' ('Drinking Song', *Sir John in Love,* R. Vaughan Williams) 'Ave Verum Corpus' (Viadana), plus own choice

Adjudicators: Cyril Anthony, D.T. Davies, Rhoslyn Davies

9 choirs   including Tredegar Orpheus, Froncysyllte, Trelawnyd, Morlais, B.P. Llandarcy, Penrhyn, and Rhymney Silurian. This was a formidable line-up.

Result: 1. Rhymney Silurian (Glynne Jones) [231] 2. Morlais (Ferndale) [215], 3. B.P. Llandarcy [212]

1961 Dyffryn Maelor (Rhosllannerchrugog)

not under 80 voices

Prizes: £200; £100

Test pieces: 'Y Refali' ('The Reveille', Elgar), 'Nidaros' (Daniel Protheroe)

Adjudicators: W. Matthews Williams, Arwel Hughes, Meirion Williams

2 choirs

Result: 1. Treorchy (John H. Davies)   90 + 93 = 183

                   2. Morriston Orpheus (Eurfryn John)   83 + 86 = 169

The Orpheus were now conducted by their former accompanist Eurfryn John, who had succeeded the legendary Ivor Sims. Sims had died on 6 April 1961, aged 64, having achieved two firsts with Morriston United, and seven with the Orpheus.

Treorchy's winning prize of £200 exactly covered the costs of travel and an overnight stay. Morriston chose to stay three nights in Liverpool at a cost of £600, which their second prize of £100 barely disturbed. In the light of Treorchy's age profile – they had twenty young men under the age of 25, and about an equal number over 40, the remainder all in the 25–40 age group – the *Rhondda Leader* wondered 'when – if ever – the victory march of this choir is likely to be halted.' It would soon find out.

Second competition, under 80 voices

Prize: £100

Test pieces: 'Dychwelyd '(Bryceson Treharne), 'Y Gwyntoedd' (E.T. Davies)

Adjudicators: E. J. Williams, John Hughes, W.S. Gwynn Williams

Result: 1. Froncysyllte, 2. Trelawnyd, 3. Penrhyn

1962 Llanelli

not under 80 voices

Test pieces: 'Chwyth, chwyth aeafol wynt' (J. Owen Jones), 'Prospice' (D. Vaughan Thomas)

Adjudicators: John Hughes, W. Matthews Williams, Mansel Thomas

4 choirs

Result:
1. Rhosllannerchrugog*	95 + 96 = 191
2. Treorchy	92 + 90 = 182
3. Morriston Orpheus	88 + 85 = 173
4. Manselton	86 + 84 = 170

* 130 choristers on stage

Having come within a single mark of Treorchy on their first appearance under Colin Jones in 1959, here Côr Meibion y Rhos beat them. It was characteristic of the man, and of the changed atmosphere since the sulphurous rivalries of an earlier era, that the first person on stage to congratulate the young Colin Jones was Treorchy's John H. Davies.

Second competition, under 80 voices

Test pieces: 'De Profundis' (Vincent Thomas), 'Y Ffoadur' (D. Tawe Jones)

Adjudicators: Mansel Thomas, D. T. Davies, Arwel Hughes

5 choirs

Result:
1. Rhymney Silurian (Glynne Jones)	86 + 84 = 170
2. Pontarddulais	84 + 80 = 164
3. London Welsh	82 + 81 = 163
4. B.P. Llandarcy	80 + 82 = 162
5. Morlais, Ferndale	78 + 76 = 154

1963 Llandudno

not under 80 voices

Prize: £200

Test pieces: 'Salm Bywyd' (Haydn Morris), 'Agnus Dei' (Jacobus Kerle)

Adjudicators: W. Matthews Williams, John Hughes, Graham Thomas

2 choirs

Result:	1. Pontarddulais (Noel Davies)	84 + 90 = 174
	2. Pendyrus (Glynne Jones)	79 + 82 = 161

This was Pontarddulais' first appearance in the chief competition. In 1960 the local youth choir decided to transform themselves into a male choir under their conductor Noel Davies. They soon had a membership of over a hundred but competed under 80 voices in 1962, coming second to Glynne Jones's Silurians. 'Bont' turned the tables the following year, by which time Glynne Jones was conducting Pendyrus. Pontarddulais would go on to become one of Wales' finest competitive choral organisations and chalk up more victories than any other in the history of the National Eisteddfod.

Second competition, under 80 voices

Prize: £100

Test pieces: 'Brain Owain' (Bryceson Treharne), 'Y Carwr Ffyddlon' (Vincent Thomas)

Adjudicators: Arwel Hughes, D. T. Davies, James Williams

6 choirs

Result:	1. Froncysyllte	91 + 93 = 184
	2. Rhymney Silurian	90 +88 = 178
	3. Trelawnyd	89 + 87 = 176
	4. Dunvant Excelsior	88 + 86 = 174

1964 Swansea

Male choirs not under 80 voices

Prizes: £500; £150; £50

Test pieces: 'Y Pren ar y Bryn' (William Mathias), 'Arglwydd Da, nid wyf deilwng' ('Domine non sum dignus,' T.L. de Victoria), 'Paracelsus' (Bantock), the last two both unaccompanied

Adjudicators: Meredith Davies, Peter Gellhorn, Elfed Morgan

6 choirs

Result:	1. Treorchy (John H. Davies, accompanist. Tom Jones)	90 + 89 + 90 = 269
	2. Pontarddulais (Noel Davies, acc. Elwyn Sweeting)	89 + 88 + 89 = 266
	3. Pendyrus (Glynne Jones, acc. Bryan Davies)	89 + 88 + 88 = 265

4. Morriston Orpheus (Eurfryn John,
   acc. Jennie Sims)   89 + 87 + 87 = 263
5. Manselton   88 + 84 + 86 = 258
6. Rhosllannerchrugog   86 + 85 + 86 = 257

One of the epic contests in the history of the National Eisteddfod for the then unprecedented prize of £500. This is the only occasion when all the leading large choirs in Wales at the time, all National winners, faced each other. The competition was listened to by 8,000 in the pavilion and 30,000 on the 'maes'. It was touch and go whether Treorchy's conductor would make it, being confined to bed with a chill after watching Glamorgan's cricketers beat the Australians at St Helen's earlier in the week. He had to miss the final rehearsals. Rhos sang first and Treorchy second; as soon as they had finished John Davies staggered off the podium to be wrapped in a blanket and immediately driven back home to the Rhondda. Meredith Davies was a renowned choral and orchestral conductor; Peter Gellhorn, who had conducted at Carl Rosa, Covent Garden and Glyndebourne and was currently director of the BBC Chorus, stepped to the microphone to say 'Canu bendigedig' ('Wonderful singing'), and Elfed Morgan, music organiser for Carmarthenshire, delivered the adjudication. The spry and rhythmic 'Y Pren ar y Bryn' was a recent work by William Mathias, dedicated to Glynne Jones and the Silurian Choir who had brought off a National hat-trick before Glynne moved to Pendyrus in 1962. After its exposure here it became a favourite competition and concert piece among better choirs. When Pontarddulais won at Llanelli in 2014 they sang 'Y Pren ar y Bryn' and the de Victoria motet as they had done in 1964. (For further details on the 1964 contest see chapter 8 in Part One)

Second competition, for choirs under 80 voices
Prize: £150; £75; £25
Test pieces: 'Cytgan y Gwrthryfelwyr' ('The Rebels' Chorus', Semiramide, Meyerbeer), 'Cyfod F'anwylyd' (Robert Smith)
Adjudicators: Ieuan Rees Davies, Peter Gellhorn, J. Sutton Owen
6 choirs
Result: 1. Myrddin, Carmarthen [176], 2. Rhymney Silurian [170], 3. Froncysyllte [168], 4. Trelawnyd [163], 5. Joint – Dunvant Excelsior and Ferndale Imperial [162]

The Ferndale 'Imps' had been preoccupied with providing the 'Men of Harlech' soundtrack to the film *Zulu* (the Zulus had 'a good bass section but no top tenors' according to Ivor Emmanuel's Private Owen), starring and produced by local Blaenllechau boy Stanley Baker, and which received its Welsh première at the Olympia Cinema in Cardiff on 23 March 1964 with the 'Imps' – and Ivor Emmanuel – in attendance.

1965	**Newtown**	
over 70 voices		
Prizes:	£500; £250; £100	
Test pieces:	'O Mae Hi'n Braf' ('Prisoners' Chorus,' *Fidelio*, Beethoven), 'Y Sipsiwn' (William Mathias), 'Cytgan y Pererinion' ('Pilgrims' Chorus', *Tannhauser*, Wagner)	
Adjudicators:	Rae Jenkins, Maurice Jacobson, D.T. Davies, Gerallt Evans	
2 choirs		
Result:	1. Pontarddulais	87 + 89 + 84 = 260
	2. Rhosllannerchrugog	85 + 86 + 85 = 256

In 1965 Pontarddulais achieved the unprecedented clean sweep of the National, Pontrhydfendigaid and Cardigan semi-nationals, and the Miners' Eisteddfod. They repeated this feat three years later.

Second competition, under 70 voices		
Prizes:	£100; £60; £30	
Test pieces:	'Hai Noni No' (Bryceson Treharne), 'Di Rosyn, Dos' (Meirion Williams), 'Mentra Gwen' (arr. E.T. Davies)	
Adjudicators:	G. Peleg Williams, M. Jacobson, Enid Parry	
4 choirs		
Result:	1. Dolgellau	86 + 85 + 87 = 258
	2. Pontypridd	81 + 87 + 86 = 254
	3. Myrddin	83 + 84 + 84 = 251

1966 Port Talbot

over 70 voices	
Prizes:	£500; £250
Test pieces:	'Angladd y Marchog' (W. Matthews Williams), 'Gogonedda Di, Arglwydd Nef' ('Confitemini Deo', Palestrina), 'Mordaith Cariad' (T. Hopkin Evans)

Adjudicators: Elfed Morgan, Peter Gellhorn, Terry James

3 choirs

Result:

1. Pendyrus	89 + 87 + 92 = 268
2. Morriston Opheus	85 + 85 + 88 = 258
3. Manselton	86 + 83 + 87 = 256

Second competition, 40–70 voices

Prize: £200, £100

Test pieces: 'Ysbryd yw Duw' (J. Morgan Nicholas), 'Seren Bethlehem' (T. Hopkin Evans)

Adjudicators: Terry James, Peter Gellhorn, Meirion Williams

9 choirs

Result: 1. Cwmbach, 2. Trelawnyd

Glee, under 40 voices

Test pieces: 'Cân Pwca' (Thomas Dunhill), 'Gobaith' (Ieuan Rees-Davies)

Adjudicators: Dilys Elwyn Edwards, Peter Gellhorn

2 choirs

Result: 1. Morlais, Ferndale, 2. Llandeilo'r Fan

1967 Bala

over 70 voices

Test pieces: 'Moliant fo i Dduw Anfeidrol' (Bach), 'Yna Plant yr Hebreaid' ('Pueri Hebraeorum', Palestrina), 'Y Gwyntoedd' (E.T. Davies)

Adjudicators: Mansel Thomas, Kenneth Bowen, Meirion Williams

4 choirs

Result:

1. Treorchy (John Cynan Jones)	276
2. Pontarddulais (Noel Davies)	274
3. Dunvant	254
4. Rhos Orpheus	253

After a record (subsequently overtaken by Pontarddulais) of 8 firsts and 3 seconds, this was Treorchy's last appearance at the National Eisteddfod.

Second competition, 40–70 voices

Test pieces: 'Dana Dana' (Lajos Bárdos), 'Y Gariad Gollwyd' (D. Vaughan Thomas), 'Deryn y Bwn' (arr. E.T. Davies)

Adjudicators: Gerallt Evans, D.G. Evans, Caleb Jarvis

4 choirs

Result: 1. Trelawnyd, 2. Brythoniaid

Glee, under 40 voices

Test pieces: 'O Eneth Lân' (Hassler), 'Pan fwyf mewn bedd' (Oliver Edwards)
Adjudicators: Clydwyn Jones, Meirion Williams
5 choirs
Result: 1. Llanerchymedd (Anglesey), 2. Great Sutton (Ellesmere Port)

1968 Barry

over 70 voices

Test pieces: 'Dies Irae' (*Requiem*, Cherubini, to be sung in Latin) plus 2 own choices, one from 16-17th century, the other by a 20th century Welsh composer, in a 25-minute programme
Adjudicators: Meirion Williams, Dilys Elwyn Edwards, Douglas Robinson
3 choirs
Result: 1. Pontarddulais $95 + 93 + 95 = 283$
2. Pendyrus $96 + 90 + 95 = 281$
3. Dunvant $87 + 85 + 82 = 254$

This decision, and Glynne Jones' public denunciation of the adjudicators as fools, led to Pendyrus' withdrawal from the Eisteddfod for over 40 years until, ten years after Jones's death, they reappeared in 2010 under Stewart Roberts. See chapter 9 for a fuller account.

Second competition

Test pieces: 'Hwn yw Dydd Geni Crist ein Iôr' ('Hodie Christus Natus Est', Palestrina), 'Difyr yw Gweld' ('Feasting I Watch', Elgar), plus own choice by a 20th-century Welsh composer
Adjudicators: Mansel Thomas, Anthony Randall, Douglas Robinson
4 choirs
Result: 1. Cwmbach $90 + 88 + 90 = 268$
2. B.P. Llandarcy $83 + 77 + 80 = 240$
3. Rhymney Silurian $76 + 78 + 80 = 234$
4. Myrddin $74 + 80 + 72 = 226$

Cwmbach's margin of victory makes it the most crushing in Eisteddfod history.

Glee, under 40 voices

Test pieces: 'Teg a Difwyn, Gwir a Gau' ('Fair and Ugly, False and True', Travers), 'Hwn yw fy ngorchymyn' (Tallis)
Adjudicators: Dilys Elwyn Edwards, Douglas Robinson
2 choirs
Result: 1. Morlais, Ferndale, 2. Cambrian, Clydach Vale

1969 Flint

over 70 voices

Test pieces: 'Chwyth, Chwyth Aeafol Wynt' (J. Owen Jones), 'Cyn Cau Llygaid' ('Close Thine Eyes', Ieuan-Rees Davies), 'De Profundis' (Vincent Thomas)

Adjudicators: Mansel Thomas, Elfed Morgan, Roy Bohana

3 choirs

Result: 1. Rhosllannerchrugog, 2. Morriston Orpheus, 3. Cwmfelin (Llanelli)

Second competition

Test pieces: 'Salm 23' (Schubert), 'Y Fedwen Arian' ('The Silver Birch', arr. Alexandrof), 'Y Bugail' (E.T. Davies)

Adjudicators: Terry James, Rowland Wyn Jones, Meirion Williams

6 choirs

Result: 1. Brythoniaid, 2. Cwmbach, 3. Mynydd Mawr

Glee, under 40 voices

Test pieces: 'Y Gwcw Fach' (Haydn Morris), 'Matona fy Anwylyd' (di Lasso)

Adjudicators: Elfed Morgan, Roy Bohana, Terry James

Result: 1. Barrog (Penybont-fawr), 2. Llangefni, 3. Great Sutton (Ellesmere Port)

1970 Ammanford

over 70 voices

Test pieces: 'Salm 148' (Arwel Hughes), 'Arglwydd Da, nid wyf deilwng' (de Victoria), 'Prospice' (D. Vaughan Thomas)

Adjudicators: Dilys Elwyn Edwards, Douglas Robinson, Anthony Randall

1 choir

Result: 1. Pontarddulais

Second competition

Test pieces: 'Ynys Hedd' (Elfed Morgan), 'Mentra Gwen' (arr. E.T. Davies), 'Cytgan yr Helwyr' ('Huntsmen's Chorus', *Der Freischütz*, Weber)

Adjudicators: Arthur Vaughan Williams, Megan Jones, Douglas Robinson

8 choirs

Result: 1. Mynydd Mawr, 2. Brythoniaid, 3. Cwmbach
Also competing were Bargoed, Blaenavon, Burry Port, Froncysyllte and Rhymney Silurians.

Glee

Test pieces: 'Di Rosyn, Dos' (Meirion Williams), 'Dana, Dana' (Lajos Bárdos)

Adjudicators: Irwyn Walters, Douglas Robinson

4 choirs

Result: 1. Morlais, Ferndale, 2. Llandybie, 3. Traeth, 4. Gleision Teifi

1971 Bangor

over 70 voices

Test pieces: 'O Mae Hi'n Braf' ('Prisoners' Chorus', Beethoven), 'Yr Hen Lanc' (Kodály), 'Y Pren ar y Bryn' (Mathias)

Adjudicators: Arwel Hughes, Kenneth Bowen, Meirion Williams

3 choirs

Result: 1. Rhosllannerchrugog [137], 2. Llanelli [129], 3. Morriston Orpheus [128]

This was the last 'National' appearance to date of Morriston Orpheus, seven times winners between 1937 and 1960.

Second competition

Test pieces: 'Y Sipsiwn' (Mathias), 'Cysga Di' (arr. E.T. Davies), 'Cân Ymdaith' ('Marching Song', Seiber)

Adjudicators: Kenneth Bowen, Gerallt Evans, Gerald Davies

6 choirs

Result: 1. Brythoniaid, 2. Mynydd Mawr, 3. Penrhyn
Also competing were Trelawnyd, Traeth and Ferodo (Caernarfon)

Glee, under 40 voices

Test pieces: 'Nos a Bore' (Mathias), 'Robin Ddiog' (arr. E.T. Davies), 'Coelcerthi' (R. Maldwyn Price)

Adjudicators: Gerallt Evans, Kenneth Bowen, Meirion Williams

3 choirs

Result: 1. Moelwyn (Blaenau Ffestiniog)

1972 Haverfordwest

over 70 voices

Test pieces: 'Gloria' (Mathias), 'Yna Plant yr Hebreaid' ('Pueri Hebraeorum', Palestrina)

Adjudicators: Dilys Elwyn Edwards, Gerallt Evans, Douglas Robinson

2 choirs

Result: 1. Pontarddulais, 2. Llanelli

Second competition

Test pieces: 'Cytgan y Gwrthryfelwyr' ('Rebel Soldiers Chorus', *Il Profeta*, Meyerbeer), 'Ysbryd yw Duw' (J. Morgan Nicholas)

Adjudicator: Arnold Lewis, William Mathias, Douglas Robinson

6 choirs

Result: 1. Ferodo (Caernarfon), 2. Dunvant, 3. Mynydd Mawr

Glee

Test pieces: 'Robin Ddiog' (arr. E.T. Davies), 'Cân Pwca' (Thomas Dunhill)

Adjudicators: Alun John, Douglas Robinson

7 choirs

Result: 1. Moelwyn (Blaenau Ffestiniog), 2. Morlais (Ferndale), 3. Gyrlais (Ystradgynlais)

1973 Dyffryn Clwyd (Ruthin)

over 70 voices

Test pieces: 'Brain Owain' ('The Ravens of Owain', Bryceson Treharne), 'O Chwi Bobloedd' ('O vos omnes', Victoria)

Adjudicators: Elwyn Jones, Gerallt Evans, Terry James

3 choirs

Result: 1. Dowlais (D. T. Davies), 2. Brythoniaid (Meirion Jones), 3. Tredegar Orpheus (Ieuan Davies)

With this victory D. T. Davies (1900–1983) completed a remarkable hat-trick of wins with Dowlais choirs: Dowlais Ladies (1928, 1934 and 1935), Dowlais United (Chief Choral, Fishguard, 1936) and now Dowlais Male Choir. This achievement of three firsts in the three major choral competitions remains unique in the history of the National Eisteddfod.

Second competition, 41–70 voices

Test pieces: 'Y Carwr Ffyddlon' ('The Faithful Lover', Vincent Thomas), 'Jubilate Amen' (H. Kjerulf)

Adjudicators: Roy Bohana, Terry James, Elfed Morgan

7 choirs

Result: 1. Trelawnyd, 2. Ferodo (Caernarfon)

Other contestants included Penrhyn, Canoldir, Dunvant and Brymbo.

Glee, under 40 voices
Test pieces: 'Dau o Seraphim' (Victoria), 'Tydi a Roddaist' (Arwel Hughes)
Adjudicators: Elwyn Jones, Owain Arwel Hughes, Arnold Lewis
Result: 1. Penybont-fawr, 2. Great Sutton

1974 Carmarthen

over 70 voices
Test pieces: 'Cân yr Ysbrydion' ('Song of the Spirits over the Waters',
                Schubert), 'Mordaith Cariad' (Hopkin Evans)
Adjudicators: Alun John, Gerallt Evans, Dilys Elwyn Edwards
6 choirs
Result: 1. Pontarddulais (Noel Davies)   93 + 90 = 183
                2. Rhos (Colin Jones)   90 + 84 = 174
                3. Dowlais (D.T.Davies)   87 + 83 = 170
                4. Mynydd Mawr (J Rhyddid Williams)   81 + 82 = 163
                5. Brythoniaid (Meirion Jones)   80 + 81 = 161
                6. Llanelli (Denver Phillips)   78 + 81 = 159

Had Canoldir not withdrawn, there would have been seven choirs competing, a post-war record for the 'chief'. There were seven at Cardiff (2008) and Ebbw Vale (2010).

Second competition, 40–70 voices
Test pieces: 'Salm 23' (Schubert), 'De Profundis' (Vincent Thomas)
Adjudicators: John H. Davies, Kenneth Bowen, Brian Hughes
6 choirs
Result: 1. Pontypridd   84 + 88 = 172
                2. Traeth   83 + 86 = 169
                3. Trelawnyd   81 + 84 = 165
                Also competing were Rhymney Silurian [163], Dunvant [162] and Caldicot [155].

Pontypridd were conducted by Joyce Durston (1964–77) and accompanied by Dorothy Ingram. In 1989 Pontypridd's Dorothy Davies-Ingram (1977–89) became the first woman to conduct the 1000 Welsh Male Voices Festival at the Royal Albert Hall.

Glee, under 40 voices

Test pieces: 'Y Delyn Aur' (arr. D. Pughe Evans), 'Yr Hufen Melyn' (Caradog Roberts)

Adjudicators: Rowland Wyn Jones, Peter Gellhorn, Roy Bohana

9 choirs

Result:
    1. Gwalia (London)   91 + 89 =180
    2. Penybont-fawr   85 + 87 =172
    3. Adar Tawe   85 + 86 =171

Also competing were Rhos Cwmtawe [168], Gyrlais [165], Caron [164], Ferndale [163], Llandybie [163], Clawdd Offa [156].

1975 Bro Dwyfor (Criccieth)

Test pieces: 'Dies Irae' (*Requiem*, Cherubini), 'Y Gwyntoedd' (E.T. Davies)

Adjudicators: Arnold Lewis, Brian Hughes, Roy Bohana

1 choir

Result: Mynydd Mawr were the only contestants, and were awarded the second prize of £200

Second competition

Test pieces: 'Seren Bethlehem' (T. Hopkin Evans), 'Cân Buddugoliaeth' (Mansel Thomas)

Adjudicators: Owain Arwel Hughes, Arnold Lewis, Roy Bohana

6 choirs

Result: 1. Caernarfon [170], 2. Trelawnyd [166], 3. Gwalia [165]

Glee, under 40 voices

Test pieces: 'Y Sipsiwn' (Mathias), 'Christus Redemptor '('Hyfrydol', arr. Mansel Thomas)

Adjudicators: Alun John, Rowland Wyn Jones, John Stoddart

8 choirs

Result: 1. Rhos, Cwmtawe [174], 2. Bro Glyndŵr (Corwen) [173], 3. Moelwyn [170]

1976 Cardigan

over 40 voices

Test pieces: 'Meibion yr Anial' (T. Hopkin Evans), 'Geiriau Olaf Dafydd' ('Last Words of David', Randall Thompson)

Adjudicators: Owain Arwel Hughes, David Clover, Rowland Wyn Jones

2 choirs

Result:
    1. Pontarddulais   97 + 97 = 194
    2. Llanelli   91 + 87 = 178

Second competition

Test pieces: 'Y Ganfed Salm' ('Psalm 100', George Stead), 'Di Rosyn, Dos' (Meirion Williams)

Adjudicators: J. Raymond Williams, Haydn James, Alun John

6 choirs

Result: 1. Caernarfon, 2. Traeth

Glee, under 40 voices

Test pieces: 'Yr Hen Lanc' ('The Batchelor', Kodaly), 'Dydd Da fy Mherl' ('Bonjour mon coeur', di Lasso)

Adjudicators: Alun John, Rowland Wyn Jones, John Stoddart

10 choirs

Result: 1. Colwyn, 2. Penybont-fawr

1977 Wrexham

over 70 voices

Test pieces: 'Salm 148' (Arwel Hughes), 'O Berffaith Nos' ('O Perfect Night', Edward German), 'Cytgan y Morwyr' ('Sailors Chorus', *The Flying Dutchman*, Wagner)

Adjudicators: George Guest, Alun Guy

3 choirs

Result: 1. Brythoniaid (Meirion Jones) [270], 2. Llanelli (Eifion Thomas) [267], 3. Trelawnyd (Goronwy Wynne) [261]

Second competition

Test pieces: 'Bywyd y Bugail' (Brian Hughes), 'Innsbruck' (Heinrich Isaak), 'Rhyfelgan Rhufain' ('Roman War Song', *Rienzi*, Wagner)

Adjudicators: Brian Hughes, Rowland Wyn Jones

8 choirs

Result: 1. Froncysyllte [268], 2. Brymbo [257], 3. Canoldir, Birmingham [256]

Glee

Test pieces: 'Cytgan y Cynllwynwyr' ('Zitti, Zitti', 'Conspirators' Chorus', *Rigoletto*, Verdi), 'Sanctus' (*Requiem*, Cherubini)

Adjudicators: Alun Guy, John Stoddart

6 choirs

Result: 1. Penybont-fawr, 2. Moelwyn, 3. Ardudwy

1978 Cardiff

over 70 voices

Prize: £300

Test pieces: 'Breuddwyd Llewelyn ap Gruffydd' (Alan Bush), 'Y Peunod' ('The Peacocks', Kodály), 'Nos a Bore' (Mathias)

Adjudicators: George Guest, Brian Hughes

Result: 1. Pontarddulais   89 + 88 + 90 = 267

                 2. Llanelli   88 + 87 + 90 = 265

Second competition, 40–70 voices

Test pieces: 'Ysbryd yw Duw' (Morgan Nicholas), 'Cytgan yr Herwyr' ('Bandits Chorus', *Ernani*, Verdi), 'Epilog' (Mervyn Burtch)

Adjudicators: Roy Bohana, Eirug Thomas

9 choirs

Result: 1. Dunvant   86 + 90 + 86 = 262

                 2. Colwyn   87 + 86 + 85 = 258

                 3. Traeth   85 + 84 + 87 = 256

                 4. Canoldir   84 + 86 + 85 = 255

                 5. Ferodo, Caernarfon 85 + 84 + 83 = 252

                 6. Brymbo   83 + 83 + 81 = 247

                 7. Ystradgynlais   82 + 85 + 87 = 244

                 8. Barry   82 + 79 + 81 = 242

                 9. Cowbridge   79 + 81 + 80 = 240

Led by T. Arwyn Walters (1970–2000), another gifted product of the unofficial music academy that was Gowerton Grammar School, Dunvant's triumph in this riveting contest marked the dawn of a golden era in the history of this long-established (1895) choir from the western outskirts of Swansea, an area where they claim singing comes as naturally as tax evasion, where it dissolves into the Gower. The Broadmead and Derlwyn housing developments in the 1970s saw a substantial rise in choir recruitment; Dunvant RFC's success propelled it into the first rank of Welsh rugby clubs at the same time. Following victory at Cardiff, Dunvant with enhanced numbers moved up into the chief male voice category which they promptly won. In these years (1978–85) they won the BBC Wales Male Choir of the Year Award twice, the Miners' Eisteddfod three times, the two Pantyfedwen Eisteddfodau (Pontrhydfendigaid and Cardigan), and the Cornish Open Championship. In 1985 they took 114 choristers to Canada along with a promising young north Wales bass-baritone called Bryn Terfel. Arwyn

Walters was succeeded in 2000 by Tim Rhys-Evans, later of Only Men Aloud, under whom they won at the Sir Benfro (St David's) National in 2002. Colwyn, who came second in 1978, moved up into the chief category the following year and won it. Dunvant did the same in 1980.

Glee, under 40 voices

Test pieces: 'Nefol Ogoniant' ('Cum Sancto Spiritu', *Gloria,* Vivaldi, arr. Arwel Hughes), 'Dana Dana' (Lajos Bárdos),'Y Ferch o Blwyf Penderyn' (arr. Alun Guy)

Adjudicators: John Hywel, J. Glynne Evans

3 choirs

Result: 1. Penybont-fawr, 2. Gyrlais, 3. Onllwyn

1979 Caernarfon

over 70 voices

Test pieces: 'Castîlia' (Daniel Protheroe), 'Ti a Addolwn' ('Adoremus Te', Palestrina)

Adjudicators: T. Gwynn Jones, George Guest, Arthur Hefin Jones

4 choirs

Result:

1. Colwyn (Neville Owen)	89 + 89 = 178
2. Brythoniaid (Meirion Jones)	88 + 89 = 177
3. Joint – Trelawnyd	88 + 85
Llanelli	87 + 86 = 173

This victory marked a remarkable progression for Colwyn who won the glee competition under 40 voices in 1976, came second in the second category in 1978, and in 1979 won the 'chief.'

Second competition

3 choirs

Test pieces: 'Mintai Briodas' (Kjerulf), 'Difyr yw gweld' ('Feasting I Watch,' Elgar)

Adjudicators: Roy Bohana, George Guest, T. Gwynn Jones

3 choirs

Result:

1. Penrhyn	84 + 87 = 171
2. Traeth	83 + 85 = 168
3. Bro Glyndŵr (Corwen)	82 + 84 = 166

Glee

Prize: £100 & Welsh Association of Male Choirs Cup

Test pieces: 'Mae'r awel yn fain' ('The winds whistle cold,' Herbert Howells), 'Di Rosyn, Dos' (Meirion Williams)

Adjudicators: Arthur Hefin Jones, John Hywel, Gwyn L. Williams

4 choirs

Result: 1. Moelwyn, 2. Ardudwy, 3. Madog

1980 Dyffryn Lliw (Gorseinon)

over 70 voices

Test pieces: 'Gwledd y Gwleddoedd' (Arnold Williams), 'Cytgan y Pererinion' ('Pilgrims Chorus', *Tannhauser*, Wagner)

Adjudicators: Roland Morris, Valerie Ellis, Alun Guy, Delme Bryn Jones

4 choirs

Result: 1. Dunvant [168], 2. Canoldir (Birmingham) [167], 3. Swansea [164], 4. Colwyn [163]

Second competition

Test pieces: 'Tair Cân Hwngaraidd' ('Three Hungarian Folksongs' arr. Seiber), 'Mordaith Cariad' (T. Hopkin Evans)

Adjudicators: John Huw Davies, Alun Guy, Dilys Elwyn Edwards

4 choirs

Result: 1. Mynydd Mawr (J. Rhyddid Williams) [171], 2. Ystradgynlais [169], 3. Joint – Marazion Apollo (Cornwall) and Myrddin [164]

Entirely Welsh-speaking Côr Meibion Mynydd Mawr was based on the mining villages of Tumble and Cross Hands in the anthracite coalfield of east Carmarthenshire. Founded in 1965, and drawing on a long and robust choral tradition in the area – its ranks included the melodious *noson lawen* favourites 'Jac a Wil' (Davies) – it rapidly attained chief male voice status. But the decline of the coal industry in the Gwendraeth valley, culminating in the closure in 1989 of the Cynheidre colliery, which had employed over a thousand men in the 1970s, and an inability to rejuvenate an ageing membership, brought home to Mynydd Mawr the realisation that they could no longer compete in the senior class. They did not renounce competition however, and went on to attain success at under 70 voices.

Glee

Test pieces: 'Dilys Wamal' (arr. Eric Thiman), 'Arglwydd Da, nid wyf deilwng' (Victoria)

Adjudicators: Haydn James, Aldon Rees, J. Glynne Evans

8 choirs

Result: 1. Gwalia (Swansea) [86], 2. Llandybie [84], 3. Rhos Cwmtawe [81]

1981 Machynlleth

over 70 voices

Test pieces: 'Henffych Gorff Diymwad' ('Ave Verum Corpus,' Viadana), 'Y Pysgotwyr' (T. Maldwyn Price)

Adjudicators: G. Peleg Williams, Richard Elfyn Jones, Alun Guy

5 choirs

Result:

1. Pontarddulais	92 + 89 = 181
2. Canoldir	87 + 90 = 177
3. Llanelli	87 + 87 = 174
4. Colwyn	84 + 88 = 172
5. Brythoniaid	86 + 84 = 170

Llanelli, accompanied by Clive Phillips, were the largest choir, staging 129, Canoldir (Birmingham) the 'smallest' with 93.

Second competition

Test pieces: 'O Mae Hi'n Braf' ('Prisoners' Chorus', *Fidelio*, Beethoven), 'Dychwelyd' (Bryceson Treharne)

Adjudicators: T. Gwynn Jones, Alun Davies, John Stoddart

4 choirs

Result: 1. Caernarfon, 2. Mynydd Mawr, 3. Bro Glyndŵr

Glee

Test pieces: 'Nos a Bore' (Mathias), 'Cyn Cau Llygaid' ('Close Thine Eyes', Ieuan Rees-Davies)

Adjudicators: Alun Davies, Maureen Guy, John Stoddart

3 choirs

Result: 1. Penybont-fawr, 2. Bro Aled, Llansannan, 3. Madog

1982 Swansea

Test pieces: 'Brenin yr Wybren' ('King of Worlds,' Dard Janin), 'Y Pren ar y Bryn' (Mathias)

Adjudicators: George Guest, Kenneth Bowen, Dilys Elwyn Edwards, Haydn James

3 choirs

Result:
1. Pontarddulais   87 + 92 = 179
2. Dunvant*   88 + 87 = 175
3. Canoldir   86 + 84 = 170

*123 choristers on stage

Second Competition

Test pieces: 'Yr Alwad Adre' ('Crossing the Bar,' Caradog Roberts), 'Bywyd y Bugail' (Brian Hughes)

Adjudicators: Brian Hughes, George Guest, Heward Rees

2 choirs

Result:
1. Caldicot   84 + 86 = 170
2. Mynydd Mawr   82 + 84 = 166

Glee

Test pieces: 'Trugaredd Duw' (Kodály), 'Jubilate Amen' (Kjerulf)

Adjudicators: Eirug Thomas, Valerie Ellis, Gerallt Evans

1 choir

Result: 1. Eifl (Caerns.)

1983 Ynys Môn

Test pieces: 'Yn y dafarn lon' ('Quando sumus in taberna', *Carmina Burana*, Carl Orff), 'Seren Bethlehem' (T. Hopkin Evans)

Adjudicators: George Guest, Brian Hughes, Alun Guy

1 choir

Result: 1. Trelawnyd (Geraint Roberts)

Second competition

Test pieces: 'Cytgan y Morwyr' ('Sailors Chorus', *Flying Dutchman*, Wagner), 'Oleuni Mwyn' (W. Bradwen Jones)

Adjudicators: Rhys Jones, John Huw Davies, T. Gwynn Jones

7 choirs

Result: 1. Traeth, 2. Brythoniaid, 3. Joint – Caernarfon and Maelgwn

Glee

Test pieces: 'Sanctus' (*Requiem*, Cherubini), 'Y Sipsiwn' (Mathias)

Adjudicators: John Peleg Williams, Alun Guy, Brian Hughes

8 choirs

Result: 1. Bro Glyndŵr, Corwen, 2. Highfield, Flint, 3. Runcorn

1984 Lampeter

over 70 voices

Test pieces: 'Cytgan y Pererinion' ('Pilgrims' Chorus', Joseph Parry), 'Di Rosyn, Dos' (Meirion Williams)

Adjudicators: George Guest, Alun Guy, Eileen Price, T. J. Williams

4 choirs

Result: 1. Llanelli   90 + 92 = 182

                2. Canoldir   89 + 86 = 175

                3. Ystradgynlais   88 + 86 = 174

                4. Aberafan   87 + 85 = 172

Second competition

Test pieces: 'Seiniwch y Corn' ('Sound an Alarm,' *Judas Maccabeus*, Handel), 'Matona fy anwylyd' (di Lasso)

Adjudicators: T.J. Williams, Helena Braithwaite, John Stoddart

1 choir

Result: 1. Mynydd Mawr

Glee

Test Pieces: 'Serenâd y Gondolîr' ('Gondelfahrer', Schubert), 'Henffych Iesu' ('Ave Verum', Mozart)

Adjudicators: Alun Guy, Gareth Glyn, George Guest

10 choirs

Result: 1. Eifl   89 + 88 = 177

                2. Gwalia (Swansea)   87 + 87 = 174

                3. Gyrlais (Ystradgynlais) 88 + 84 = 172

                4. Rhymney Silurian   85 + 86 = 171

                5. Myrddin   84 + 86 = 170

                6. Llandybie   83 + 86 = 169

                7. Caron   83 + 85 = 168

                8. Joint – Rhos Cwmtawe   83 + 83

                        Penybont-fawr   82 + 84 = 166

               10. Blaenporth   82 + 83 = 165

1985 Rhyl

over 70 voices

Prize: £400

Test piece: 'Gloria Hyd y Nef i'r Arglwydd' (Mansel Thomas), plus 2 own choices

Adjudicators: John Stoddart, George Guest, Gerallt Evans

1 choir

Result: 1. Trelawnyd (Geraint Roberts)

214

Second competition

Test pieces: 'Wrth Afonydd Babilon' ('By Babylon's Wave', Gounod), 'Ave Verum Corpus' (Byrd)

Adjudicators: T. Gwynn Jones, George Guest, Eirug Thomas

6 choirs

Result:

1. Brythoniaid	85 + 89 = 174	
2. Traeth	85 + 88 = 173	
3. Eifl	87 + 85 = 172	
4. Colwyn	83 + 88 = 171	
5. Joint – Flint	85 + 84	
Maelgwn	84 + 85 = 169	

Glee

Test pieces: 'Â Llawenydd, Cenwch' ('With a Voice of Singing,' Martin Shaw), 'Harddwch' (Cecil Cope)

Adjudicators: J. Hywel Williams, Alun Guy, Brian Hughes

Result: 1. Moelwyn, 2. Llangwm, 3. Glyndŵr

1986 Fishguard

Test pieces: 'Yna Plant yr Hebreaid' ('Pueri Hebraeorum,' Palestrina), 'Breuddwyd Llewelyn ap Gruffydd' (Alan Bush)

Adjudicators: Gerallt Evans, Kenneth Bowen, George Guest

1 choir

Result: Llanelli

Second Competition

Test pieces: 'Ti a Addolwn' ('Adoremus Te,' Palestrina), 'Nos a Bore' (William Mathias)

Adjudicators: Brian Hughes, Eric Jones, Richard Elfyn Jones

3 choirs

Result: 1. Gwalia (London Welsh), 2. Whitland, 3. Bridgend

Glee

Test pieces: 'Henffych Gorff Diymwad' ('Ave Verum, 'Viadana), 'Clychau'r Gôg' (Gareth Glyn)

Adjudicators: Alun Davies, Gareth Glyn, John Stoddart

4 choirs

Result: 1. Llangwm, 2. Maesteg Gleemen, 3. Tenby

1987 Porthmadog

not under 61 voices

Prize:	£500
Test pieces:	'Arglwydd Da, nid wyf deilwng' (Victoria), 'Nidaros' (D. Protheroe)
Adjudicators:	George Guest, John Daniel, Brian Hughes
5 choirs	

Result:

1. Rhosllannerchrugog	92 + 88 = 180
2. Brythoniaid	89 + 89 = 178
3. Traeth	89 + 85 = 174
4. Caernarfon	86 + 87 = 173
5. Trelawnyd	86 + 84 = 170

Second competition, 41–60 voices

Test pieces:	'Castilia' (D. Protheroe), 'Dydd da fy mherl' (di Lasso)
Adjudicators:	as above
3 choirs	
Result:	1. Colwyn, 2. Moelwyn, 3. Eifl

Glee

Test pieces:	'Rhyfelgan Rhufain' ('Roman Warsong', *Rienzi*, Wagner), 'Y Gariad Gollwyd' (D. Vaughan Thomas)
Adjudicators:	as above
8 choirs	

Result:

1. Maesteg Gleemen	88 + 84 = 172
2. Bro Glyndwr	84 + 85 = 169
3. Llangwm	86 + 82 = 168
4. Ardudwy	82 + 85 = 167
5. Bro Aled	87 + 79 = 166
6. Morlais	82 + 83 = 165
7. Joint – Dyffryn Nantlle	82 + 80
Penybont-fawr	80 + 82 = 162

1988 Newport

Test pieces:	'Y Pysgotwyr' (T. Maldwyn Price), 'Molwch yr Arglwydd' (Dilys Elwyn Edwards)
Adjudicators:	John Cynan Jones, John S. Davies, Eric Jones
2 choirs	

Result:

1. Froncysyllte	88 + 87 = 175
2. Swansea	88 + 86 = 174

Second competition

Test pieces: 'Y Glöwr' (Dulais Rhys), 'Dana Dana' (Lajos Bárdos)

Adjudicators: George Guest, John Cynan Jones, Richard Elfyn Jones

3 choirs

Result:
1. Risca	92 + 90 = 182	
2. Mynydd Mawr	88 + 88 = 176	
3. Caldicot	86 + 87 = 173	

Glee

Test pieces: 'Henffych Iesu' ('Ave Verum', Mozart), 'Deryn y Bwn' (arr. Mervyn Burtch)

Adjudicators: Eric Jones, John S. Davies, John Cynan Jones

6 choirs

Result:
1. Rhymney Silurian (Ralph Williams)	88 + 92 = 180	
2. Llangwm	85 + 87 = 172	
3. Morlais	83 + 82 = 165	
4. Joint – Eifl	79 + 81	
Cwm Garw	81 + 79 = 160	
6. Maesteg Gleemen	80 + 79 = 159	

Following Glynne Jones' defection to Pendyrus in 1962, Rhymney Silurians' baton was taken up by Paul Bailey. He in turn was succeeded by Ralph Williams, who by 2015 was four years away from completing half a century as the Silurians' musical director.

1989 Dyffryn Conwy (Llanrwst)

over 61 voices

Test piece: 'Croesi'r Anial' ('Crossing the Plain,' T. Maldwyn Price), plus 2 own choices

Adjudicators: Noel Davies, Roland Morris, Heward Rees

5 choirs

Result:
1. Traeth	85 + 85 + 88 = 258	
2. Penrhyn	89 + 83 + 85 = 257	
3. Caernarfon	83 + 81 + 86 = 250	
4. Rhosllannerchrugog	79 + 77 + 83 = 239	
5. Swansea	77 + 80 + 75 = 232	

Second competition, 40– 60 voices

Test pieces: 'O Cyfod Haul' ('Arise o Sun,' Maude Craske-Day), 'Wele Gysegredig Wledd' (Viadana)

Adjudicators:	Roland Morris, Noel Davies, Richard Elfyn Jones	
Result:	1. Flint	83 + 85 = 168
	2. Bro Glyndŵr	84 + 82 = 166
	3. Ardudwy	81 + 83 = 164
	4. Maelgwn	81 + 82 = 163
	5. Colwyn	79 + 78 = 157

Glee

Test pieces:	'Ffarwel i'r Bardd' (T. Osborne Roberts), 'Fy Nghoedwig Werdd' ('A Finnish Forest,' arr. Bryan Davies)	
Adjudicators:	Noel Davies, John S. Davies, Richard Elfyn Jones	
12 choirs	(15 choirs entered, but three – Morlais, Dyffryn Nantlle and Llanrwst – withdrew)	
Result:	1. Godre'r Aran (Eirian Owen)	86 + 87 = 173
	2. Bro Aled	83 + 85 = 168
	3. Rhymney Silurian	81 + 84 = 165
	4. Moelwyn	81 + 83 = 164

Also competing: Llangwm [163], Penybontfawr [163], Eifl [161], Lleisiau'r Frogwy [160], Dyffryn Ceiriog [156], Maesteg Gleemen [150], Gwynionydd [150], Cwm Garw [147].

1990 Cwm Rhymni

over 61 voices

Prize:	£500
Test piece:	'Salm 23' (Mathias), plus own choice in a 12–15 minute programme
Adjudicators:	Roland Morris, Dilys Elwyn Edwards, Gregory Rose
2 choirs	
Result:	1. Penrhyn [86], 2. Brythoniaid [84]

Second competition

Test Piece:	'Nos-gân yn y Coed' ('Nachtgesang im Walde,' Schubert), plus own choices
Adjudicators:	Roland Morris, George Guest, Gregory Rose
1 choir	
Result:	1. Whitland

Glee

Test pieces:	own choice in a programme 10–12 minutes in length
Adjudicators:	Roland Morris, Dilys Elwyn Edwards, Gregory Rose

5 choirs

Result: 1. Llangwm, 2. Rhymney Silurian, 3. Rushmore Oddfellows, Aldershot

1991 Bro Delyn (Mold)

Test piece: 'Invictus' (Daniel Protheroe), plus 2 own choices

Adjudicators: A.J. Heward Rees, Gwyn Morris, Elwyn Jones

6 choirs

Result: 1. Rhos Orpheus (John Glyn Williams) [259], 2. Caernarfon (Menai Williams) [252], 3. Penrhyn (Alun Llwyd) [251], 4. Trelawnyd (Geraint Roberts) [249], 5. Brythoniaid (Meirion Jones) [248], 6. Traeth (Gwyn L.Williams) [245]

Second competition

Test piece: 'Gloria' (*12th Mass*, Mozart) plus 2 own choices

Adjudicators: as above

6 choirs

Result: 1. Flint (Rodney T. Jones) [170], 2. Aberystwyth (Margaret Maddock) [167], 3. Colwyn [166], 4. Ardudwy [164], 5. Bro Glyndwr [162], 6. Mynydd Cynffig (Kenfig Hill) [160]

Glee

Test pieces: 'Gwcw Fach' (Haydn Morris), 'Trugarhâ di wrthyf' (Victoria)

Adjudicators: as above

5 choirs

Result: 1. Godre'r Aran [173], 2. Penybont-fawr [170], 3. Llangwm [165]

1992 Aberystwyth

Test pieces: 'Salm 148' (Arwel Hughes), 'Y Gwyntoedd' (E.T. Davies), plus own choice

Adjudicators: Roland Morris, Royston Havard, Brian Hughes

3 choirs

Result: 1. Trelawnyd (Geraint Roberts)   90 + 87 + 88 = 265

2. Llanelli   87 + 90 + 86 = 263

3. Caernarfon   88 + 85 + 87 = 260

Second competition

Test Pieces: 'Mordaith Cariad' (T. Hopkin Evans), 'Tair Cân Hwngaraidd' ('3 Hungarian Folk Songs', arr. M. Seiber), plus own choice

Adjudicators: Roy Bohana, Alun Guy, Royston Havard

4 choirs
Result:
1. Aberystwyth (Margaret Maddock)   85 + 89 + 89 = 263
2. Flint (Rodney T. Jones)   85 + 88 + 87 = 260
3. Mynydd Mawr   83 + 81 + 85 = 249
4. Llanfair Caereinion   81 + 85 + 80 = 246

Glee
Test pieces: 'Yn Enw yr Iesu' (J. Hændl), 'Y Sipsiwn' (Mathias)
Adjudicators: Alun Guy, Roland Morris, Brian Hughes
9 choirs
Result:
1. Godre'r Aran   92 + 90 = 182
2. Bro Glyndwr   82 + 85 = 167
3. Bro Aled   80 + 86 = 166
4. Joint – Gwalia (Swansea)   82 + 82
    Eifl   81 + 83 = 164

Also competing, Madog, Caron, Gwalia (London Welsh), Penybont-fawr.

1993 Builth

Test piece: 'Gorfoleddus Gân' (Michael Head), plus own choice
Adjudicators: Richard Elfyn Jones, Noel Davies, Rhidian Griffiths
1 choir
Result: 1. Llanelli

Second competition
Test piece: 'Requiescat' (Mansel Thomas), plus own choices
Adjudicators: as above
3 choirs
Result: 1. Faerdre (Clydach) [84], 2. Aberystwyth [82], Brythoniaid [80]

Glee
Test piece: 'Wele gysegredig wledd' (Viadana), plus own choices
Adjudicators: Brian Hughes, Noel Davies, Rhidian Griffiths
5 choirs
Result: 1. Godre'r Aran, 2. Llangwm, 3. Penybont-fawr

1994 Neath

Test pieces: 'Cân yr Ysbrydion dros y Dyfroedd' ('Song of the Spirits over the Waters,' Schubert), 'Cysga di fy mhlentyn tlws' (arr. E.T. Davies)

Adjudicators: John S. Davies. John Hugh Thomas, Jean Stanley Jones

1 choir

Result: 1. Pontarddulais

Second competition

Test pieces: 'Y Refali' ('The Reveille', Elgar), 'Mawr yw yr Arglwydd' (J. Morgan Nicholas)

Adjudicators: George Guest, John S. Davies, John Hugh Thomas

2 choirs

Result: 1. Caernarfon, 2. Faerdre (Clydach)

Glee

Test pieces: 'Arwelfa' (arr. Arwel Hughes), 'Mintai Briodas' (Kjerulf), 'Robin Ddiog' (arr. E.T. Davies)

5 choirs

Adjudicators: John S. Davies, John Hugh Thomas, Jean Stanley Jones

Result: 1. Llangwm, 2. Rhymney Silurian, 3. Glynneath, 4. Joint – Tonna and Onllwyn

1995 Colwyn Bay

Test piece: 'Y Pren ar y Bryn' (Mathias), plus own choice

Adjudicators: Richard Elfyn Jones, Frank Smith, Anthony Hose

3 choirs

Result: 1. Rhos (Tudor Jones), 2.Trelawnyd, 3. Penrhyn

Second competition

Test piece: 'Rhyfelgyrch Oroveso' ('Oroveso's Campaign', *Norma*, Bellini), plus own choices

Adjudicators: Gwyn L. Williams, Frank Smith, Jeffrey Wynn Davies

3 choirs

Result: 1. Caernarfon, 2. Flint, 3. Colwyn

Glee

Test piece: 'Jubilate Amen' (H. Kjerulf), plus own choices

Adjudicators: John A. Daniel, Anthony Hose, Frank Smith

10 choirs

Result: 1. Ardudwy (Harlech), 2. Llangwm, 3. Ar Ôl Tri (Cardigan)
                Also competing: Dwyfor, Eifl, Maesteg Gleemen, Penybont-fawr, Bro Aled, Lleisiau'r Frogwy, Betws-yn-Rhos

1996 Llandeilo

Test piece: 'Y Greadigaeth' ('The Creation', Willy Richter), plus own choices

Adjudicators: Royston Havard, Carlo Rizzi, Jeffrey Wynn Davies

5 choirs

Result: 1. Llanelli, 2. Traeth, 3. Rhos Orpheus, 4. Joint – Morriston RFC and Brythoniaid

Second competition

Test piece: 'Cytgan y Milwyr' ('Soldiers' Chorus', *Faust*, Gounod)

Adjudicators: As above

6 choirs

Result: 1. Caernarfon, 2. Mynydd Mawr, 3. Aberystwyth, 4. Mynydd Islwyn (Blackwood, Gwent), 5. Caerfyrddin, 6. Dyffryn Aman

Glee

Test piece: 'Heibio Aeth' ('Passing By', Edward Purcell), plus own choices

Adjudicators: Rhian Samuel, Mervyn Burtch, Carlo Rizzi

5 choirs

Result: 1. Maesteg Gleemen, 2. Ar Ôl Tri, 3. Llandybie, 4. Ardudwy, 5. Caron

1997 Bala

Test piece: 'Geiriau Olaf Dafydd' ('Last Words of David', Randall Thompson), plus 2 own choices

Adjudicators: Huw Tregelles Williams, John Harper, Jean Stanley Jones

2 choirs

Result: 1. Traeth (David Davies), 2. Rhos Orpheus (John Glyn Williams)

Second competition, 41–60 voices

Test piece: 'Sigla fy Enaid' ('Rock-a my Soul', arr. Gwyn Arch) plus 2 own choices

Adjudicators: John Hugh Thomas, Nigel Perrin, John Harper

3 choirs

Result: 1. Aberystwyth (Margaret Maddock), 2. Caernarfon (Menai Williams), 3. Mynydd Islwyn (Graham Davies)

Glee, under 40 voices

Test piece: 'Clychau'r Gôg' (Gareth Glyn), plus 2 own choices

Adjudicators: Huw Tregelles Williams, John Harper, Jean Stanley Jones

9 choirs

Result: 1. Ar Ôl Tri (Wyn Lewis), 2. Llangwm, 3. Ardudwy

1998 **Bridgend**

Test piece: 'Salm 150' (Goff Richards), plus own choices

Adjudicators: John S. Davies, Jonathan Greaves-Smith, Alun Guy

1 choir

Result: 1. Llanelli (Eifion Thomas)

Second competition

Test piece: 'Cytgan yr Helwyr'/'Llawenydd yr Heliwr' ('Huntsmen's Chorus'/ 'Joy of the hunter', Weber)

Adjudicators: Alun Guy, Richard Elfyn Jones, Jonathan Greaves-Smith

5 choirs: 1. Mynydd Mawr (Alun Rhyddid Williams), 2. Penrhyn, 3. Aberystwyth

Glee

Test piece: 'Emyn y Greadigaeth' (Beethoven)

Adjudicators: as above

7 choirs

Result: 1. Ar Ôl Tri, 2. Llanfair Caereinion, 3. Hogia'r Ddwylan

1999 **Ynys Môn**

Test pieces: 'Salm 100' (George Stead) plus own choices, to include an operatic chorus and a piece by a Welsh composer

Adjudicators: Eirian Owen, John Pryce Jones, Helena Braithwaite

3 choirs

Result: 1. Trelawnyd (Geraint Roberts), 2. Caernarfon (Menai Williams), 3. Rhos (John A.Daniel)

Second competition

Test piece: *Serenâd y Gondolîr* ('Gondelfahrer', Schubert)

Adjudicators: Helena Braithwaite, Eirian Owen, Brian Hughes

5 choirs

Results: 1. Llangwm (Bethan Smallwood), 2. Brythoniaid, 3. Flint

Glee

Test piece: *Y Duw roes inni fywyd* ('The God who gave us life', Randall Thompson)

Adjudicators: Helena Braithwaite, John Pryce Jones, Brian Hughes

Result: 1. Hogia'r Ddwylan (Ilid Anne Jones), 2. Ar Ôl Tri, 3. Penybont-fawr

2000 Llanelli

Test piece:	Dies Irae (Cherubini, *Requiem*) plus own choices
Adjudicators:	Iwan Edwards, Jeffrey Wynn Davies, Terry James, Terence Lloyd
1 choir	
Result:	1. Llanelli (Eifion Thomas)

Second competition

Test piece:	'Cytgan y Morwyr' ('Sailors' Chorus', *Flying Dutchman*, Wagner)
Adjudicators:	as above
3 choirs	
Result:	1. Llangwm, 2. Aberystwyth, 3. Joint – Aberafan and Mynydd Mawr

Glee

Test piece:	*Hafan Gobaith* (Delyth Rees, arr. Valerie Hoppe), plus own choice
Adjudicators:	as above
9 choirs	
Result:	1. Ar Ôl Tri, 2. Hogia'r Ddwylan, 3. Bois y Castell

2001 Denbigh

Test pieces:	'Gwledd y gwleddoedd' (Arnold Williams), plus own choice
Adjudicators:	Richard Elfyn Jones, Huw Williams, Mair Carrington Roberts
3 choirs	
Result:	1. Caernarfon (Menai Williams), 2. Trelawnyd (Geraint Roberts), 3. Dunvant (Tim Rhys-Evans)

In 1999 Caernarfon was the first choir ever in the chief male voice choir category to be conducted by a woman (Menai Williams). In 2001 Menai Williams became the first woman to win it.

Second competition

Test piece:	'Cytgan yr Offeiriaid' ('O Isis and Osiris', *Magic Flute*, Mozart), plus own choice
Adjudicators:	Delyth Hopkins Evans, Huw Williams, Richard Elfyn Jones
5 choirs	
Result:	1. Godre'r Aran (Eirian Owen), 2. Llangwm (Bethan Smallwood), 3. Penrhyn (Owain Arwel Davies)

Glee

Test piece: 'Mae'r Dydd yn Cilio' ('The Long Day Closes', Arthur Sullivan), plus own choice

Adjudicators: Richard Elfyn Jones, Huw Williams, Alun Guy

6 choirs

Result: 1. Hogia'r Ddwylan (Ilid Anne Jones), 2. Ar Ôl Tri (Wyn Lewis), 3. Lleisiau'r Frogwy (Gareth Glyn)

2002 Tyddewi (St David's)

over 45 voices

Prize: £750

Test piece: 'Pan Seinio'r Utgorn Arian' ('Arouse Ye', *I Puritani*, Bellini) and own choices

Adjudicators: Jean Stanley Jones, Eric Jones, Huw Tregelles Williams

3 choirs

Result: 1. Dunvant (Tim Rhys-Evans), 2. Traeth (Annette Bryn Parri), 3. Dowlais (Gareth Ellis)

Second competition, under 45 voices

Test piece: 'Carol yr Alarch' (Gareth Glyn), plus own choice

Adjudicators: as above

3 choirs

Result: 1. Ar Ôl Tri, 2. Haverfordwest, 3. Hogia'r Ddwylan

Open competition, any number above 20 voices

Prize: £750

Test piece: A 15-minute programme including a piece by a Welsh composer from 1980

Adjudicators: as above

2 choirs

Result: 1. Brythoniaid (John Eifion), 2. Llanelli (Eifion Thomas)

2003 Meifod (Powys)

over 45 voices

Test piece: 'Cytgan y Carcharorion' ('O welche Lust', 'Prisoners' Chorus,' *Fidelio*, Beethoven) and own choice

Adjudicators: D. Eifion Thomas, Alun Guy, Brian Hughes

3 choirs

Result: 1. Caernarfon (Menai Williams), 2. Maelgwn, 3. Traeth

Second competition, under 45 voices

Test piece: 'Cytgan yr Herwyr' ('Bandits' Chorus', *Ernani*, Verdi), plus own choice

Adjudicators: as above

5 choirs

Result   1. Hogia'r Ddwylan (Ilid Anne Jones), 2. Ar Ôl Tri, 3. Penybontfawr

Open competition

Prizes: £1000; £600; £400

Test pieces: own choice

Adjudicators: as above

4 choirs

Result: 1. Pontarddulais (Clive Phillips), 2. Llangwm, 3. Froncysyllte, 4. Penrhyn

Clive Phillips had succeeded Noel Davies as conductor of Pontarddulais the previous year. Under Noel Davies they had achieved a record eleven firsts and two seconds (to Treorchy in 1964 and 1967) at the National Eisteddfod, won at Llangollen twice, the Cardigan semi-national ten times (1964–1976), the Miners' Eisteddfod six times (1965–87) and Pontrhydfendigaid semi-national twice (1965, 1968).

2004 Newport

over 45 voices

Prizes: £750; £450; £300

Test piece: 'Cytgan y Pererinion' ('Pilgrims' Chorus', *Tannhauser*, Wagner), plus 2 own choices

Adjudicators: Huw Willliams, Adrian Partington, Gwyn L. Williams

3 choirs

Result: 1. Bridgend (John Jenkins), 2. Maelgwn, 3. Caldicot

Second competition, under 45 voices

Test piece: 'Soldiers' Chorus' (*Il Trovatore*, Verdi), plus 2 own choices

Adjudicators: as above

3 choirs

Result: 1. Ar Ôl Tri, 2. Meibion y Machlud (Cowbridge), 3. Victoria Welsh (Melbourne, Australia)

Open, choirs of more than 20 voices

Prizes: £1000; £600

15-minute programme

Adjudicators: as above

2 choirs

Result: 1. Pontarddulais (Clive Phillips), 2. Risca (Martin Hodson)

2005 Bangor

over 45 voices

Prizes: £750; £450; £300

Test piece: 'Y Pren ar y Bryn', plus own choice

Adjudicators: Eirian Owen, John S. Davies, Geraint Roberts

2 choirs

Result: 1. Maelgwn (Trystan Lewis), 2. Penrhyn (Owain Arwel Davies)

Second competition, not over 45 voices

Test piece: 'Clychau'r Gog' (Gareth Glyn)

Adjudicators: as above

8 choirs

Result: 1. Ar Ôl Tri (Wyn Lewis), 2. Hogia'r Ddwylan, 3. Maesteg Gleemen

Open, choirs of more than 20 voices

Prizes: £1000; £600; £400

15-minute programme

Adjudicators: as above

2 choirs

Result: 1. Brythoniaid (John Eifion), 2. Llangwm

2006 Swansea

Over 45 voices

Prize: £750

Test piece: 'Arglwydd da, nid wyf deilwng' (T.L. de Victoria)

Adjudicators: Delyth Hopkins Evans, Alun Guy, Huw Tregelles Williams

2 choirs

Result: 1. Bridgend (John Jenkins), 2. Morriston RFC (D. Huw Rees)

Second competition, 20–45 voices

Prize: £750

Test piece: 'Â llawenydd, cenwch' ('With a voice of singing', Martin Shaw), plus own choices

Adjudicators: as above

7 choirs

Result: 1. Ar Ôl Tri (Wyn Lewis), 2. Bois y Castell (Nia Clwyd), 3. Hogia'r Ddwylan (Ilid Anne Jones)

Open competition, over 20 voices

Prize: £1000

15-minute programme

2 choirs

Result: 1. Pontarddulais (Clive Phillips), 2. Llanelli (Eifion Thomas)

The venue of this Eisteddfod was the bleak site of the demolished Felindre Tinplate Works where a large number of past and present members of these two choirs had sweated over many decades.

2007 Flint

over 45 voices

Prize: £750

Test piece: 'Mawr yw yr Arglwydd' (J. Morgan Nicholas) in a 15-minute programme

Adjudicators: R. Allan Fewster, Tim Rhys-Evans, Menai Williams

1 choir

Result: 1. Traeth (Annette Bryn Parri)

Second competition, 20–45 voices

Prize: £750

Test piece: 'Sanctus' (Gounod)

Adjudicators: as above

6 choirs

Result: 1. Ar Ôl Tri, 2. Bro Aled, 3. Llangwm

Open competition

Prize £1000; £600; £400

Adjudicators: as above

4 choirs

Result: 1. Trelawnyd (Geraint Roberts), 2. Rhosllannerchrugog, 3. Penrhyn, 4. Hogia'r Ddwylan

2008 Cardiff

over 45 voices

Prize £750; £450; £300

Test piece: 'Y Greadigaeth' ('The Creation', Willy Richter), plus own choice

Adjudicators: Pat Jones, Helena Braithwaite, Richard Elfyn Jones
7 choirs
Result: 1. Pontarddulais (Clive Phillips), 2. Brythoniaid, 3. Traeth

The competition was reminiscent of the mighty contest of 1964 in Swansea in that all seven competing choirs were previous National winners of the 'chief': in order of singing, Maelgwn, Pontarddulais, Llanelli, Bridgend, Brythoniaid, Traeth and Dunvant.

Second competition, 20–45 voices
Prize: £750; £450; £350
Test piece: Rhyfelgan Rhufain' ('Roman Warsong', *Rienzi*, Wagner), plus own choice
Adjudicators: as above
7 choirs
Result: 1. Côr Meibion Taf, Cardiff (Robert Nicholls), 2. Maesteg Gleemen (Alun Hodges), 3. Bois y Castell (Nia Clwyd)

2009 Meirion and District (Bala)

over 45 voices
Test piece: 'Oleuni Mwyn' (W. Bradwen Jones), plus own choice
Adjudicators: Alun Guy, John S. Davies, Jean Stanley Jones
5 choirs
Result: 1. Maelgwn (Trystan Lewis), 2. Brythoniaid, 3. Flint

Second competition, 20–45 voices
Test piece: 'Cytgan yr Helwyr' ('Huntsmen's Chorus', Weber), plus own choice
Adjudicators: as above
6 choirs
Result: 1. Ar Ôl Tri (Wyn Lewis), 2. Taf, 3. Llangwm

2010 Ebbw Vale (Blaenau Gwent)

over 45 voices
Test piece: 'Heriwn, wynebwn y wawr' (Gareth Glyn), plus own choices
Adjudicators: Geraint Roberts, Lyn Davies
7 choirs
Result: 1. Taf (Rob Nicholls), 2. Llanelli (Eifion Thomas), 3. Pendyrus (Stewart Roberts)
   Also competing were Bridgend, Brythoniaid, Dunvant, and Traeth

Like the 2008 contest, all seven choirs were previous National winners, though 44 years had elapsed since Pendyrus, absent from the National stage from 1968, last won it. Rob Nicholls' Taf, having won the second competition at their first attempt in 2008, repeated this feat in the 'chief'.

> *Second competition, 20–45 voices*
> Test piece: 'Salm 23' (Eric Jones), plus own choice
> Adjudicators: as above
> 3 choirs
> Result: 1. Ar Ôl Tri, 2. Bechgyn Bro Taf (Cardiff), 3. Chepstow

2011 Wrexham

> *over 45 voices*
> Test piece: 'Cytgan y Carcharorion' ('Prisoners' Chorus, *Fidelio*,
>   Beethoven), plus own choices
> Adjudicators: Dafydd Lloyd Jones, Gwawr Owen, D. Eifion Thomas
> 3 choirs
> Result: 1. Rhos (Aled Phillips), 2. Taf (Rob Nicholls), 3. Maelgwn
>   (Trystan Lewis)

> *Second competition, 20–45 voices*
> Test piece: 'Benedictus' (Robat Arwyn), plus own choices
> Adjudicators: as above
> 6 choirs
> Result: 1. A'ni'ma'to (Cardiff) (Elis Griffiths), 2. Llangwm, 3. Dwyfor

2012 Vale of Glamorgan

> *over 45 voices*
> Test piece: 'Bywyd y Bugail', (Brian Hughes), plus own choices
> Adjudicators: Richard Elfyn Jones, Lyn Davies
> 4 choirs
> Result: 1. Rhos (Aled Phillips), 2. Taf (Rob Nicholls), 3. Llanelli (Eifion
>   Thomas), 4. Pendyrus (Stewart Roberts)

Pendyrus' accompanist Gavin Parry was completing 40 years unbroken service with one choir, a record shared with Margaret Davies (Beaufort), Anne Phillips (Rhos Orpheus), the late Alwen Lloyd Elston (Cymau), and Grês Pritchard (Traeth). There may be others, but not many.

Second competition, 20–45 voices

Test piece: 'Cennin Aur' (Mansel Thomas), plus own choices

Adjudicators: as above

5 choirs

Result: 1. Llangwm (Bethan Smallwood), 2. Ar Ôl Tri, 3. Eschoir (London Welsh),

2013 Sir Ddinbych (Denbighshire)

over 45 voices

Test pieces: 'Geiriau Olaf Dafydd' ('Last Words of David', Randall Thompson)

Adjudicators: Eric Jones, Catrin Wyn Hughes, David Davies

1 choir

Result: 1. Rhos (Aled Phillips)

Second competition, 20–25 voices

Test pieces: 'Cytgan y Milwyr' ('Soldiers' Chorus', *Il Trovatore*, Verdi)

Adjudicators: as above

5 choirs

Result: 1. Llangwm, 2. Bro Aled, 3. Flint

2014 Sir Gâr (Llanelli)

over 45 voices

Test pieces: 'Salm 100' (George Stead), plus own choice

Adjudicators: Huw Williams, Iwan Edwards, Beryl Lloyd Roberts

3 choirs

Result: 1. Pontarddulais (Clive Phillips), 2. Taf (Rob Nicholls), 3. Llanelli (Eifion Thomas)

Pontarddulais' own choices were 'Arglwydd Da, nid wyf deilwng' ('Domine non sum dignus,' T.L. de Victoria) and 'Y Pren ar y Bryn' (Mathias), two of the three pieces they sang when they came second to Treorchy in the epic encounter fifty years earlier in Swansea.

Second competition, 20–45 voices

Test piece: 'Sanctus' (*Requiem*, Cherubini)

Adjudicators: as above

3 choirs

Result: 1. Ar Ôl Tri (Wyn Lewis), 2. Bois y Castell (Nia Clwyd), 3. Meibion y Machlud (Eric Dafydd)

A *frisson* of excitement tinged with alarm rippled through the Pavilion when fearless Welsh rugby hero J.P.R. Williams was spotted in the ranks of Cowbridge choir Meibion y Machlud ('Sons of the Setting Sun'). It is not certain whether the journalist who asked the great J.P.R. whether he would consider exchanging one of his 52 Welsh caps for a National Winner's medal is still alive.

2015 Meifod (Montgomeryshire and the Marches)
      over 45 voices
      Test pieces: own choices in a 15-minute programme
      1 choir
      Adjudicators: Julian Wilkins, Robat Arwyn, Menai Williams
      Result: 1. Taf (Rob Nicholls)

      Second competition
      Test pieces: own choices in a 12-minute programme
      Adjudicators: as above
      8 choirs
      Result: 1. Bois y Castell (Nia Clwyd), 2. Machynlleth (Aled Myrddin), 3. Llangwm (Bethan Smallwood)

In 1987 Maesteg Gleemen won the Glee competition out of 8 choirs, only two of which came from south Wales, singing Wagner's 'Roman War Song'. In 2015 Bois y Castell of Llandeilo were the *only* south Wales choir among 8 competitors and won it, after 12 years of dogged attempts, with the same piece. It was a personal triumph for founder-conductor Nia Clwyd, one of the six female conductors in the competition. Since contralto Ffion Hâf, also of Llandeilo, won the Blue Riband the same afternoon, it was a good eisteddfod for the Tywi valley's men *and* women.

Unless the Eisteddfod changes its mind, this would be the last occasion for competing choirs to be categorised according to size. Where there had in the past been three male voice competitions, from 2016 there will be only one, for choirs of any number above 20. It does not mean there will be no more 'battles of the giants,' but there are now opportunities for giant-*killers*. It marks the end of an era and the beginning of a new one.

Bibliography

Books and articles

John Asquith, *Sea of Voices: the story of Côr Meibion Morlais* (2011)

Dudley Baines, 'The Onset of Depression', in P. Johnson (ed.), *Twentieth Century Britain: Economic, Social and Cultural Change* (1995)

Terry Budd, *Canton RFC Male Voice Choir 20th anniversary 1993–2013* (2013)

Gerald Cumberland, *Written in Friendship* (1923)

John Davies, *Hanes Cymru/History of Wales* (1991/1993)

John H. Davies, 'Rhondda Choral Music in Victorian Times,' in K.S. Hopkins (ed.) *Rhondda Past and Future* [1975]

D. Dowe, 'The workingmen's choral movement in Germany before the First World War', *Journal of Contemporary History*, 13 (1978)

W.L. Evans and W. Bodger, *Pontnewydd Male Choir: a brief history 1904–79* (1979)

Hywel Teifi Edwards, *Eisteddfod Ffair y Byd Chicago 1893* (1990)

Gareth Evans, *Dunvant: portrait of a community* (1992)

Harry Evans, 'Welsh Choral Singing' in T. Stephens (ed.) *Wales Today and Tomorrow* (1907)

Ralph Ellison, 'In a Strange Country,' in John F. Callahan (ed.), *'Flying Home' and other stories* (1998)

Ferndale Male Voice Choir: 30 Years of Music Making 1949–79 (1979)

Didier Francfort, *Le Chant des nations: musiques et cultures en Europe 1870–1914* (2004)

Rhidian Griffiths, 'Isaac Jones, music printer and publisher,' *The Book in Wales*, no. 5, 2003

'O Gwmgiedd i Chicago, teyrnged i Daniel Protheroe 1866-1934', *Cerddoriaeth Cymru /Welsh Music*, vol.9 no.7, 1994–5

'Y Gân Orchfygol', in Hywel Teifi Edwards (ed.) *Cwm Rhondda* (1995)

'Cerddor yr Haf: Gwilym Gwent (1834-1891)', in H.T Edwards (ed.), *Ebwy, Rhymni a Sirhywi* (1999)

'"Arweinydd trwy ras Duw": Harry Evans (1873-1914)' in H.T.Edwards (ed.), *Merthyr a Thaf* (2001)

Philippe Gumplowicz, *Les Travaux d'Orphée, deux siècles de pratique musique amateur en France* (2nd ed. 2001)

Trevor Herbert and Gareth Elwyn Jones (eds.), *Wales between the Wars* (1988) *Wales since 1945* (1995)

Martin Hodson, *Risca Male Choir: the first forty years 1970–2010* (2012)

Colin Hughes, *Mametz: Lloyd George's Welsh Army at the Battle of the Somme* (1990)

Vaughan Hughes, *Cymru Fawr* (2014)

Alwyn Humphreys, *Yr Hunangofiant* (2006)

John Isaac and Leslie Sims, *A History of Cwmbach Male Choir 1921–2001* (2001)

J. Geraint Jenkins, *Drefach-Felindre and the Woollen Industry* (1976)

Cyril Jones (compiler), *History in the Making: Pendyrus Male Choir 1924–2008* (2008)

Elfed Jones, *Côr Meibion y Penrhyn Ddoe a Heddiw* (1984)

Emyr Jones, *Canrif y Chwarelwr* (1964)

Eric Jones, *Maestro: cofiant Noel Davies: a biography* (2007) *Brethren, Sing On! A History of Pontarddulais Male Choir 1960–2010* (2010)

Glynne Jones, 'The end of the Cartrefle dynasty,' *Welsh Music*, 3 no. 6, Spring 1970 'Harry Evans 1873–1914', *Welsh Music*, 4, no. 5, Winter 1973/4

Ieuan Gwynedd Jones, 'The City and its villages' in R.A. Griffiths (ed.), *The City of Swansea* (1990)

Krisztina Lajosi and Andreas Stynen (eds), *Choral Societies and National Movements in Europe* (2015)

Gareth H. Lewis, 'The Welsh Choral Tradition: fact and myth', *Welsh Music*, 5 no. 4 (Winter 1976-7)

Carl Llewellyn, 'The *Lusitania* Catastrophe and the Welsh Male Voice Choir,' *Merthyr Historian*, vol. 17, 2004

E.D. Mackerness, *A Social History of English Music* (1964)

R.G.Mainwaring, D.G. Richards, J.C. Evans, *A Hundred Years of Harmony: Dunvant and its Male Choir 1895–1995* (Dunvant, 1995)

David Morgans, *Music and Musicians of Merthyr and District* (1922)

Morriston Orpheus Choir: Golden Jubilee 1935–85 souvenir brochure (1985): *75th Anniversary 1935–2010 concert brochure* (2010)

Reginald Nettel, *Music in the Five Towns 1840–1914* (1944)

Meurig Owen, *North Wales Male Voice Choirs* (2009)

Pendyrus Golden Jubilee Festival brochure 1924–74 (1974)

Dean Powell (compiler), *Musical Rhondda* (2000) *Treorchy Male Choir* (2001)

Dean Powell, 'Treorchy Male Choir: the early years', *Excelsior: The Voice of the Treorchy Male Choir*, 2007

'Rhondda Glee Society: rivals in song', *Excelsior*, 2010

'The Royal Welsh Male Choir: a history', *Excelsior*, 2011

Daniel Protheroe, *Nodiadau Damweiniol a D'rawyd o Dro i Dro* (1924)

Alun John Richards, *Tinplate in Wales* (2008)

D. Gerwyn Richards (ed.), *Côr Meibion Llanelli 1964–1989: 25th Anniversary* (1989)

Dave Russell, *Popular Music in England 1840–1914: a social history* (rev.ed.1997)

Rhos Male Voice Choir First American Tour 1967 souvenir brochure (1967)

Dulais Rhys and Frank Bott, *To Philadelphia and Back: the life and music of Joseph Parry* (2010)

Dai Smith, *In the Frame: memory and society 1910-2010* (2010)

Peter Stead, 'Amateurs and Professionals in the Cultures of Wales' in G.H. Jenkins and J.B. Smith (eds.), *Politics and Society in Wales 1840–1922: essays in honour of Ieuan Gwynedd Jones* (1988)

Robert Stradling and Meirion Hughes, *The English Musical Renaissance 1840–1940* (rev. ed. 2001)

Gwyn Thomas, *Y Pethau Diwethaf* (1975)

John Hugh Thomas, 'Music' in R.A. Griffiths (ed.), *The City of Swansea* (1990)

Wynford Vaughan Thomas, *Madly in All Directions* (1967)

Alun Trevor, *Cofio Cantorion: The Welsh Imperial Singers* (1991)

Côr Meibion Trelawnyd 1933–1983 souvenir brochure (1983)

Glen Tucker (compiler), *Côr Meibion Aberafan Port Talbot 1966–91* (1991)

C.H. Dudley Ward, *History of the Welsh Guards* (1920)

Eugen Weber, *Peasants into Frenchmen – the modernisation of rural France 1870–1914* (1977)

A. Tudno Williams, *E.T. Davies, arloeswr cerdd* (1981)

Daniel G. Williams, *Black Skin, Blue Books: African Americans and Wales 1845–1945* (2012)

Gareth Williams, *Valleys of Song: Music and Welsh Society 1840–1914* (rev. ed. 2003)

'"How's the tenors in Dowlais?" The choral culture of the south Wales coalfield c.1880-1930', *Transactions of the Honourable Society of Cymmrodorion*, 2004 (2005)

'Citadel of Song: Merthyr's Choral Culture c.1870-1970', *Merthyr Historian*, vol.20, 2009

'"Then came we singing": Gwyn Thomas's world of music', *Llafur*, vol.11, no.3, 2014 (2015)

'Cythraul y Canu yn Oes Aur y Corau Mawr,' *Y Traethodydd*, Ebrill [April] 2015

Gwilym Williams, *Cwmbach Male Choir: half a century of song 1921–71* (1971)

Huw Williams, *Canu'r Bobol* (1978)

Ieuan M. Williams, *Côr Meibion Pontarddulais 1960–85: Pontarddulais Male Choir* (1986)

Raymond Williams, *Border Country* (1960; Library of Wales, 2006)

Ivor Wynne Jones, *The Cairo Eisteddfod and other Welsh adventures in Egypt* (2003)

Theses

David R. Jones, 'Advocate of change and tradition in Wales: W.S.Gwynn Williams 1896–1978' (Ph.D. thesis, Bangor University, 2007)

Gwawr E. Jones, '*The Mighty Mam*: Clara Novello Davies a byd cerddoriaeth broffesiynol yng Nghymru' (Ph.D. thesis, Bangor University, 2015)

Susan Skinner, 'The Cornish Male Voice Choir: a history of the relationship between music, place and culture' (Ph.D. thesis, University of Plymouth, 2014)

Christopher R. Wiltshire, 'The British Male Voice Choir: a history and contemporary assessment' (Ph.D. thesis, University of London, Goldsmith's College, 1993)

Periodicals

Y Cerddor Cymreig

Y Gerddorfa

Y Cerddor

Y Cerddor Newydd

Welsh Music / Cerddoriaeth Cymru

Musical Times

Musical Herald

Musical Opinion

The Sackbut.

Index

(The years refer to specific mention in the Results section in Part 3)